KNACK™
MAKE IT EASY

CLEAN HOME,
GREEN HOME

CLEAN HOME, GREEN HOME

The Complete Illustrated Guide to Eco-Friendly Homekeeping

KIMBERLY DELANEY

KNACK™
MAKE IT EASY

Guilford, Connecticut
An imprint of The Globe Pequot Press

KNACK™
MAKE IT EASY

Cover photos by (from left to right) Emin Ozkan/shutterstock, Sandra Rugina/shutterstock, Willam Milner/shutterstock, Dusan Zidar/shutterstock
Photo research by Anna Adesanya
Additional photo research by Mary Rischer

Text design by Paul Beatrice
Special Photography by Carole Drong

Library of Congress Cataloging-in-Publication Data
Delaney, Kimberly.
  Knack clean home, green home : the complete illustrated guide to eco-friendly homekeeping / Kimberly Delaney.
    p. cm.
  ISBN 978-1-59921-389-7
1. House cleaning. 2. Green products. I. Title.
TX324.D443 2009
648'.5--dc22
                                    2008031978

Printed in China

10 9 8 7 6 5 4 3 2 1

To my breaths of clean fresh air—my daughter Riley and husband Kevin

Acknowledgments

Thanks to editor Maureen Graney for the thought-provoking and inspiring brainstorm sessions that kicked off this project, and editor Katie Benoit for her insightful feedback and excellent organization throughout the process. Thanks to Anna Adesanya for her creativity and resourcefulness in providing the photos for the book. Thanks also to my friends and family—and especially my mother, Marcia Bird—for their support and help in testing out and thinking through ideas, recipes, and techniques that went into this book.

CONTENTS

INTRODUCTION
The Green-Cleaning Mind-set

With more news coming out about dangerous toxins in common household products, it's easy to feel either a little overwhelmed or a little over it. After all, if some of the most common and best-selling household products have hazardous chemicals in them, what can we do about it? Luckily, one of the simplest ways to have a big impact on the health of your family and the environment is to green your cleaning. Contrary to what many people assume about green cleaning, it actually doesn't have to cost any more, take more time, or mean you have to compromise on what you think of as clean. But green cleaning does require a shift in how we define *clean*.

"Clean" in the conventional sense means free of dirt and germs. It's about how the surfaces and objects in your home look. Are the appliances shiny? The cupboards free of fingerprints? The windows clean and clear? When you go green, the definition of clean expands, and, by this definition, many chemical-laden products might not be considered cleaners at all. A clean green home is still one that is free of dirt and germs, but it's also free of toxic pollution.

1. Green cleaning is about air quality

The difference between green-cleaning and just cleaning can be boiled down to the simple rule that when

What Is a Toxin?

What is a toxin? A chemical that irritates your skin, burns your eyes, or causes human illness or injury when inhaled, swallowed, or absorbed through the skin. While any chemical can be toxic if you drink the whole bottle, the toxins we refer to in this book are those that have been shown to have or are strongly suspected of having health or environmental consequences even when used according to the directions on the package.

you finish green-cleaning a room, the air should be as clean or cleaner than when you started. That means no more toxic chemicals to shine surfaces or remove dirt or grease. Using products that pollute the air is not cleaning. It's polluting.

In the green-cleaning mind-set, sleeping in a clean bedroom means the shelves and furniture are well dusted, the mirror and windows are streak-free, the blinds and draperies are clean, as are the floor and area rugs. It also means the furniture is hardwood and finished in sealants or varnishes that don't pollute. The bedding is free of anti-wrinkle chemicals and perhaps even the comforter is clean wool or organic cotton. In short, the room is free of dirt and the air is healthy and fresh.

Consider exposure

We know that we most likely will not keel over from breathing in one toxic glass cleaner or spraying a little weed killer on our landscaping. But it's important to think in terms of "exposure." We're not just spraying one chemical cleaner or one pesticide on any given day. In fact, the average person is exposed to 100 different chemicals a day—and that's just in personal care products. That average person hasn't even started to clean yet.

Although it's easy to believe that if a product is on the shelf at your grocery store, it must be safe, studies show that this is not necessarily the case. Unfortunately, only a very few of the 85,000 chemicals in use today have even been tested for safety. Many that have been tested and found to cause health problems are still used in the products we buy. In addition, many scientists believe that household toxins are one of the big reasons why asthma and allergies are on the rise.

While there is clearly a lot we don't know, there is also enough that we do know about these toxins to limit our exposure. With that in mind, one of the goals of this book is to provide information you need to know to help reduce your exposure to these chemicals as you create your clean green home.

Breaking Down the Terms

- Carcinogens can cause cancer or worsen it by stimulating the spread of cancer cells.
- Neurotoxins can attack the nervous system and can cause brain damage with prolonged exposure.
- Endocrine disrupters can disrupt the body's hormonal and reproductive system.
- Teratogens can affect fetal development, causing birth defects.
- Mutagens can permanently alter genetic code in a cell.
- Immunotoxins can damage the immune system, either making it underactive and leaving you vulnerable to illness, or overactive, as in an autoimmune disorder.

The importance of dusting

Far from being rocket science, you'll find that one of the most important green-cleaning steps you can take is really just dusting. This is because the dust gives toxins something to stick to so our exposure is prolonged. Breathing in all this dust means these toxins may now linger in your body, where some attach to fat and build up for decades. Eventually we may transfer these toxins to our children in breast milk. Studies have found that controlling dust reduces our exposure to household toxins. That's why consistent dusting and using a vacuum with a quality filter designed to capture these particles might be the best tools you have to detox your home.

2. Green cleaning is about reducing

The green-cleaning mind-set also finds ways of cleaning that help reduce energy, water, and other resource consumption. Rather than buying a separate cleaner for every job, you'll have just a few, and even some you make yourself from a short list of basic ingredients like vinegar and vegetable-based soap. You might fill the sinks instead of letting the water run to hand-wash the dishes, or you could buy an energy-efficient washer when your old one dies.

Maintaining what you already own

You are also looking to extend the life of things you already have and keep appliances running as efficiently as possible. For example, dust buildup on a ceiling fan can cause unnecessary wear and could ultimately break it. Mineral deposits in your dishwasher can interfere with the water flow so that you need to use either a harsher detergent or more water to rinse the dishes to get the level of clean you desire. Dusty lightbulbs get hotter so they need to be replaced faster. They also shed less light so you need to turn on more lamps and use more electricity to light your home. Neglecting to replace your dirty furnace filters can mean expensive heating bills. The longer you keep these things clean and well-maintained the more efficiently they run and the longer they stay out of the landfill.

3. The self-cleaning home

While we can't promise that following the advice in this book will make your home clean itself, it will likely reduce the time it takes to clean. That's because the green-cleaning mind-set is also about taking proactive steps to keep your home cleaner, longer, eliminate the need for harsh chemical products and make cleaning easy. When rooms are cluttered, preparing to clean them takes about as long as cleaning them—so you've doubled the time you need to spend on the job. Throughout the book, we suggest ways of setting up rooms to make them as easy to clean as possible. The easier it is to clean, the more often you'll be able to do it, even with a busy schedule.

For example, you might set up your entryway so it is designed to contain the dirt, jackets, shoes, bags, mail, and whatever else you bring in from the outside world so it won't spread all over your house. And each of those items get a designated bin or basket, hook or shelf that's easy to remove when you want to clean the entryway.

When it comes to making cleaners, almost all of the recipes in this book require a few of the eight or so basic cleaning ingredients, a spray bottle, and a good shake. A few others require you to mix a powder like baking soda and liquid soap to make a paste. None require exotic ingredients and all can be mixed up in just a few minutes.

As you explore this book, you will no doubt find a few recipes to start with and a few jobs that you'd rather tackle with a store-bought green cleaner. With that in mind, each section of the book highlights the ingredients you'll want to look for and those you want to avoid in that product category. You'll also learn how to tell a truly green cleaner from a purely "green-washed" product (see page 10) so your shopping will be easier.

This book is meant to be a guide in exploring green cleaning. If you want to go further, check the resource section for Web sites and books that will help. The book can be read from front to back, or just flip to the room you want to clean. Go at your own pace. Each step you take to green your cleaning will reduce your exposure to toxins. Even if you just replace three cleaners with home-made recipes, you're doing something great for your family and the environment. And don't forget that one of the satisfying rewards of green cleaning is that when you're finished, you can take a deep breath of clean, fresh air and reward yourself for your green efforts!

HOUSEHOLD PRODUCT LABEL PRIMER

Crack the code to recognize toxins at a glance

A big part of making the shift to green cleaning is to redefine how we understand clean. Sure, a spotless kitchen counter and polished bath faucet are visual signals that a home is clean. But what about what we don't see? What chemicals are we exposing ourselves to through inhalation, skin absorption, or even ingestion? Green cleaning starts with the great news that you can have your spotless countertop and polished bath faucet without dirtying your air, your body, or the environment.

Extreme Hazard

POISON: MAY BE FATAL IF SWALLOWED OR INHALED.

- "Poison" is the strongest signal word you'll find on household products and it is not common on cleaners.

- Meaning: Highly toxic.

- Found on: Some car products such as antifreeze as well as paint or varnish removers and insecticides.

- To use this product safely you would need major ventilation and safety gear. Better yet, find something less toxic for the job.

Highly Toxic

DANGER: CAUSES SEVERE BURNS/CORROSIVE.

- "Danger" is the second strongest signal word.

- Meaning: Spills or ingestion could cause permanent tissue damage to the skin, mouth, throat, and stomach or the product could be very flammable.

- Found on: Cleaning products designed for tough jobs like some oven, toilet bowl, or drain cleaners, and also bleach and spray adhesives.

- "Corrosive" means the product can eat away at different types of materials, including human tissue.

Reading labels can seem daunting—sodium laureth what? But once you know what you're looking for—and what you're not—you'll be able to confidently choose the products you want in your home. Thanks to the Federal Hazardous Substances Act (FHSA), you can usually tell how toxic a product is in one glance at the label. FHSA requires manufacturers of hazardous household substances to use a simple code that ranges from "poison" to "caution" to tell consumers how dangerous the product can be to their health. These labels usually also include directions on how to use the products safely and what to do if there's an accident.

Reading labels is essential since the average home contains 3–10 gallons of hazardous products that we use for everything from cleaning our homes, cars, and bodies to caring for our furniture and ridding our gardens of pests. It's not surprising that 90 percent of all accidental poisonings happen at home. But researchers are also finding that, even when used safely, certain household chemicals are absorbed by our bodies and never leave. Instead we carry them around with us in our fat tissues or bloodstreams where they have more time to cause damage to our cells and our health, possibly contributing to the rise in asthma rates as well as other chronic diseases.

Use the graphics in this chapter for easy reference to buy the cleanest and safest products for your home and health.

Medium hazard

WARNING: FLAMMABLE.

- "Warning" is a common signal word on cleaning products.

- Meaning: Flammable or moderately toxic, but not likely to produce permanent damage if handled properly.

- Found on: some toilet bowl cleaners, flea sprays, and other cleaning products.

- This product is flammable which means it can catch fire easily with increased temperature or a nearby spark. Another word to look for is combustible.

Low to Medium Hazard

CAUTION: IRRITANT.

- "Caution" is the most common label on cleaning products.

- Meaning: Slightly toxic, which tells you that you can ingest more before the product is fatal. This does not tell you about long-term risks like cancer.

- Found on: dishwasher detergent, glass cleaner, all-purpose cleaners, sealant, insecticide, rat poison, and other products.

- An irritant means prolonged or repeated use can cause injury to the area of the body that is in contact with it.

THE DIRTY 8
Your cheat sheet for toxins you don't want in your home

Wouldn't it be great to be able to recognize and understand all those unpronounceable words on ingredient lists so we could keep the worst of them out of our homes? Here's a great place to start: The Dirty 8 are some of the most common and toxic chemicals you'll find in your cleaning and medicine cabinets.

These first four ingredients are very common in household products, so both your family's exposure and the environment's exposure may be high. For example, antibacterial ingredients are now found in over 700 product categories, including everything from sponges and cutting boards to mattresses and mascara. Yet the EPA finds soap and water as or more effective in killing bacteria. Fragrance is so common that we have to look harder to find unscented products than

Antibacterials

Major polluter

- Antibacterial products contain EPA-registered pesticides and they may be contributing to a rise in resistant bacteria.

- Studies show that the most common, triclosan, is contaminating our waterways and has been linked to reproductive malformations in fish.

- When triclosan is exposed to sunlight and chlorinated water, it can convert to dioxin, a known carcinogen.

- These products have not been proven safe or effective. Regular washing with soap and water is as or more effective for killing bacteria.

Artificial Fragrance

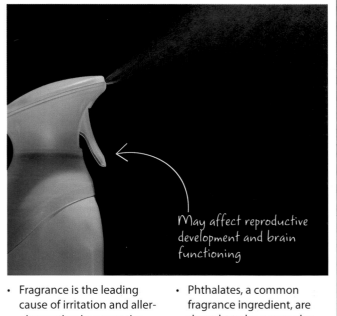

May affect reproductive development and brain functioning

- Fragrance is the leading cause of irritation and allergic reaction in cosmetics.

- Most artificial fragrance ingredients are petroleum-based, a nonrenewable resource, and they do not readily biodegrade in the environment.

- Phthalates, a common fragrance ingredient, are thought to be a reproductive toxin and are linked to the feminization of boys.

- Toluene, another common fragrance ingredient, is a neurotoxin that can damage the liver, kidney, and brain.

scented ones. But manufacturers are not required to list the ingredients that go into those scents.

Phosphates, which soften the water so detergents clean more effectively, are relatively low on the toxic scale for our immediate exposure. But because of their severe impact on the environment, most laundry detergent companies and some states have banned them. Still, phosphates persist as an ingredient in almost all automatic dishwashing detergents.

Sodium hydroxide, also known as lye, is one of the reasons oven and drain cleaners are so immediately toxic. It is an extreme respiratory, skin, and eye irritant bottled in a spray container for oven cleaners, making it very difficult to avoid body contact.

Buying products that are free of these ingredients requires a little extra label scrutiny, but the benefits of not using them far outweigh the costs of using them. Once you find a few brands you trust, you'll have no problem making greener choices for your home and family.

Phosphate

Polluting waterways and killing off fish

Sodium Hydroxide

Extreme irritant

- Phosphates are found in almost all automatic dish-washing detergents and some all-purpose cleaners.

- They soften water and help detergents clean.

- But they are also fertilizers that cause excessive algae bloom, polluting waterways and killing off fish and vegetation.

- The problem is so wide-spread that phosphates have been mostly phased out in laundry detergents and some states have banned them completely.

- Sodium hydroxide is found in drain, metal, and oven cleaners and is also called lye, caustic soda, white caustic, and soda lye.

- Sodium hydroxide's toxic effects are immediate. It can cause severe damage to eyes, skin, and mucous membranes, as well as to the digestive system.

- Tests on people showed respiratory irritation with only two to fifteen minutes of exposure.

- Animals have gone blind with very minimal exposure.

3

THE DIRTY 8 (CONTINUED)
Four more toxins to avoid

The last four of the Dirty 8 include chemicals that are called synthetic surfactants and solvents. Surfactants are also called "surface active agents" reduce water surface tension and basically make the water wetter. This enables the detergents to lather up, spread out, penetrate stains, and wash them away. Surfactants are not always specified on product labels but are usually petroleum-based. One surfactant; to look for is al-kyl polyglycoside. It is plant-based, which makes it a greener surfactant. Petroleum-based surfactants can be contaminated with known carcinogens, and they are not well regulated by the government.

APEs (alkylphenol ethoxylates), DEAs (diethanolamines), and SLS (sodium lauryl sulfate) are all surfactants that are commonly used in household products. SLS and its cousin

APEs

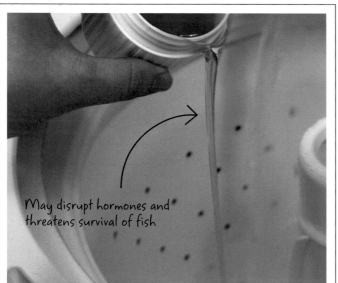

May disrupt hormones and threatens survival of fish

- APEs are a family of synthetic surfactants found in laundry detergents, disinfectants, all-purpose cleaners, and hard surface cleaners.

- Though APEs do not have severe immediate toxic effects, they are suspected long-term endocrine disrupters that have been linked to the stimulation of breast cancer cell growth.

- Researchers have found APEs in 69 percent of nationwide water samples.

- They may be reducing the reproduction and survival rates of salmon and other types of fish.

Diethanolamines (DEA) and Triethanolamines (TEA)

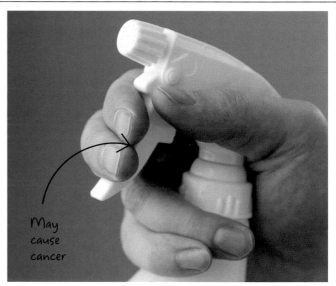

May cause cancer

- DEA and TEA are synthetic surfactants that also work to neutralize acids to make products less irritating to skin.

- They are found in all-purpose cleaners, hand dishwashing liquids, detergents, stain removers, and personal care products.

- They are carcinogenic, skin, eye, and respiratory irritants, and very slow to biodegrade in the environment.

- DEA and TEA react with nitrites that are often used as preservatives but not listed on labels and form nitrosamines, a family of known carcinogens.

SLFS (sodium laureth sulfate) are especially pervasive in personal care products, such as body washes, shampoos, and soaps. Yet, workers who interact with these two chemicals are told to avoid body contact because they are toxic. They have also been found to be contaminated with 1,4-dioxane, a strongly suspected carcinogen.

Solvents are also important toxins to be aware of. Solvents are common ingredients in many household cleaning and paint products because they keep other ingredients from separating and the product in its liquid state. They also dissolve dirt without leaving a film or other residue. However, because they're soluble in fat, they are easily absorbed by the body and can enter the brain, where they may cause damage. Solvents also contaminate waterways and soil.

Butyl cellosolve is just one of the many toxic solvents you'll find in everyday household use. A few of the others to look for and avoid are: ethyl cellosolve, ethylene glycol, petroleum distillates, petroleum hydrocarbons, hexane, toluene, benzene, xylene, and perchloroethylene (PERC).

Sodium Lauryl/Laureth Sulfate (SLS and SLFS)

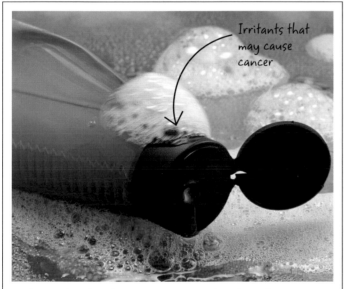

Irritants that may cause cancer

- These related surfactants are found in any type of product that produces lather.

- They can cause severe skin and eye irritation and have been linked to abnormal eye development in children.

- Studies show they can react with other ingredients in these products to produce carcinogenic nitrosamines and dioxin.

- They have also been found to be lethal to fish at low levels of exposure.

Butyl Cellosolve

Can cause damage to brain and nervous system

- Synthetic solvent found in all-purpose, glass, and abrasive cleaners. It's also found in auto products, floor polish, inks, leather goods, paint thinners, pesticides, and home furnishings.

- Butyl cellosolve is a known neurotoxin.

- It is also a suspected blood, kidney, and liver toxin, and endocrine disrupter.

- Its immediate toxic effects include eye, nose, throat, and lung-tissue irritation.

GREEN LABEL PRIMER
Know the label claims you can trust and those you can't

Products can look green, smell green, and have a lineup of good-looking certification seals telling us they don't support animal abuse, contain toxins, or harm the environment. But not all of these seals are created equally. This does not mean that the companies who use them aren't being truthful, but that the most reliable seals are those that are well-defined and well-regulated by third-party organizations.

Knowing how a claim term like "organic" is defined can make a big difference in your purchasing decisions. Does it mean all ingredients are organic, or just a few? What if the ingredients are organic but synthetic chemicals are part of the processing? Currently *USDA-certified Organic* is the most specific and best-regulated measure of organic products.

USDA Organic

Green Seal

- This certifies that fruits, vegetables, meat, and poultry are free of synthetic pesticides, fertilizers, antibiotics, genetic engineering, irradiation, and sewage sludge.

- There are three levels of organic certification: 100 percent Organic contains only organic ingredients and can bear the USDA logo.

- Organic products that contain 95 percent organic ingredients can also use the logo.

- Products that contain 70 percent organic ingredients can't use the USDA logo but can use the independent certifier's logo.

- This certifies that cleaning, personal care, and paper products are environmentally sound from manufacturing to disposal.

- Green Seal cleaners can't contain toxic ingredients and especially do not contain known mutagens, reproductive toxins, or carcinogens.

- Certified products can't be combustible or contain ingredients that pollute the air.

- Any fragrance must be listed on product labels and the product must be biodegradable.

"Nontoxic" is another slippery term. One manufacturer's toxin is another's "safe" food additive. *Green Seal* is a third-party testing organization that is working to standardize what it means for a product to be nontoxic throughout its life cycle, from manufacturing to disposal.

For animal testing, the major gray area is that companies that don't test on animals themselves may subcontract to labs or suppliers that do. The Coalition for Consumer Information on Cosmetics (CCIC) is working to standardize and regulate what it means to not test on animals with their *Leaping Bunny Program*. CCIC consists of the Humane Society and

Beauty without Cruelty, along with other animal protection groups from around the world.

Wood is another murky topic in the green world. Wood products are thought of as more natural and green than, say, plastics. But, without regulation, harvesting wood can mean a whole host of environmental woes, including clear-cutting and illegally harvesting endangered woods like teak. The *Forest Stewardship Council* (FSC) helps to identify wood from well-managed forests that are held to strict environmental and social standards.

Leaping Bunny

- Found on cleaners as well as skin care products, oral hygiene products, sun care products, and cosmetics.

- Certifies that the product was produced in compliance with the Corporate Standard of Compassion for Animals developed by CCIC.

- Certified manufacturers do not conduct animal testing for their products or for the individual ingredients that go into those products.

- They also do not subcontract any firms to perform animal testing of ingredients, formulations, or finished products on their behalf.

Forest Stewardship Council

- FSC certifies that wood is harvested from "well-managed" forests.

- That means the wood is harvested in a way that is environmentally responsible in terms of the type of wood harvested and the rate of harvest, among other factors.

- FSC forests must also be socially responsible with respect to protecting workers' rights, indigenous land rights, and the rights of people who live in surrounding areas.

- Genetically engineered wood is not FSC wood.

ANATOMY OF A GREEN PRODUCT
Judging a green product by its packaging

You can tell a lot about a product by its packaging, and even its lack of packaging. Here are some telltale signs of a not-so-green product: Product is double or triple wrapped, packaged in nonrenewable materials like vinyl with brightly colored glossy labels, and packaging is neither made of recycled materials nor recyclable in most locations. In fact, statistics show that if every home restricted their purchasing to products with minimal or no packaging, 5.5 billion pounds of garbage would be kept out of the landfills.

The "chasing arrows" logo enclosed in a circle means that the packaging contains recycled materials. For paper products, federal standards indicate that a product should con-

Postconsumer Waste Recycled

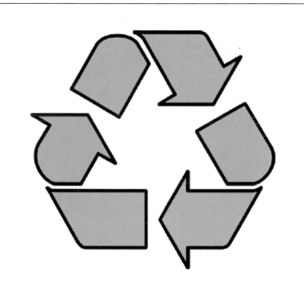

- Packaging made from PCW recycled materials means that it uses paper or metal that was used by consumers and then recycled.

- Non-PCW recycled is generally the waste material from manufacturing new products.

- Choose those with the highest percentage of PCW recycled materials you can find.

- Ideally PCW recycled paper will also be Processed Chlorine Free (PCF) meaning the paper was not bleached with chlorine, a process that pollutes both air and waterways.

Recyclable

- Packaging for green products should also be easily recyclable.

- That means it will be made of paper or either #1 or #2 plastics, which are the easiest to recycle no matter where you live.

- Green products should also have only minimal or no packaging.

- Think twice before buying a blanket made of organic cotton packaged in cardboard and then wrapped in PVC, which is rarely recyclable.

tain at least 30 percent postconsumer waste (PCW) to display this logo. The greenest packaging is made from 100 percent PCW recycled materials and is also recyclable. PCW means the product is made from materials that have already been used and placed into the recycling bin by consumers and then transformed into this new material. Recycled material that is not PCW usually is waste from the manufacturing process itself—scraps of unused materials left over from creating new products. Buying PCW recycled goods is an im-

portant step in closing the recycling loop. The existence of recycling programs depends on there being a market for recycled materials. Without that market, those programs would disappear.

Green packaging also uses nontoxic coloring. Since conventional inks and dyes are petroleum-based and give off volatile organic compounds (VOCs) that pollute the air, green manufacturers are turning to plant- and especially soy-based inks and dyes that give off far less VOCs.

Inks and Dyes

- Conventional inks and dyes are typically petroleum-based, which is a non-renewable resource.

- They also have high levels of VOCs that can mix with other pollutants in the air to form smog.

- Soy inks and dyes have substantially less VOC emissions.

- They are also easier to recycle because they can be removed from the paper much more effectively than petroleum inks. Therefore, less hazardous waste is created in the process.

Buying Bulk

- Green products should be available in larger containers.

- Buying bulk can save you money, and it reduces the amount of fossil fuels and energy to transport the products to sell and to dispose of or recycle.

- You are also reducing the amount of waste you're sending to the landfill or recycling center.

- Hang on to your smaller shampoo bottles and other containers so you can easily refill them from larger bottles.

WHAT'S IN A PRODUCT'S CLAIM?

See through the "green washing"

When you scan the shelves of green home products, typical claims include *biodegradable*, *nontoxic, eco-friendly*, and *natural*. Some products use their labels to let you know that they are free from certain chemicals or that their ingredients come from plants, not petroleum sources. Unfortunately, a number of companies are capitalizing on the green wave by making claims on their labels that suggest their products are green when they aren't. This is called "green washing."

Many of these claims are so nonspecific or even contradictory that they really don't tell you anything about the product. For example, since there is no agreed-upon and regulated definition for *eco-friendly*, the claim may identify a green

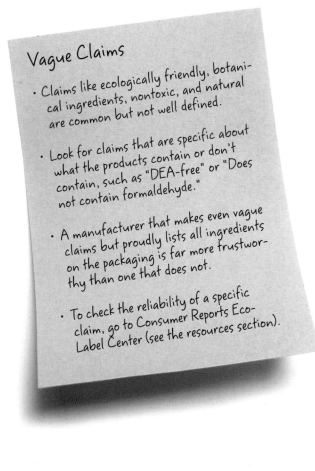

Vague Claims

- Claims like ecologically friendly, botanical ingredients, nontoxic, and natural are common but not well defined.

- Look for claims that are specific about what the products contain or don't contain, such as "DEA-free" or "Does not contain formaldehyde."

- A manufacturer that makes even vague claims but proudly lists all ingredients on the packaging is far more trustworthy than one that does not.

- To check the reliability of a specific claim, go to Consumer Reports Eco-Label Center (see the resources section).

Biodegradable

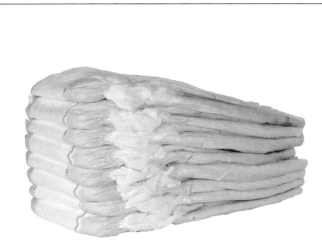

- Most products will biodegrade eventually give or take one hundred years, so look for claims that are time-specific.

- However, keep in mind that products like disposable diapers that go directly to the landfill will generally not readily biodegrade.

- Landfill waste is not exposed to the natural conditions it needs to break down.

- Look for materials that are "compostable." Your compost heap will be much more effective than the landfill in breaking down the material.

product held to strict environmental standards, or it may be a green-washing claim for a product that contains one organic ingredient and forty synthetic ingredients, some of which are toxic. Since ingredient lists are hardly ever complete or understandable, we need to know how to read these claims for content.

The most specific and defined claims are the most preferable—think "Made from recycled materials" vs. "100 percent postconsumer waste-recycled." The latter tells you volumes that the former leaves out. It's important to also be educated about which chemicals have already been banned from certain product categories. For example, aerosol cans that claim "No CFCs" are guilty of green washing since CFCs were banned in the 1970s. Read the entire label so you can catch conflicting claims, such as a cleaner that swears it is nontoxic on the front yet bears a hazardous product warning on the back.

In general, look for products that make very specific claims and stand behind them by proudly displaying their ingredient lists.

Stating the Obvious

Contains no brussel sprouts!

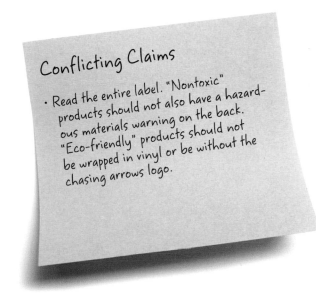

Conflicting Claims

- Read the entire label. "Nontoxic" products should not also have a hazardous materials warning on the back. "Eco-friendly" products should not be wrapped in vinyl or be without the chasing arrows logo.

- Be wary of products that claim to be free of chemicals that are generally not found in that product class.

- "Phosphate-free" on automatic dishwashing detergents tells you a lot about the product because most do contain phosphates.

- The same claim on laundry detergent is meaningless because phosphates have been largely phased out of that product class.

- Similarly, some products make claims that are not applicable to their category, such as "organic" nail polish.

BACK TO BASICS
Essential inexpensive green-cleaning ingredients for your home

One of the biggest myths about "going green" is that it costs a lot more than doing things the conventional way. When it comes to green cleaning, the exact opposite is true. In fact, it can be far less expensive to clean without toxins than it is to clean with them.

Of course, you could spend the 10 to 30 percent extra to replace each of your conventional cleaners with a green one. Yet, having so many distinct products is unnecessary, and it's cheaper and just as easy to create your own out of just a few ingredients you probably already have in your home.

As your grandmother (or hers) already knows, these basic ingredients work great. Plus, you won't have to worry about

White Distilled Vinegar

- Vinegar disinfects, loosens dirt, and deodorizes. It also removes mineral deposits, stains, and tarnish, and eliminates static cling when added to the rinse cycle.

- Look for white distilled vinegar with 5 percent acetic acid. Dark vinegars stain.

- Alternative: Lemon juice works to cut grease or polish metal. You can buy bottled lemon juice, but you'll use more than if you squeeze.

- Do not use on acid-sensitive surfaces such as marble.

Baking Soda

- Baking soda is just abrasive enough to make a great scrubber that won't damage most surfaces.

- It also eats odor and works as a deodorizer for carpets, refrigerators, and drains. Add it to the wash cycle to soften fabric.

- Mixing this alkaline with acidic vinegar will make it fizz and speed up your cleaning. This is great for toilets and to clear blocked drains.

- Look for baking soda that is "pure" or "100 percent sodium bicarbonate."

whether a green-marketed product is actually green or wonder about ingredients that aren't listed on the label. The recipes you'll find throughout this book are based on these essential ingredients so you can buy in bulk to save money and packaging.

As you get started, there may be some products you choose to buy for convenience or because you like how they work. In each section, this book will note what to look for when buying green so you can choose the best products with ease and confidence.

Castile Soap

- Castile soap means soap made only from vegetable oil instead of animal fat.

- Diluted castile soap can be used as an all-purpose cleaner, laundry or dish soap, spot remover, and body washer.

- Look for "Pure Castile" that is non-petroleum-based and does not contain detergents. The greenest choices use organic ingredients and come in 100 percent postconsumer-waste recycled packaging.

- Buying in bulk is a great idea because castile soap is so versatile.

Borax and Washing Soda

- These alkaline minerals are like baking soda but stronger and more caustic, so wear gloves and store out of reach of children.

- Add either borax or washing soda to your wash for extra cleaning and brightening or use to scrub extra-stubborn stains on counters or bathtubs.

- Use borax to disinfect and whiten cloth diapers or as a highly effective mold killer and toilet bowl cleaner.

- Mix washing soda and baking soda to clean dirty (non-self-cleaning) ovens.

ANTIBACTERIAL ARSENAL

Healthy, safe ingredients to combat germs

An easy way to save money and do something great for your health and the environment is to avoid antibacterial cleaning products and replace them with regular use of nontoxic soap and water, vinegar, and essential oils. Research shows that antibacterial products don't work any better than regular soap and water in eliminating germs. Yet their cost to the environment and our health can be great.

Most antibacterial products contain antimicrobial pesticides, of which triclosan is the most common. Triclosan has been found in 57.6 percent of U.S. waterways, making it one of the most prevalent contaminants out there. Even more compelling, researchers have found a strong link between triclosan and dioxin, considered by many to be one of the most dangerous chemicals ever tested and highly carcino-

Soap and Water

- Experts agree that soap and water are just as effective as but less harmful than antibacterial products.

- Soap reduces surface tension of water and creates a thin film around dirt molecules, bacteria, and even viruses. It captures them and transports them down the drain.

- Soap and water can effectively clean everything from your table and countertops to carpet and fabric stains.

- Look for vegetable-based, non-petroleum, detergent-free, and fragrance-free soaps. Use warm water for fighting germs.

Vinegar

- Although not an EPA-registered pesticide, studies show that distilled white vinegar kills 99 percent of bacteria, 82 percent of mold, and 80 percent of germs.

- For best results, soak or spray and leave vinegar on the affected area. Only rinse

on delicate surfaces.

- Vinegar can be used to disinfect laundry, household filters, cutting boards, and just about anything.

- Keep a spray bottle of straight vinegar handy to clean up any problem areas quickly and easily.

genic. Studies show that triclosan is often contaminated with dioxin and can convert to dioxin when exposed to sunlight or treated with chlorine in water treatment plants. If that's not enough, strong evidence suggests that the overuse of antibacterial products is causing an increase in allergies and the creation of drug-resistant bacteria.

For a greener approach, washing your hands and home regularly and incorporating these natural products into your cleaning regimen are all you need for a healthy home.

ZOOM

When washing your hands, use regular, nontoxic soap, such as castile or glycerin. Make sure you lather up for a full fifteen to twenty seconds. The soap bubbles surround the bacteria and take it with them when they're rinsed down the drain. Rinse thoroughly. Use a clean towel to dry your hands and remove any remaining bacteria.

Tea Tree Oil

- Tea tree oil is a fungicide and antibacterial that has been used for centuries.

- It's potent, so a little goes a long way. Anti-mold spray needs only 1 teaspoon tea tree oil to 2 cups water.

- Adding a few drops to soap and water can enhance antibacterial effects.

- Look for "100 percent pure essential oil" rather than "fragrant," "perfume," or "aromatherapy" oil, which may mean synthetic. The bottle should be dark amber or blue glass for a longer shelf life.

Lavender Oil

- Lavender is a great choice if you don't like the smell of tea tree oil.

- Lavender-scented cleaning products give you the added benefit of calming and mood-lifting aromatherapy.

- Add a few drops to a vaporizer to fight colds and infections, Add to all-purpose or glass cleaner or dilute with water to make an antibacterial spray.

- Watch out for synthetic versions and buy only 100 percent essential oil in dark glass containers.

SPONGES AND SCRUBBERS

Go natural for nontoxic cleaning tools that are better for the environment

For such a simple product, the array of sponges and scrubbers now available is mind-boggling. When searching for the right sponge, avoid ones that say *antibacterial, odor free, fights germs,* or make any other claim that suggests they might be laden with pesticides (see page 2). Yet, sponges can collect bad bacteria that might pose a health risk, which is why some experts suggest throwing out your sponge each week to prevent its spread.

But there is a less wasteful and equally effective alternative for keeping your sponges clean: Microwave your sponge for thirty seconds, and you can kill nearly all bacteria except E. coli. Microwave for a full minute, and you can kill the E. coli

Natural Cellulose Sponges

- Natural cellulose sponges are made from wood pulp.

- The empty spaces absorb liquids and anything in the liquid, including dirt and bacteria, and the surface tension of the water keeps it from leaking out until you squeeze it.

- Microwaving or replacing often is imperative so bacteria does not grow in the sponge's empty spaces.

- Even natural sponges can be coated with pesticides; be sure to read the entire label.

Loofah Sponges

- Loofah is a gourd so it's renewable, biodegradable, and not a petroleum product.

- While loofahs are more common in the bath as an exfoliating tool, a few companies are introducing them as kitchen scrubbers.

- Loofahs can collect bacteria like any sponge, so be sure to keep them dry and disinfect them regularly.

- Wet the sponge thoroughly and place in the microwave for a minute. Give it some time to cool before removing and squeezing.

and 99.9 percent of all other bacteria. If you don't have a microwave, boil the sponge for three to five minutes for the same effect. Throw the sponge out when you can see rips and tears in the surface fibers. These will only encourage the growth of bacteria.

Choosing the right sponge is a great opportunity to do something for the environment. Choose sponges and scrubbers made from renewable resources like natural cellulose or loofah and make sure they are unscented and chemical-free.

GREEN TOOLS

Multiuse Wood-Pulp Cloth

- Look for cloths made from natural wood pulp, which are odor-resistant, and more absorbent than a cotton cloth.

- Layers of fiber hold in dirt and water until you rinse them with clean water.

- Wood-pulp cloths feel like silk, but they do a great job scrubbing delicate surfaces without scratching.

- To clean: Rinse, wring out, and hang to dry after use. Throw them in the washing machine weekly and add ¼ cup vinegar to the rinse cycle to disinfect.

Hemp Abrasive Scrubbers

- Hemp is naturally coarse so it's perfect for scrubbing tough pots and pans or grout.

- Hemp is fast-growing and requires very little water and pest control.

- Hemp is naturally antibacterial, which means hemp scrubbers will outlast your sponges and cloths and need less maintenance cleaning—although it's still important to wring them out and let them dry between uses.

- Hemp is also machine-washable.

SOFT CLOTHS
Find the perfect cloth for the job and help the environment along the way

Paper towels have long been the cleaning cloth of choice. They're convenient and disposable so you don't have to deal with the muck. However, substantially reducing the use of paper towels can help in the fight to stop deforestation and reduce chemical pollution resulting from the bleaching process. If you must use paper, look for the "Processed Chlorine Free" (PCF) label and buy a recycled product with a high percentage of postconsumer waste (PCW).

Other types of cloths perform the same or better on any household cleaning job, and many of these cloths can be recycled out of old clothes—saving both the discarded paper towels and the clothing from the landfill.

Old T-Shirt

- Use cotton T-shirts to dust, polish, and wipe any surface.

- The more they've been worn and washed the better because all the finishes will have worn off, and they'll be softer and more absorbent.

- Conserve rags by starting with the cleanest job, such as the mirror, and progress to the dirtier job, such as the toilet.

- Throw dirty rags in the washer and add vinegar to the rinse cycle or washing soda to the wash cycle to disinfect.

Wool Socks

- Old wool socks make excellent dusting tools, especially if you're delegating to children.

- Rotate the sock around your hand as each side gets filled up with dust.

- To make sure the dust stays on the socks instead of

being pushed around, keep them slightly damp or use the damp dusting spray (see page 39).

- Dusting socks can be washed with the rest of your rags and reused indefinitely.

Using the right cloth can also improve the efficiency and quality of your cleaning experience. It can mean the difference between scattering the dust and actually removing the dust or achieving a semi-clean window and creating a spotless window. The key is to find the cloth that has the right properties for the job.

Flannel

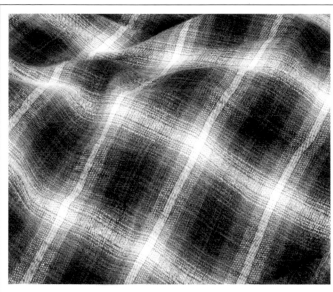

- Cotton flannel attracts dust and holds it to the fabric.

- It also makes a great polishing cloth for metal or wood because it's soft and won't scratch.

- To create dusting or polishing cloths, remove buttons and cut your old shirts into 6x9 rectangles and fold in half. As one section fills up with dust, flip or refold to a clean section.

- Throw in the washer with rags and reuse indefinitely.

Microfiber

- Microfiber has become the duster of choice for the 21st century.

- Made from polyester and nylon, it is a petroleum-based product, but its ability to trap dust and bacteria without using a cleaning solution and its reusability make it worthy of consideration even for a green household.

- Microfiber is particularly good for dusting where using any kind of moisture or cleaning solution would cause damage, such as electronics or art.

VACUUMS

Look for high-quality vacuums to improve indoor air quality

Studies show that inside air is four times dirtier than outside air, and dust is a big contributor to the problem. Your vacuum is your most important tool for controlling dust in your home. But make sure the vacuum itself has low emissions or you may be counteracting its air-cleaning benefits.

Besides cleaning the air, regular vacuuming can make area rugs and floors last longer. With the right attachments, vacuums can also be used to speed cleaning and reduce the need for cleaning products on upholstery, window treatments, mattresses, and bookshelves.

If someone in your family suffers from allergies, you'll want to stick to the models that use disposable bags to minimize

CLEAN HOME, GREEN HOME

Types of Vacuums

- Uprights used to be for carpets and canisters for hard floors, but the distinction has blurred.

- Many upright vacuums now allow you to turn the brush off and have attachments that make it easier to clean bare floors.

- Canisters generally do better for upholstery and drapes. They're easier to maneuver on stairs and under furniture.

- Choose a vacuum that's not too heavy, doesn't require you to hunch over when you use it, and has accessible attachment placement.

Bags

- Bagless vacuums collect dust and dirt in a bin, which you then empty into your garbage can.

- This helps you reduce waste and costs because there are no special bags to buy.

- However, bagless vacuums can be hard on people with

- allergies because emptying the bin can kick up a lot of dust and allergens.

- Most bagged vacuums lose suction when the bag is only partially full, which means you change the bags more often.

your contact with dust. A HEPA filter is also crucial.

If allergies are not a problem, you can reduce waste by buying a bagless vacuum. Some other types of filters work as well or almost as well as HEPA filters and cost less, so do your homework and compare ratings, such as those found in *Consumer Reports*.

Poor-quality vacuums can break easily and be expensive to fix. If you're buying a new vacuum, make sure the one you choose will last as long as possible. Look for vacuums that have washable lifetime filters and long-term warranties.

ZOOM

What's in that dust you're vacuuming? Unhealthy particles in the air can include tobacco smoke, dirt, pet dander, pollen, and dust mite waste. But HEPA filters can also trap some of the chemical off-gassing from household products. These include neurotoxic flame retardants, endocrine disrupting phthalates, as well as toxic pesticides.

Attachments

- Most vacuums come with a crevice tool, small brush, upholstery tool, and floor tool.

- Other options include motorized pet hair removal heads, car kit attachments, stair tool, and different-sized brushes and floor tools.

- Extra attachments can add to the price of your vacuum. Consider which ones will be useful and which will be clutter.

- Store the most-used attachments in a mesh bag tied to the handle of your vacuum so they're readily accessible.

Special Features
- Brush on/off switch
- Manual pile-height adjustment
- HEPA or other high-quality filter
- Low emissions
- Long-term warranty

CLEAN GREEN SMELLS
Natural ways to make your home smell clean

We all know a clean home when we smell it. But just how clean is that smell? The smell of conventional cleaning products can make you feel queasy or give you a colossal headache, and those are just the effects you notice right away.

What smells "clean" often truly isn't, and toxic cleaners—and especially air fresheners—can leave behind more trouble than they're worth. Rather than clean out the smells, most air fresheners simply mask unpleasant smells, which may include lingering dirty house smells or even ammonia from your cleaning products. It's no wonder that indoor air is so much more polluted than outdoor air.

But nature has no shortage of sweet-smelling offerings that

Lavender

- Considering that the word "lavender" comes from the Latin *lavare,* which means "to wash," lavender is a natural choice for a clean home smell.

- A vase of fresh or dried lavender on the table or positioned in front of a window on a breezy day can make your entire home smell clean.

- Lavender sachets can do wonders for a stuffy closet.

- As aromatherapy, lavender is considered a natural antidepressant and can help you fall asleep.

Eucalyptus

- A few sprigs of eucalyptus in a vase can give your home an energizing, uplifting scent.

- The smell of eucalyptus also has medicinal properties that can help with colds, congestion, and allergies.

- Fresh eucalyptus will last for twenty days or longer if you rinse and then cut the stems underwater.

- To dry eucalyptus, bind stems of a few sprigs and hang upside down in a dry and well-ventilated area.

can leave a house smelling, well, clean. Here are just a few natural products that can create the smell of the new green clean in your home.

Nontoxic Candles

- Nonpetroleum candle options include beeswax, soy, and other vegetable-based waxes.

- Aromatherapy candles should be made with 100 percent pure essential oils. Synthetic fragrances can emit toxic VOCs like neurotoxic toluene and benzene.

- Metal wicks may contain neurotoxic lead. Look for all-cotton wicks instead.

- To get the most out of pillar candles, make sure the first burn is long enough to establish a wide burn pool—at least two hours for a 2-inch and four to five hours for a 3-inch diameter candle.

Essential Oils

- Essential oils can create a subtle clean scent for your home.

- Make a diffuser by adding a few drops of the oil to a small bowl of water placed over a tea light.

- Mix up a room-freshening spray by adding 1 teaspoon of essential oil with 1 cup of water in a spray bottle.

- Make sure you buy only 100 percent pure essential oils with no synthetic ingredients.

23

THE ART OF HAND WASHING
A greener way to wash dishes by hand

When it comes to cleaning, low-tech cleaning solutions are often the greener ones, such as using vinegar instead of a product designed in a lab to clean your floors. But it's not always this obvious. Although automatic dishwashers require resources to build and distribute and they need electricity to clean, most experts agree that using an automatic dishwasher is more eco-friendly than hand washing. This is because the average dishwasher uses 3.5 gallons of water per load while the typical hand washer uses 15 to 16 gallons.

If you don't have a dishwasher—or you have an old one that requires you to basically wash the dishes before putting the dishes in the dishwasher—you can hand-wash without

Wash without Waste

- Fill one side of your sink or a plastic tub with enough clean, hot, soapy water to cover a load of dishes.

- Partially fill the other side of your sink or tub with clean rinse water.

- Without turning the water back on, wash the glass-ware, then flatware, then already-scraped plates, then pots and pans.

- Rinse and place on drying rack. Change water in sinks or tubs as needed.

Easy Dry

- Look for a rack that will fit all the dishes you use in a normal meal.

- Make sure your rack is either over the sink or on a mat that drains the water back into the sink.

- To prolong the life of your dish rack and mat, put away the dishes as soon as they are dry.

- Prevent mold and mildew by leaning the mat up against the rack to let it dry thoroughly.

wasting all this water. The key is to set up a system to reduce your water use without compromising cleanliness. Making or using nontoxic, natural dishwashing soap also helps and is a great alternative to automatic dishwashing detergent which has more of an environmental impact.

Pans

- Steel wool is tempting for scrubbing baked-on food, but it can also ruin your pans. Try this instead:

- Sprinkle ¼ cup baking soda into the bottom of the pan.

- Boil water in a teakettle or pot and fill the pan with the boiling water so that all of the baked-on food is covered.

- Let soak overnight and then wash and dry as usual.

Pots

- There's no need to wear yourself out scrubbing burned pots with this technique:

- Pour ¼ cup of regular table salt into the bottom of the pot.

- Add cold water so that all of the burned areas are covered. Stir mixture.

- Let sit overnight, then scrub, wash, and dry as usual.

AUTOMATIC DISHWASHING
Green strategies for sparkling dishes and a clean environment

Washing dishes in the dishwasher doesn't have to be a feat of massive energy-consuming proportions. With greener detergents, energy-efficient machinery, and a good strategy that everyone in your family can use, you can make washing the dishes an eco-friendly affair. If you have an ENERGY STAR–rated machine, you're already on the right path to conserv-ing resources, but it's still important that you only wash full, well-organized loads at off-peak hours, such as at night right before going to bed.

Most dishwasher detergents contain ingredients that harm the environment and are irritating to our bodies. Powdered detergents can contain phosphates that can cause algae

Detergents: What to Avoid

- Labels do not always list all ingredients, but this warning is your first cue.

- Most dish detergents are petroleum-based and contain phosphates, fragrance, color, and chlorine.

- Some contain alkyphenol ethoxylates (APEs), a suspected hormone disruptor that does not readily biode-grade and can be contaminated with the carcinogen 1,4-dioxane.

- Other common ingredients: Diethanolamine (DEA) and triethanolamine (TEA), which can react with nitrites, used as a preservative, to form nitrosamines, a carcinogen.

Detergents: What to Look for

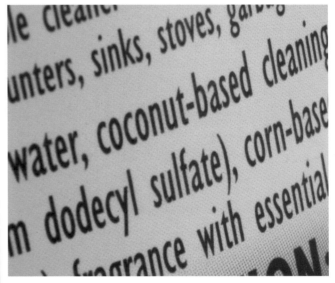

- The first indication that this is a good choice is that all of the ingredients are listed right on the bottle.

- Additionally, this is a fragrance-, chlorine-, dye-, and phosphate-free product.

- The ingredients are mostly plant- and mineral-based.

- This product is better than most, but given that all detergents are synthetic, there aren't currently completely green options in this category.

blooms in our waterways that deplete the supply of oxygen in the water and subsequently kill off other aquatic life. Phosphates already have been banned in laundry detergents, but they are still around—and legal—in dishwashing detergents. Most detergents also contain chlorine, which is especially harsh to our lungs and skin when combined with the hot water from the dishwasher. Dyes that go into brightly colored detergents may be contaminated with arsenic, lead, or other heavy metals.

Chemicals called surfactants are another concern. These agents reduce surface tension of the water (or make water wetter) so it can spread over a surface more easily. Almost all surfactants are derived from petroleum and have been shown to have neurotoxic and carcinogenic impact with prolonged exposure. According to some experts, even when products claim they contain plant-derived surfactants, they are still partially petroleum-based. But it is possible to find more eco-friendly detergents if you know what to look for.

Effective Loading: Top

- If you have a utensil tray, arrange flatware so individual pieces do not overlap or stack and water can flow freely around them.

- Place bowls and saucers down the center with enough space between them for cleaning.

- Place mugs and cups along the sides between prongs. Putting them over the prongs may lead to chipping.

- Hand-wash any glassware that is delicate or prone to falling over, such as stemmed wine glasses and champagne flutes.

Effective Loading: Bottom

- If you have a utensil basket, alternate between placing some flatware pointing up and some down so they don't stack.

- Plates will be cleaner if you mix the sizes together so the water flows more freely around them.

- Place large pieces along the sides after the center is full.

- Hand-wash wood, cast iron, painted dishware, nonstick pans, crystal, and silver.

SHINY SINKS
The dirt on sink cleanliness

We do more cleaning in the kitchen sink than anywhere else in the house. Yet, the sink itself is often one of the more neglected areas in most people's cleaning routines. Without regular cleaning, dirt can build up on the sink, in the seams that join the sink and the counter, and around the faucet. With neglect, the drain can emit odors and become clogged.

How clean can your dishes be if the sink you washed them in is downright grimy? Even with the hottest water and soap, your sponge may be hanging out in a pool of water over a dirt-filled seam, creating the ultimate bacteria-breeding environment.

Because the sink gets so much use, it's a smart idea to give

Stainless Steel

- Cleaning tools: Baking soda, warm water, and three soft cloths.

- Mix ¼ cup of baking soda with a quart of warm water until dissolved.

- Wash sink using solution and a soft cloth. Use a toothbrush for seams and hard-to-get areas of the sink.

- Rinse and wipe dry with a clean soft cloth.

- Finish by polishing with a dry cloth. If you have hard water, use a solution of half vinegar and half water to polish surface.

Porcelain

- Cleaning tools: Castile soap, warm water, and a soft towel or sponge.

- Wash entire sink with sudsy water, paying particular attention to where the sink meets the counter and the drain opening where dirt can get caught.

- Rinse inside of sink with water and use a clean damp cloth to wipe the outside of the sink while minimizing drips to the floor.

- Don't use abrasive pads, wire brushes, or abrasive cleaners that can scratch the surface.

it a good cleaning every week. This will ensure that the sink stays clean and that it never becomes so big a job that you feel like you have to buy a toxic product to scrub it clean. In choosing how you will clean the sink, consider its surface. Maintain its shine and avoid scratching or causing unnecessary wear with overly harsh cleaners or scrubbers. Also, a simple act of drain maintenance each week will keep your drains clean, clear, and odor-free all year.

KITCHEN

Faucet

- Wipe faucet daily with a clean sponge and towel dry.

- Remove mineral deposits by spraying faucet with equal parts vinegar and water and polishing with a soft cloth.

- For a weekly deeper clean, use an old toothbrush to get into all of the crevices around the base, handle, and spout.

- Start with mild dishwashing detergent. If crevices do not come clean, make a paste with baking soda and water and scrub.

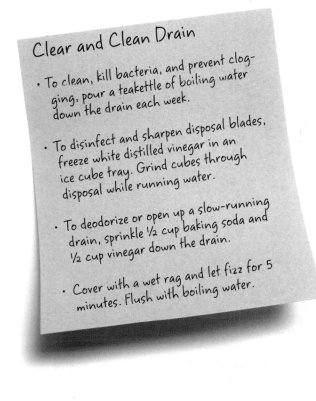

Clear and Clean Drain

- To clean, kill bacteria, and prevent clogging, pour a teakettle of boiling water down the drain each week.

- To disinfect and sharpen disposal blades, freeze white distilled vinegar in an ice cube tray. Grind cubes through disposal while running water.

- To deodorize or open up a slow-running drain, sprinkle ½ cup baking soda and ½ cup vinegar down the drain.

- Cover with a wet rag and let fizz for 5 minutes. Flush with boiling water.

SPOTLESS COUNTERTOPS
Keep your food safe with clean countertops

Keeping countertops clean is serious business because that's where all of your food prep happens. The most obvious danger is the spread of bad bacteria, like Salmonella, that can happen when you don't clean up after slicing raw chicken or missing the bowl when you crack an egg. Daily countertop cleaning along with frequent hand-washing and the use of

cutting boards are important steps in minimizing the risk.

But in a typical busy house, countertop use is not limited to food prep. Counters can be holding zones for everything from mail to antifreeze as well as sites of art and science projects, temporary toddler holding, and flower arranging. Since each of these activities can leave their mark and contaminate

Proactive Steps

- Using cutting boards for everything from carving meat to cutting lemons helps keep your countertops sanitary and in good condition.

- Keep separate glass cutting boards that fit in the dishwasher for raw meat cutting or wooden ones only used for this purpose.

- Wood cutting boards are generally resistant to bacteria and are great for fruits and vegetables, but they don't go in the dishwasher.

- Choose renewable or recycled materials such as bamboo, recycled plastic, or reclaimed Corian.

Cutting Board Care

Scrub with the grain

- Plastic and glass boards should be washed with soap and hot water or run through the dishwasher after every use.

- Wood and bamboo boards should be hand-washed with castile soap and a scrub brush after use.

- To disinfect, routinely coat with antibacterial spray and let dry without rinsing.

- To get deep in the crevices, periodically sprinkle coarse salt on the board and scrub with a cut lemon.

food, it's important to keep the counters as clean as possible. But how you clean them is as important as how often you clean them. Instead of trading bacteria for toxic cleaner residue, use homemade cleaning solutions to keep your counters clean and your food safe.

Use this easy-to-make all-purpose cleaner for nontoxic daily maintenance for most counter types, and this natural antibacterial spray for extra safety.

Easy Counter Clean

- Countertops should be washed every evening.

- Most countertop surfaces, including concrete, butcher block, and stainless steel, will clean well with just castile soap and water.

- Plastic, laminate, or Corian counters can handle an all-purpose cleaner (see above). Don't use an abrasive scrubber or it may scratch.

- Don't forget to wash backsplashes, especially behind the sink and stove.

pH Neutral Cleaning

- Stone, marble, and tile counters require pH-neutral cleaners, like mild dishwashing soap and water.

- Never use acidic cleaners like vinegar or lemon juice on these surfaces because they can be etched by the acid.

- Use a soft bristled brush to dislodge debris from grout. Avoid abrasive pads or cleaners. Studies have found elevated radon emissions from a limited number of granite countertops. If you have granite, it's a good idea to have them tested (see page 156).

KITCHEN

APPLIANCES
Eco-friendly cleaning for the long haul

Regular cleaning of your major kitchen appliances can extend their life spans because dirt and grime don't have a chance to build up and cause damage.

As with everything else, there seems to be a product for every job and every type of appliance in the kitchen, and many are extremely toxic. In fact, oven cleaners are one of the top three most corrosive household products and should be avoided. Corrosive substances can cause severe burning to your eyes, skin, and throat if ingested. Many oven cleaners also contain the known carcinogen benzene and sodium hydroxide, which can cause scarring and blindness. Luckily, with today's self-cleaning function, there is little need for such a harsh product.

Stainless-steel appliances look sleek but need to be cleaned

Refrigerator

Shelves slide out

Removable drawers

- Remove all food from your refrigerator and all shelves and bins.

- Wipe down interior with a sponge dipped in castile soap and water. Use a scrubber for problem spots.

- Wash each component in the sink and dry before reassembling. Add an open box of baking soda to absorb odors and change boxes every three months.

- Use soap or all-purpose cleaner (see page 31) to wipe down external doors and handles.

Dishwasher

- If your dishwasher smells or loses efficiency, it's time to clean it.

- Use warm, soapy water and a sponge to scrub the door and inside cavity. A toothbrush works well in dirty crevices.

- Remove the bottom rack and clean around the drain area.

- Place a cup of vinegar in the top rack and run the dishwasher through a rinse cycle. This will help disinfect, cut grease, and eliminate hard-water deposits that can clog the drain.

often to battle fingerprints. Many stainless-steel-specific cleaners are extreme irritants to the eyes, skin, and lungs, and quite a few of these come in spray bottles that seem to invite contact with these areas.

You can cut the risk involved with appliance cleaning by using the cleaning features on the appliance and the most basic, nontoxic cleaning solutions.

For cleaner coffee, first soak the removable parts and carafe in 2 teaspoons baking soda dissolved in water for a few hours. Wash and dry them normally. Then, fill the water reservoir with white vinegar, and run the vinegar through the machine. Repeat twice with vinegar and then do the same with water to rinse.

Oven

- If your oven smokes, clean it immediately. Otherwise clean it every few months.

- Remove racks and soak in warm sudsy water for three hours or overnight.

- Self-cleaning ovens: Simply switch to *clean* mode. When it's done and cooled, wipe interior with a damp cloth.

- Non-self-cleaning: Create a paste with ¾ cup baking soda, ¼ cup salt, and ¼ cup water, and coat interior. Let stand overnight then scrape with a plastic spatula. Wipe clean with a damp cloth. Replace salt with washing soda for extra dirty ovens.

Stove

- Most stove surfaces need only all-purpose cleaner (see page 31) and a sponge or cloth.

- Glass stovetops often have a protective coating, so use castile soap and water or equal parts vinegar and water to cut grease.

- Electric burners have removable plates that need to be soaked and washed by hand monthly to keep them safe and sparkling.

- Wash grates or pans for gas burners by hand as well, and clean off any spill as soon as it cools.

CABINETS

Keep storage areas sanitized for a healthy kitchen

Along with a shiny sink, clean cabinet doors go a long way toward making a kitchen appear sparkling clean. Sticky fingers leave behind dirt and bacteria, especially around the handle. Routine wiping helps ensure that food and grime don't build up and damage the surface of the door. Make this a part of your daily kitchen maintenance routine.

But there is more to cleaning the cabinets than just the doors. Keeping the insides clean is crucial. Food and liquid spills can attract insects and rodents and even encourage the growth of mold that contaminates stored food and dishes, as well as the air.

Under the kitchen sink, where you may store cleaning prod-

This area gets the dirtiest

Clean Doors

- Wash cabinet doors with warm soapy water and dry with a towel to avoid streaking.

- Pay particular attention to fingerprints in the area around the handle.

- Open the door and wipe down the other side.

- Handles and hinges can collect grime, so once a season it's a good idea to unscrew them and soak them in warm water and dish soap for thirty minutes. Use a brush to scrub lightly, dry, and reattach.

Shelf Liners

- Removable shelf liners help speed your cabinet cleaning. Take them out carefully and shake crumbs and dust into the sink.

- Avoid adhesive vinyl liners, which will pollute your cabinet air, and thus your food and dishes, with toxic VOCs.

- Cork is a great option because it provides some cushion to minimize breakage.

- Other natural fabrics that are machine-washable are also good choices.

ucts along with garbage and compost pails, is another area that needs at least an occasional thorough cleaning. Because of the plumbing here, this is a good place to check for leaks. If you notice dampness, take care of the problem right away. Leaks account for an average of 14 percent of household water use and dark, wet cabinets can get moldy fast. Lining the floor of this cabinet with old baking trays or non-vinyl shelf liner paper can make this job easier because these surfaces are washable. If you're switching to green cleaning, you'll want to dispose of old toxic cleaners appropriately and give the undersink cabinet a deep detox.

Moths and other pests hang out here

Deep Clean

- Deep-clean once a season or more if you have problems with pests or mold.

- Empty cabinets and place items away from your work area. Remove shelf liners to wash or wipe down with warm sudsy water.

- Use a handheld vacuum or a sponge to remove crumbs and dirt.

- Wash shelves and walls with soap and water. Let dry before replacing liners and other items.

Under the Sink Detox

- Empty the cabinet and pour flour, kitty litter, or sand to soak up any liquid that remains from your old cleaners. Let sit for five minutes.

- Scrape mixture with a piece of cardboard into a used plastic bag.

- Use dish or laundry detergent, water, and a brush to scrub the interior of the cabinet. Leave the doors open to dry.

- To control spills, place old baking sheets under your new green cleaners and wash sheets as needed.

TOXIC PLASTICS
Your cheat sheet for choosing the safest plastics

Plastics are under scrutiny for leaching unhealthy chemicals into our food and water and for the mountains of waste they create in our landfills, oceans, and roadsides. Yet there's no doubt that many daily tasks such as packing a lunch or quenching our thirst when we're out of the house would be much less convenient without plastic. Knowing how to sort by number empowers you to know which to cut and which to keep.

Although plastic is the poster child for the green mantra "reduce, reuse, recycle," it is also where the cycle most obviously breaks down. Plastic made from recycled materials uses 70 percent less energy than when made from scratch, and recycling reduces the plastic content of landfills. But not all

Bad Plastic #3

- Some cling wraps and soft bottles are #3 PVC or V (polyvinyl chloride).

- PVC contains endocrine-disrupting phthalates that make it pliable, and vinyl chloride, which is a known carcinogen.

- PVC leaches toxins into food, especially when used to heat fatty foods.

- Use glass containers with covers instead of cling wrap and avoid buying products in plastic containers marked #3. Or, look for safer plastic #4 LDPE (low-density polyethylene).

Bad Plastic #6

- #6 PS (polystyrene) includes Styrofoam take-out containers and meat and baked good packaging. In its hard clear form, it's used for take-out and disposable plastic cups and utensils.

- #6 is made with carcinogenic benzene and leaches possible carcinogen and endocrine-disrupting styrene into food.

- This plastic is generally not recyclable so it's best to avoid it all together.

- If your favorite take-out place uses it, bring your own container, and ask them to find a safer plastic.

plastics are recyclable everywhere, and some are not recyclable at all. In 2005, only 6 percent of the plastic used in U.S. cities made it into the recycling stream.

Reuse is also problematic because many plastics are designed for just a single use. Any good environmentalist will want to reuse that container at least a few times before finally recycling or throwing it out. But microwaving single-use plastic is a big risk because studies show that chemicals from the plastic can leach into your food. Single-use containers labeled "microwave safe" are generally misleading because the label simply means that the container won't melt in the microwave. It's safe for the container and for your microwave to reuse these plastics, but it might not be safe for you. To be extra careful, it's best to do all of your microwaving in non-plastic containers

Of all the "3Rs," reducing is the most important. To support the planet and your health, minimize the amount of plastic you buy. This cheat sheet will help you do it.

Bad Plastic #7

- #7 is usually polycarbonate and found in most baby bottles as well as large water bottles, reusable food storage containers, and the liners in food cans.

- Polycarbonate plastic leaches bisphenol A (BPA), which is thought to be a reproductive and hormonal toxin.

- Studies show that leaching increases with heat, yet heating is common with bottles and storage containers.

- Switch to glass containers and bottles or find bottles that are polycarbonate- and BPA-free.

Safer Plastics

- #1 PET or PETE (polyethylene terephthalate) is found in soda and other drink bottles, and ketchup, salad dressing, peanut butter, and other food jars.

- It is not known to leach toxins and is widely recyclable.

- #2 HDPE (high-density polyethylene) is found in milk, water, and juice bottles along with yogurt and other tubs, cereal box liners, and shopping bags.

- It is not known to leach toxins and is widely recyclable.

LIGHT FIXTURES
For a clean eating area, start at the top

Light fixtures are often neglected because, when we sit at the table and look up, we don't see all the dust and grime that has accumulated on top or in the crevices. A coating of dust on a lightbulb can diminish the quality and amount of light coming from the fixture by up to 25 percent. If that bulb is under a dusty shade, the reduction in light is even more dramatic. Routine dusting and cleaning also gives you the opportunity to regularly inspect your fixtures, drastically reducing the chance that they become a fire hazard due to frayed wiring or other damage.

Like it or not, another reason for dusting your fixtures regularly is to minimize the amount of dust you eat. Think about

Dust

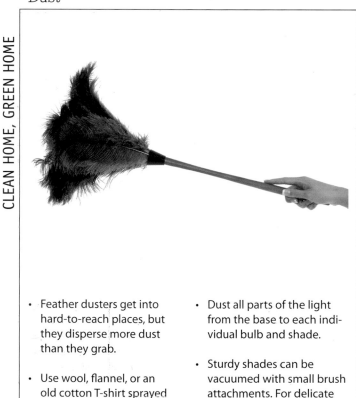

- Feather dusters get into hard-to-reach places, but they disperse more dust than they grab.

- Use wool, flannel, or an old cotton T-shirt sprayed lightly with damp dusting spray (see page 39). Or use a microfiber cloth to capture the dust.

- Dust all parts of the light from the base to each individual bulb and shade.

- Sturdy shades can be vacuumed with small brush attachments. For delicate shades try microfiber or a soft paintbrush.

Deeper Clean

- Turn off light, place cloth over table below to catch drips, and remove shades and bulbs.

- For metal fixtures, wipe with a cloth dampened with castile soap and water. Follow with a clean damp cloth and then a dry cloth.

- For crystal or glass fixtures, dampen a cotton cloth with equal parts hot water and vinegar. Rinse as needed.

- Some crystals can be removed and hand-washed with warm soapy water and dried with a soft cloth.

those nice warm sunny days when you feel a fresh breeze coming in through your window or door. It doesn't seem so fresh when you consider that it's no doubt scattering the dust from your fixture all over your grilled corn and potato salad.

Light fixtures are the first task to tackle in your eating areas because they are at the top of the room and any dirt or dust you do scatter will be picked up by the time you wash the floors.

Remove shade

Polish: Stainless Steel and Chrome

Remove shade

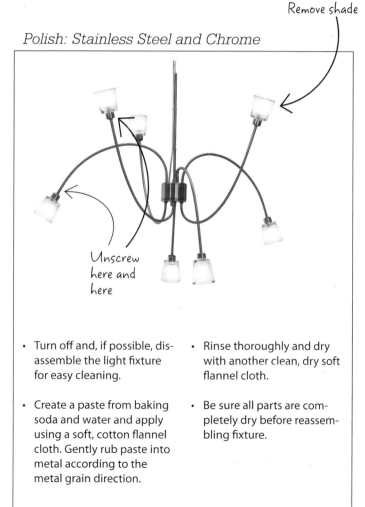

Unscrew here and here

- Turn off and, if possible, disassemble the light fixture for easy cleaning.

- Create a paste from baking soda and water and apply using a soft, cotton flannel cloth. Gently rub paste into metal according to the metal grain direction.

- Rinse thoroughly and dry with another clean, dry soft flannel cloth.

- Be sure all parts are completely dry before reassembling fixture.

Polish: Copper and Brass

- Turn off light, remove shade, and disassemble fixture.

- Create a paste from salt, flour, and vinegar.

- Apply with a soft cotton flannel cloth, wiping in the direction of the metal grain.

- Rinse each piece thoroughly and dry with another clean soft flannel cloth. Make sure the fixture is completely dry before reassembling light.

WOOD TABLES AND CHAIRS
Toxic tables make for dirty eating, so watch where you sit and eat

You may spend extra to buy your family the healthiest food available, but if your table is toxic, your eating experience is, too. Wood tables can be varnished, stained, or sealed with products that contain VOCs, and, unfortunately, these harmful chemicals don't just stay on the table. VOCs are released as gases into the air you breathe. They can have short-term effects like irritation in the eyes, nose, and throat, or headaches and nausea. They also can cause severe, long-term damage to the central nervous system, liver, and kidneys. Some VOCs are suspected or known carcinogens.

If you're in the market for a table, it's a good idea to look for low- or no-VOC tables, or buy an unfinished piece and low-

Green and Clean Table

Look for this logo

Wood Polish: What to Avoid

TOXIC HAZARD
WARNING: May be harmful if swallowed.

- Wood tables are perfect for a green home—but not all wood tables are green.

- Seek out this logo, which notes that the wood is harvested responsibly and respectfully both to the environment and the people doing the work.

- Luckily, wood tables are fairly low maintenance and will do fine with routine dusting and damp wiping to remove dust and crumbs.

- An occasional polish and wax will help protect the wood and ensure a long life.

- Most furniture polish can irritate the skin and eyes. Yet, because they are usually sprayed either by aerosol or spray bottle, skin and eyes are vulnerable.

- Many polishes contain petroleum distillates, which are neurotoxic and flammable.

- Polish can also contain carcinogenic formaldehyde.

- If you buy, look for a plant-based product that does not contain solvents, otherwise try the simple recipe on page 41 and do it yourself.

or no-VOC products to stain and seal it yourself. While you're at it, look for a table that is certified by the Forest Stewardship Council so you know the wood comes from responsibly managed forests.

But don't stop there. Keep your clean table clean by avoiding toxic cleaners. Chemicals in furniture polish can irritate eyes, skin, and lungs, and they can contain carcinogens. You can get great results with this do-it-yourself recipe and enjoy your meals knowing that your table is truly clean.

Polish recipe
½ cup white vinegar
1 teaspoon olive oil
Combine ingredients and shake well.

Polish Technique

Polish with the grain

- For natural and unfinished wood, first dust and then wash the table with a sponge dampened with mild dishwashing soap and water.

- Put a small amount—the size of a quarter to start—of polish on soft, cotton flannel cloth.

- Apply to the table, using long strokes that follow the direction of the wood grain.

- Varnished or shellacked wood finishes do not need polish.

Easy fix

To get rid of water or heat rings on your table:

- Wipe the area with a damp sponge.

- Mix mayonnaise and fireplace ash to a paste. The ash grit buffs the finish and the mayonnaise lubricates the wood.

- Dip soft cotton or flannel cloth in the mixture and rub onto area.

- Wipe the paste off with cloth. Polish the table to even out the look.

EATING AREAS

41

WAXING WOOD FURNITURE
Protect your furniture without polluting the air

Waxing is key to prolonging the life of your wood furniture. Besides making it look practically new, wax protects by creating a slick surface that an object can slide across without scratching. Wax also creates an antistatic layer so dust doesn't stick.

Yet most furniture wax contains toxic solvents, which are chemicals, such as toluene, that keep products moist. They are fat-soluble so experts believe that, when we inhale them, they go straight to the brain where they can cause damage. Many wax products also contain the known carcinogen benzene.

A safer alternative is to make your own wax or find a brand that is vegetable-based. The homemade wax recipe you see

What to Avoid

formaldehyde

nitrobenzene

perchloroethylene

phenol

cresol

toluene

xylene

- Formaldehyde and nitrobenzene are carcinogens.

- Perchloroethylene (PERC) is a toxic organochlorine solvent and probable carcinogen used most commonly in dry cleaning.

- Phenol and cresol are caustic respiratory irritants that can have immediate effects like diarrhea, fainting, and dizziness, and cause long-term damage to the kidney and liver. Phenol is a suspected carcinogen, neurotoxin, and mutagen.

- Toluene and xylene are neurotoxic solvents.

What to Look For

- In addition to the chemicals used as solvents and emulsifiers and more, most furniture wax uses a petroleum-based wax like paraffin.

- Look for paste wax made from natural ingredients like beeswax and plants like carnauba or linseed.

- Beeswax is recognized by furniture conservators as water resistant, gentle to the finish, and long-lasting.

- It will give the table a soft, satiny look that resists scratches as well as water damage.

here is one of the more involved recipes in this book partly because it requires that you actually heat and mix ingredients together instead of just pour and shake. However, because you only need to wax your furniture every 6 months to a year, I encourage you to give it a try. Beeswax is a great substitute for the more typical petroleum-based waxes. Beeswax is produced naturally by bees to make their combs and has been used for centuries by humans in everything from candles to lip balms.

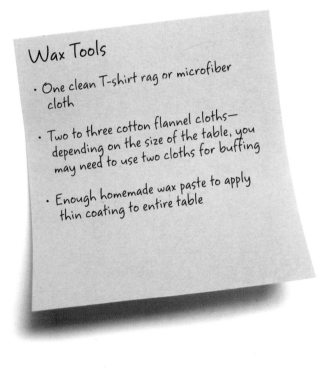

Wax Tools

- One clean T-shirt rag or microfiber cloth

- Two to three cotton flannel cloths—depending on the size of the table, you may need to use two cloths for buffing

- Enough homemade wax paste to apply thin coating to entire table

Wax Technique

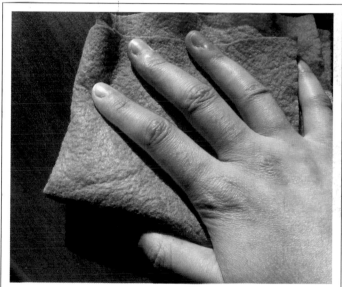

- Dust surface with a dry T-shirt or microfiber cloth.

- Dip flannel rag in wax paste. Start small. Too much wax clouds the finish.

- Coat the surface by rubbing in the direction of the grain until you've spread a thin layer evenly across the wood. Use a toothbrush and move in a circular motion to apply wax to non-flat surfaces. Let dry.

- Use a clean cloth to buff table to a shine. When the cloth starts sliding across the surface, you're done.

NON-WOOD TABLES

Keep them clean enough to eat off of with plain old soap and water

While wood is the most common table material, there are many other types of tables to choose from. Most non-wood tables require less maintenance than wood tables, but you need to pay attention to the surface and choose your cleaning solution accordingly.

For almost all surfaces, maintenance cleaning only requires a natural sponge with just a dab of dishwashing soap and water. It's important to wipe down the table after every meal to rid it of food particles. This is especially important if you have tile with grout where food can become embedded, making cleaning difficult. Beyond that, routinely wiping the dry table with a microfiber or flannel dusting rag will keep it dust-free.

Glass

- Wipe the table free of crumbs with a sponge after every meal.

- Dust the table and base once a week so it looks clean and the dust doesn't have a chance to build up.

- For sparkling clean glass, mix part white vinegar to two parts water with a dash of castile soap.

- Spray the solution on the table and wipe with newspaper or a clean T-shirt.

Tile or Stone

Scrub the grout lines

Dust build here

- Wiping the table after meals helps keep the crumbs from getting embedded in the grout.

- Wash the table with mild soapy water and a sponge, and use a toothbrush to really scrub the grout lines.

- With wood framed tile or stone table, avoid soaking the wood as you clean. Ring the sponge out and just wipe clean.

- Remember to dust the legs and pay careful attention to crevices where dust collects.

Don't forget to wipe down the legs and chairs, as well.

While tile tables have the dirt-catching grout drawback, glass tables show dirt and fingerprints easily. Glass tables look best when they're wiped free of food and then washed like a window with a vinegar and water mixture (see page 51). With clear glass tables, keeping the table frame and legs clean and free of dust is even more important since they are visible from every angle. Tables made from plastics are definitely the easiest to clean and only require the mildest of soap and wa-ter. Like all plastics, these products are petroleum-based and should be avoided where possible.

If you're in the market for a new non-wood table, choose one that is low maintenance and doesn't require special toxic cleaners. It's a great idea to buy used and save all the energy and materials that go into manufacturing new furniture. This is an especially good choice if you want the retro look of a plastic product. Another option is to buy a table made of re-cycled glass, plastic, steel, or tile.

Plastic or Formica

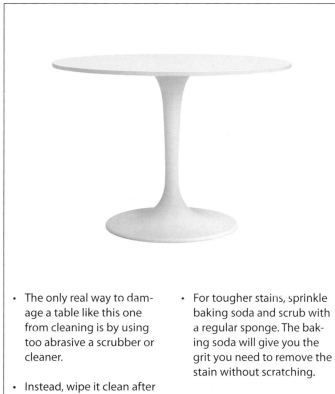

- The only real way to dam-age a table like this one from cleaning is by using too abrasive a scrubber or cleaner.

- Instead, wipe it clean after meals and wash with soapy water once a week.

- For tougher stains, sprinkle baking soda and scrub with a regular sponge. The bak-ing soda will give you the grit you need to remove the stain without scratching.

- Don't forget to wash the base.

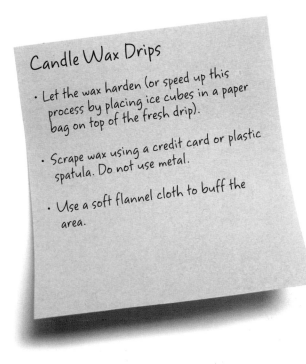

Candle Wax Drips

- Let the wax harden (or speed up this process by placing ice cubes in a paper bag on top of the fresh drip).

- Scrape wax using a credit card or plastic spatula. Do not use metal.

- Use a soft flannel cloth to buff the area.

CLEANING SILVER
Best defense against tarnish? Use it!

If you have good silver, try polishing it without the use of toxic cleaners. Most metal polishes contain neurotoxic petroleum distillates, carcinogenic formaldehyde, or respiratory-irritant ammonia. One proactive step to avoid these toxins is to use your silver more often and hand-wash your pieces after each use. By using your silver more often, you will reduce the amount of polishing you need to do. Be wary of putting good silver in the dishwasher. When silver comes into contact with stainless steel, as it might in a dishwasher, a chemical reaction could damage the silver.

A method that your grandparents probably used and that is often recommended as a green alternative to polish is simple

Silver Polish to Avoid

Metal cleaners and polishes can contain:

- Petroleum distillates – Neurotoxin

- Formaldehyde – Carcinogen

- Ammonia – Respiratory irritant

- Phenol – Respiratory irritant and suspected carcinogen

- Phosphoric acid – Eye, skin, and respiratory irritant

Silver-Polishing Toothpastes to Look For

- The most basic white toothpaste you can find is ideal for polishing silver.

- Gel toothpastes are not effective for polishing silver.

- The toothpaste should contain no baking soda and no fluoride.

- It should have nothing but natural ingredients, including flavoring.

and doesn't require elbow grease. Fill a large pan with aluminum foil, salt, baking soda, and warm water. Then submerge your tarnished silver for an hour and rinse. However, use caution and ventilate as some experts warn that this technique emits hydrogen sulfide gas, which can irritate your eyes and throat and may cause coughing or shortness of breath.

Using toothpaste is a gentler method that works easily and effectively. If you choose to use toothpaste, find one without baking soda and coloring, as some experts warn that abrasive baking soda can damage silver.

Since most recommended green methods of polishing silver involve baking soda, this is important information to consider, especially if the silver you're polishing is a family heirloom or has significant value. That said, the limited number of nontoxic polish options means that using a mild toothpaste to polish may be the best method.

Polishing Step 1: Scrub

- For quick, small jobs like necklaces or one tarnished fork, using your finger as an applicator is fine.

- Squeeze the toothpaste on your finger and rub into the piece until covered.

- For bigger jobs, squeeze the toothpaste on a toothbrush.

- Rub in a circular motion until the entire piece is covered with paste.

Polishing Step 2: Rinse

- Toothpaste polishing means instant gratification. No need to wait unless the piece is badly tarnished.

- Rinse each piece thoroughly in the sink. Use a cloth to carefully remove all toothpaste, even in nooks and crannies.

- Dry completely with a towel.

- Shine with a clean flannel cloth.

EATING CLEAN
Nontoxic food cheat sheets to help you navigate your grocery store

You've cleaned everything from your cabinets to your refrigerator, your light fixture to your table. The last thing you want to do is sit down in your clean kitchen or eating area to dine on dirty food. While buying clean foods is not as easy as one would think, there are just a few things you need to know to sort the green from the green-washed.

If you're lucky enough to have a regular farmers' market that sells locally grown organic produce, this option is by far your best bet. You not only avoid the pesticides, but you also bypass all of the energy and fossil fuels that go into the long distribution channels from farm to supermarket.

If you buy organic at your local supermarket, you are defi-

Vegetable Dirty Dozen

- Fruits and vegetables with thick, removable skin like oranges and bananas contain less pesticides so buying organic is not as important.

- But some fruits and vegetables absorb more pesticides, so it's more important to buy organic versions of these varieties.

- Fruit to buy organic: Apples, cherries, grapes, nectarines, peaches, pears, raspberries, and strawberries.

- Vegetables to buy organic: Bell peppers, celery, potatoes, and spinach.

Safest Fish and Seafood

Catfish - U.S. farmed

Oyster – Farmed

Pollock – U.S. caught from Alaska

Salmon – Wild caught from Alaska

Scallops (bay) - Farmed

Trout – Rainbow farmed

- This list is short for several reasons.

- Some fish are off the list because of high mercury levels. Mercury is neurotoxic and can severely impact a child's development.

- Other fish are off because overfishing or unsustain-

able farming have wreaked havoc on the environment and reduced fish populations.

- These fish are the safest and most sustainable, which means you can eat as much as you want.

nitely ahead of the game, but there is some controversy over whether the mainstreaming of organic is making the label less meaningful and the food less healthy. The organic movement historically championed small, pesticide-free, family-owned farms as a healthier and greener alternative to industrial farming. Yet, these days, there is an entire sector of large-scale organic farming that looks just like industrial farming, but without the pesticides. The upshot is that this food is still better for you and the environment, even if the growing process has a long way to go to be truly earth-friendly.

In the meat world, label claims can be misleading. Words like *natural, free-range*, and even *antibiotic-free,* which meant something at one time, are becoming increasingly untrustworthy. But there are other claims that are regulated, and recgonizing those will help you choose the cleanest meats, dairy products, and fish for your family. Use these cheat sheets to navigate the grocery store with confidence.

Deciphering Dairy Products

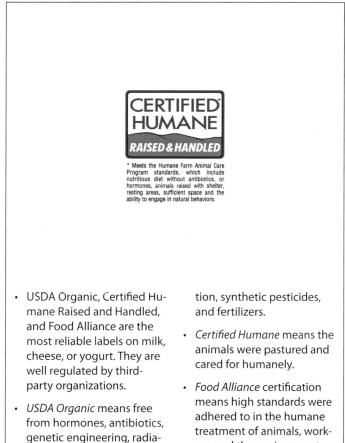

* USDA Organic, Certified Humane Raised and Handled, and Food Alliance are the most reliable labels on milk, cheese, or yogurt. They are well regulated by third-party organizations.

* *USDA Organic* means free from hormones, antibiotics, genetic engineering, radiation, synthetic pesticides, and fertilizers.

* *Certified Humane* means the animals were pastured and cared for humanely.

* *Food Alliance* certification means high standards were adhered to in the humane treatment of animals, workers, and the environment.

Meat and Poultry Labels

* In addition to the reliable labels for dairy, meat may also bear the logo for Demeter Biodynamic.

* That means no synthetic pesticides, the animals were pastured, and the farm was well managed.

* *Free range, Hormone-free, Natural,* and even *"Antibiotic free"* are not universally defined, nor regulated.

* That does not mean they're not true; there's just no way of knowing for sure. So look to see if they are backed up by reliable labels.

49

SINK AREA

Match the type of cleaner to your sink to avoid scratching

It's easy to damage your sink by using too harsh a cleanser, especially for delicate surfaces like vitreous china, brass, or copper. The key to finding the right cleaner for your sink is to start as mild as possible and add ingredients as needed.

Many glass cleaners contain dioxane, a known carcinogen, and ammonia, a respiratory irritant. Cleaning with ammonia in the bathroom is particularly dangerous since it is usually a smaller space with inadequate ventilation and because ammonia creates toxic gases when mixed with chlorine, a common ingredient in other bathroom cleaners.

Luckily, vinegar and water work great on mirrors. But there are two drawbacks that are easily overcome: the smell and

Ceramic, Vitreous China, or Fireclay

- These are the most common sink materials and the most durable. However, overly abrasive cleaners can do a lot more harm than good.

- Daily or at least weekly cleaning can be done with warm soapy water and a soft cloth.

- For deeper cleaning or to eliminate a stain, gently scrub with a mildly abrasive cleaner (see page 55) applied with a sponge or soft rag.

- If soap scum is a problem, use the advanced glass cleaner recipe (see page 51) and wipe clean.

Glass

- Wipe the sink dry after every use to reduce spotting.

- To clean, scrub the drain and any seams around the sink with mild soap and water and rinse.

- Then use glass cleaner recipe (see page 51) with a T-shirt rag or newspaper to wash the sink as you would a window or mirror.

- Abrasive cleaners will scratch the surface and make the glass surface appear dull.

50

the streaks. The vinegar smell is an easy one because it goes away in a matter of minutes, not hours like ammonia or other cleaning chemicals. If you've previously used chemical glass cleaners, you will get streaking when you first use vinegar and water. It's not the vinegar—it's the film left from your old glass cleaner that causes the streaking. Add some castile soap to the mix for the first few cleanings to avoid streaking. After that, vinegar and water will work great.

Tough Surfaces

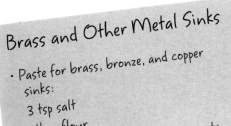

Brass and Other Metal Sinks

- Paste for brass, bronze, and copper sinks:
  3 tsp salt
  1 tbsp flour
  2 tbsp white vinegar to make a paste

- Apply with a sponge in circular motions.

- Rinse with hot water.

- Polish with soft cloth.

- Older homes may have porcelain enamel on cast-iron or steel sinks that need some special treatment.

- Do not use acidic cleaners like vinegar and lemon juice to clean these sinks, as they can cause damage.

- Instead, wash routinely with mild dish soap and warm water applied with a soft cloth or sponge.

- A mild abrasive cleaner (see page 55) can be used gently to remove stains.

51

SINK FAUCETS AND DRAINS
Know where the bacteria hides to hone your cleaning strategy

Studies show that the bathroom sink harbors about 6,300 bacteria per square inch on the faucet handles and almost 2,800 bacteria per square inch in the drain. Compare that to a garbage can with just over 400 bacteria per square inch, and you get the idea of what you're up against here.

For bathroom sinks that are used primarily for hand washing, wipe down the handles and do some drain maintenance before guests arrive, and you're all set. The other bathroom sinks, however, can become a strange tableau composed of the soap scum, toothpaste, makeup, shaving cream, and, oh yes, hair discarded from everyday living. And of this, whatever is not sticking to the faucet eventually makes its way down the drain.

Heavily used bathroom sinks need weekly cleaning. Most

Faucet

Don't forget to scrub here

- Wipe faucet and handles dry with a towel after each use. This will reduce mineral spotting and soap scum buildup.

- When you want a shine, use glass cleaner (page 51). Spray and wipe with a t-shirt rag.

- Scrub seams with mild soap and hot water to prevent mold growth and remove grime.

- Avoid abrasive cleaners in general and use soap and water instead of vinegar-based glass cleaner for porcelain fixtures or handles.

Low-flow clean

- Unscrew the spout of your faucet and remove screens, aerator, and low-flow disk. Pay attention to the order and orientation for easy reassembly.

- Use a pin to clean out holes in disk as well as screens if they need cleaning.

- Soak the pieces in vinegar for a few hours.

- Reassemble.

faucet types can be wiped with just a spray of vinegar and water and they shine and are disinfected. Brass faucets can be polished easily with baking soda and lemon or vinegar and salt on a soft cloth.

If you notice a change in the flow of the water coming from your faucet, it's probably time to clean the low-flow attachment or screens. Hard-water deposits can build up and obstruct the flow, but they'll disappear easily using the technique on page 52.

on page 52.

Clearing the Drain

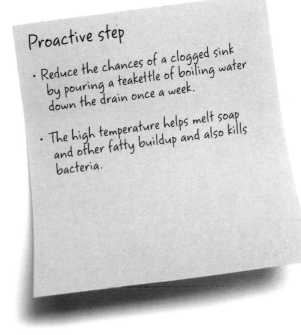

Proactive step

· Reduce the chances of a clogged sink by pouring a teakettle of boiling water down the drain once a week.

· The high temperature helps melt soap and other fatty buildup and also kills bacteria.

- Since this is one of the most germ-filled spots in the house, it's important to keep drains as clean and clear as possible.

- If it's slow to empty or you want to disinfect, pour ½ cup baking soda down the drain.

- Follow with a cup of vinegar and cover drain with a rag. Let it fizz for five minutes.

- Pour in boiling water unless your sink is glass or vitreous china, in which case, use hot water.

BATHROOM

53

TUBS AND SHOWERS
Simple ingredients for a natural clean

Admittedly, cleaning the shower isn't the first thing people want to do with their spare time. That's why there's a chemical-laden "do it easier" product for everything—from mold and mildew to soap scum and marble—and many of them claim to work "automatically." But these cleaners are labeled hazards, irritating skin and eyes, containing known carcinogens, and more. Many are spray products, yet their labels say to avoid contact with eyes, skin, and clothing. The good news is, you don't need all these pricey, unhealthy cleaners. Nontoxic ingredients like baking soda and castile soap work just as well.

One of the biggest cleaning challenges in the tub and shower is the persistent growth of mold. The going wisdom is that bleach kills mold, but mold remediators and even the

Oily Rings

Oily rings can show up here

- Oily rings are usually residue left from oily bath products, which can also make your tub slippery.

- Wash the tub with this mildly abrasive cleaner (see page 55) warm water, and a rag or sponge whenever you use the products.

- If you have tile around your tub and find oily residue there as well, clean immediately.

- Oil can penetrate the grout and encourage mildew growth. Consider switching to less oily bath products.

Grout Mildew

Mildew is tough to remove from caulk

Mildew is everywhere

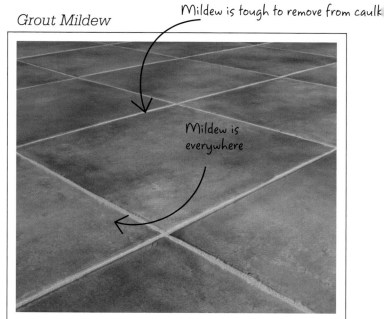

- If you have moldy grout, consider installing a fan, opening the window every time you shower, and towel dry the surround and tub after use.

- Spray affected areas with tea tree oil antibacterial spray (see page 15) or straight vinegar.

- Do not rinse. Repeat daily for a week while also keeping the entire area as dry and well ventilated as possible.

- Scrub area with a soft bristled brush and mild abrasive cleaner (see page 55).

EPA will tell you that bleach is the wrong product for the job. If you've ever used bleach to treat mold, you probably noticed that it went away for a while and then returned in the exact same spot. That's because you only bleached the mold—you didn't kill it.

Instead of using bleach, the most important thing you can do to battle mold is to keep your bathroom and shower as dry as possible in between uses. If necessary, open a window or install an exhaust fan and dry the affected area after each use.

Soap Scum

Look for soap scum here

- Minerals from your water mix with soap to form soap scum that shows up as a cloudy, gritty film.

- To reduce soap scum, wipe the tub dry after each use.

- To clean, skip the baking soda recipe above, which is mineral and alkaline—possibly contributing to the problem. Use a more acidic cleaner like equal parts vinegar and water.

- Use vinegar sparingly and never if you have porous stone like marble or limestone.

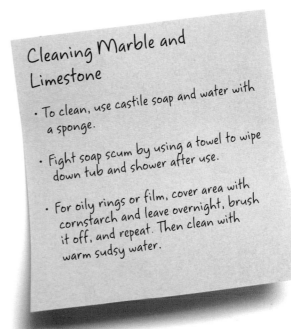

Cleaning Marble and Limestone

- To clean, use castile soap and water with a sponge.

- Fight soap scum by using a towel to wipe down tub and shower after use.

- For oily rings or film, cover area with cornstarch and leave overnight, brush it off, and repeat. Then clean with warm sudsy water.

BATHROOM

BATH FAUCETS AND SHOWERHEADS
Finish off a deep clean with a healthy shine

The most common faucets and showerheads, made of chrome or stainless steel, don't hide their dirt and spots very well. A good way to keep them shiny is to wipe them dry after use and occasionally clean with dishwashing liquid or the same vinegar mixture you use on the mirror (see page 51). If your fixtures are porcelain, be sure to avoid abrasive cleaners

and minimize your use of acids like vinegar, which can cause damage to the surface.

How frequently you need to deep-clean your fixtures depends on your water. Hard water can leave mineral water deposits that can obstruct the water flow and appears as a white film or spots on your faucet and showerhead. Both are

Scrub here

Bath Faucet

Porcelain handles need milder cleaner

Tub Drain

- Dry faucet after use to keep it shiny and reduce hard-water spotting.

- For chrome and other shiny metal, use glass-cleaning mixture of vinegar, water, and a touch of castile soap and polish with a dry cloth for the best shine.

- If your faucet or part of it is porcelain, use mild dish-washing soap and water. Vinegar may cause damage.

- Scrub seams and design details with a toothbrush to prevent dirt buildup and mold growth.

- Clean hair out of tub drain/strainer to prevent dirt and bacteria buildup and clogs.

- Pour a teakettle of boiling water down the drain once a week to melt away any buildup and inhibit bacteria growth.

- Then scrub the strainer with warm soapy water and a toothbrush.

- For a deeper clean, sprinkle ½ cup baking soda and pour 1 cup vinegar down the drain. Cover for five minutes with a rag. Follow with boiling water.

CLEAN HOME, GREEN HOME

easy to clean naturally and with minimal effort.

Pay attention to leaks while you clean. Your leaky faucet can lose up to 20 gallons a day, which can add up to a huge waste of water over time. Fix leaks immediately.

If your showerhead was installed before 1992, it most likely has a high flow rate. Try installing a low-flow showerhead to conserve water, and make good choices, such as taking shorter showers and not letting the water run unnecessarily.

Clogged Showerhead: Step 1

- Hard-water mineral deposits can clog showerheads and obstruct the flow of water.

- Fill a plastic bag with 2 cups straight white distilled vinegar.

- Slip bag over showerhead and secure with a rubber band so showerhead is completely submerged in vinegar.

- Leave on overnight. In the morning, scrub the showerhead with a toothbrush and warm soapy water.

Stubborn Clogs: Step 2

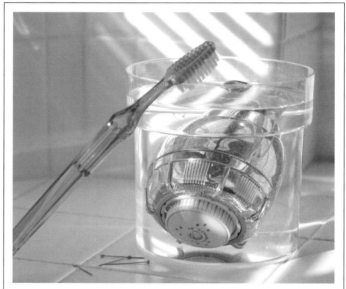

- It's a good idea to turn off the water to your house in case the pipe breaks.

- Unscrew showerhead.

- Older showerheads may be rusted, so wrap it in a towel and use a wrench to gently unscrew it.

- Remove any low-flow disk and clean it and shower-head openings with a pin; rinse. Soak in vinegar for four hours then scrub again with toothbrush and soapy water.

- To reattach, scrub any rust off the pipe. You may need to remove and replace old sealant tape to prevent leaking. Screw on showerhead.

BATHROOM

SHOWER DOORS AND CURTAINS
Eliminate mold problems and go PVC-free

It's hard to feel clean when your shower is surrounded by grime and mold. It's also not the best situation for your respiratory system, as you breathe in these mold spores. Therefore, it's important to take some quick measures to decrease your health risks and maintain an overall clean shower.

Ventilation in the form of opening windows and turning on bath fans is crucial to fighting mold. Ventilation is especially effective when you also squeegee the door dry or shake the water from the curtain and spread it open after each use.

Washable shower curtain liners make cleaning easy, but the most widely available shower curtain liners are made from PVC (see page 36), which contains a known human carcino-

Proactive Step

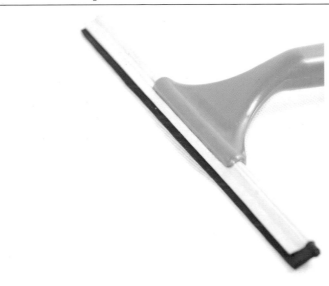

- To keep your shower door clean and clear, you don't need a daily dose of toxic, "automatic" shower cleaners.

- Get a squeegee that fits the type of door you have in terms of size and whether it's flat or curved.

- After each use, drag the squeegee in straight lines from top to bottom to wipe away soap scum and thoroughly dry the glass.

- Overlap each pass so you don't end up with streaks or lines.

Door Track

Mold and grime build up here

- If you use a squeegee on your shower door, water may pool in your door track, creating optimal conditions for mold growth.

- Use a towel to absorb water after use and leave the door open for further drying.

- To clean, use mild dishwashing soap and a toothbrush to get into hard-to-reach places.

- Wipe down the entire doorframe with soapy water and rinse. Dry and polish with a towel and clean soft cloth.

gen, endocrine disrupter, and mutagen. To avoid PVC, you can forego the liner all together and buy a mildew-resistant and water-repelling hemp shower curtain or a tightly woven cotton curtain. If you must have a liner, try nylon. It's a better option than PVC, but it is one that is made from nonrenewable resources.

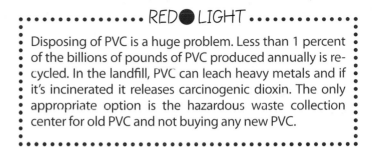
Proactive Step

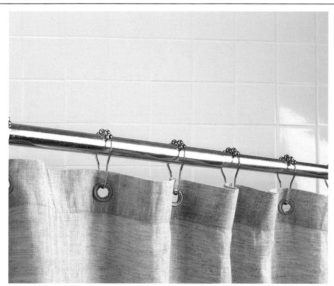

- If your bathroom tends to stay moist and mold is a problem, invest in a hemp shower curtain.

- Hemp is a hardy fiber that does not need pesticides or much water to grow.

- A hemp curtain can be used without a liner. It will get wet as you shower, but the water won't leak through to the floor.

- Unlike vinyl liners and curtains, hemp dries quickly and is naturally resistant to mold and bacteria.

Clean Liner

Detach here

- Vinyl liners keep water in the tub, but their tendency to stay stuck to the tub means the shower and tub stay wet longer.

- Although petroleum-based, nylon liners dry faster and contribute to a mold-free shower without polluting the air.

- After each use, shake out and spread the liner to help dry.

- To wash, remove the liner from hooks and throw in the washing machine. Wash in hot water if mold is present.

BATHROOM

TOILETS
You don't need a toxic hazard to get the toilet clean

Because we think of toilets as the dirtiest spots in the house, highly toxic toilet cleaners are an easy sell. Acid-based toilet bowl cleaners are in the top three of the most toxic household products available because they contain caustic ingredients that easily burn eyes, skin, and internal tissues.

Bad bacteria like E. coli and salmonella may be lurking in

your toilet, but the majority of the bacteria you have there is harmless. Harmless bacteria live on your skin, in your gut, in your garden, and all over your home. In fact, there is increasing evidence that exposure to bacteria may actually be good for us early in life because it helps strengthen our immune systems. This is not to say we should not clean our toilets and

What to Avoid

- Toilet bowl cleaners are corrosive and can cause damage and scarring if they come in contact with eyes, skin, and respiratory system.

- Many contain either bleach or ammonia.

- Products containing ammonia shouldn't be mixed with other cleaners containing

bleach. Products with chlorine don't mix with acidic cleaning ingredients. The reaction creates chlorine gas that damages your lungs.

- They also contain synthetic fragrances and toxic surfactants like sodium laureth sulfate, which may be contaminated with carcinogenic 1,4-dioxane.

Toilet Bowl

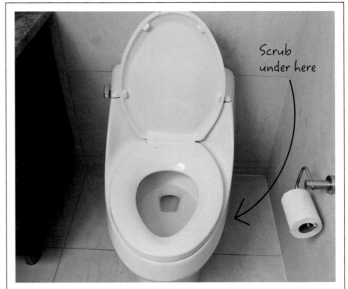

Scrub under here

- Toilet bowls should be cleaned every week, but not with toxic cleaners.

- Castile soap and baking soda will work fine because the baking soda provides enough grit for effective scrubbing and the soap and water does the cleaning.

- To kill bacteria, use baking soda and vinegar. Let fizz for five to ten minutes.

- Scrub the bowl thoroughly with a toilet brush. Get as far down the opening and as close up under the rim as possible. Then flush.

bathrooms, but that we don't need the 275 EPA-registered pesticides found in antimicrobial products to do it.

To kill even the worst of the bacteria, including E. Coli, we need hot soapy water and consistency. It's also a good idea to flush with the toilet seat down to make sure whatever bacteria you do have in your toilet does not get scattered around on other surfaces, towels, or toothbrushes. And, of course, wash your hands often and thoroughly.

Surface

Dust accumulates here

Dust and grime accumulate here

- Use all-purpose cleaner (see page 31) and a rag to wipe the exterior of the toilet.

- Start at the top to remove dust on the back and sides of the tank. Next, wipe the lid and seat and then the exterior of the bowl and base.

- Dirt and grime can collect at the base, so make sure you wipe it clean all the way around.

- For wooden seats, use mild soap and water and wipe dry.

Hard-Water Rings

- Pour a cup of white vinegar into your toilet bowl and scrub.

- Let sit for one hour.

- Scrub again and flush.

- Do not use vinegar with any product containing chlorine, including bleach.

BATHROOM

CLEAN SLEEP
Insomnia? Switch to cleaner sheets

If you're having trouble sleeping or you just want to do something great for the environment and your indoor air quality, consider a complete bedding makeover. At the top of the list: Invest in some certified organic cotton sheets and not simply because they're trendy. Nonorganic sheets are usually treated with large amounts of formaldehyde, a known carcinogen that makes them resist stains and wrinkles. Form-

aldehyde has also been linked to insomnia, of all things, and never completely washes out of your sheets.

Skyrocketing demand for organic cotton has led to an increase in production of about 76 percent a year since 2000. Organic cotton is now being grown in eighteen countries. Look for organic cotton products labeled "fair trade" or "sweatshop free" and opt for undyed sheets to further reduce your

Cleaner Mattresses

Organic cotton and wool stuffing

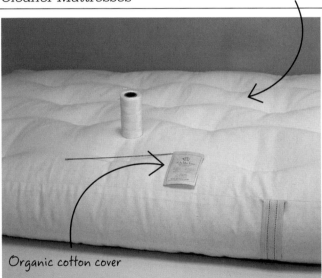

Organic cotton cover

- Stuffing: Organic cotton and wool or natural latex are sustainable nontoxic choices.

- Flame retardants: Skip the PBDEs and look for wool, a natural flame retardant that meets government standards.

- Extras: Look for unbleached and untreated cotton and wool to reduce chemical exposure even further. Avoid pesticide-laden "antibacterial" mattresses.

- Vacuum mattress regularly to rid it of allergens like dead dust mites and their feces.

Organic Futons

- Futons can be a great alternative to conventional mattresses and are often less expensive.

- Stuffing: Look for 100 percent organic cotton surrounded by fire-resistant wool.

- Fabric: Organic cotton, wool, or hemp fabrics make a healthy natural cover.

- Cleaning: It's a good idea to have a removable futon cover for easy cleaning and, again, organic cotton is a good choice. Be sure to wash cover and vacuum futon regularly.

chemical exposure. "Green Cotton" labels indicate that the cotton was not grown organically but chemicals were not added during the manufacturing process.

If you're considering a new mattress, avoid the flame retardant chemical PBDE. While this highly polluting and dangerous chemical no doubt stops fires, there are other nontoxic alternatives that do the same thing, including wool. Some mattresses and sheets labeled "antibacterial" are also coated in pesticides and other toxins.

Green Sheets

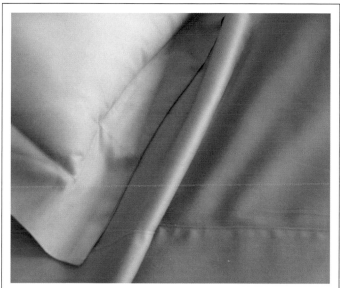

- Look for sheets that are 100 percent organic cotton, meaning they haven't been grown with pesticides and synthetic fertilizers.

- Even with organic sheets, it's important to make sure they have not been treated with harsh chemicals in manufacturing.

- Buy unbleached and undyed sheets or look for colored sheets with natural dyes free of heavy metals and formaldehyde.

- Avoid anything that says easy-care, wrinkle-free, or permanent press which means formaldehyde. Wash all sheets before using them.

Bamboo Sheets

- Bamboo is a green option because it grows fast—reaching full height in less than five years—and generally without pesticides.

- Bamboo is becoming increasingly affordable, but is sometimes sold as a mixture of bamboo and conventional cotton.

- This is greener but not ideal since conventional cotton is such a pesticide-intensive crop.

- Look for 100 percent bamboo or bamboo and organic cotton mixes with natural dyes and no extra chemical treatments.

COMFORTERS AND PILLOWS
Enjoy some clean and cozy eco-friendly options

Sleeping clean means that when you curl up with your comforter and a soft pillow, you don't breathe in harsh chemicals or mold. A simple step to combat both mold and harsh chemicals is to hang your comforters and pillows out in the sunshine for a few hours a month. This will give chemicals a chance to offgas away from you. Down or wool comforters are great because they absorb your body's moisture as you sleep, so you don't wake up sweaty as you might with synthetic materials. A few hours in the sun naturally dries, whitens, and sanitizes them. Another easy step is to buy an untreated, organic cotton protector for your current pillow or comforter that will limit your exposure to allergens and chemicals.

If you're buying new, consider other options besides down.

Comforter Choices: Organic Wool

- Wool comforters give you the same cozy fluffiness of down and also wick away moisture from your body so they keep you warm and dry.

- Dust mites are less attracted to wool, so it's a great choice for bedding.

- As with all bedding, check with the manufacturer to make sure the wool has not been treated with extra pesticides or other harsh chemicals.

- Avoid dry-cleaning your wool comforter. Hand-wash with a mild detergent and line-dry if possible.

Clean Down

- Down can pack a lot of allergens because it typically contains at least some feathers from geese and ducks that were raised in unsanitary conditions.

- Clean down or other eco-down may be ozonated to get rid of any bacteria or mold and washed in extremely hot water to clean it.

- Look for products with organic cotton covers.

- Avoid dry cleaning. Hand-wash with a mild detergent and line-dry (see page 108)

Most goose and duck down are by-products of factory-farmed animals killed for meat. While some organic farmers do sell their feathers, it's difficult to track the sources of any given comforter. "EcoDown" or other "clean" down products are generally made up of regular down that has been cleaned to reduce allergens and toxins. "Hypodown" is regular down mixed with fibers from plants.

Wool is an excellent eco-choice for bedding because it naturally controls moisture, repels dust mites, and resists fire. Look for wool from the PureGrow project in Northern California. PureGrow ranchers make sure there are no chemicals in the sheep's surroundings, feeds, pastures, or bodies. And the sheep are free to roam instead of restricted to small areas that can be dirty and spread disease. Comforters and pillows made from this wool are widely available.

Eco-friendly pillows are stuffed with everything from buckwheat and millet to recycled plastic soda bottles. If you can get past the not-so-luxurious images associated with sleeping on soda bottles, pillows filled with recycled material are a great way to close the recycling loop.

Natural Pillow Choices

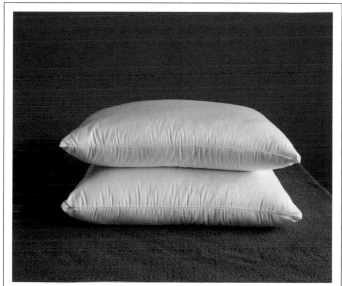

- Avoid pillows filled with synthetic petroleum-based materials like polyester.

- Kapok pillows are filled with seedpods from the kapok tree that feel a lot like down. They are generally free of allergens.

- Buckwheat is usually not certified organic because it does not require pesticides to grow.

- Buckwheat grows abundantly and makes for a supportive pillow that breathes.

Close the Loop

- The more manufacturer demand there is for recycled materials, the wider and more extensive recycling programs will become.

- Pillows made from 100 percent recycled soda bottles are hypoallergenic and as comfortable as cotton.

- Look for products that have an unbleached organic cotton cover.

- Throw pillows in the washer once a month with a mild detergent. If your washer is top loading, put two pillows in at once for balance and to reduce wear and tear on the machine.

DUST CONTROL
Reduce exposure to allergens and toxins in the home

Dust can contribute to the development and triggering of allergies and asthma, both of which are on the rise in the U.S. Since we spend about a third of our lives in the bedroom, controlling dust in our bedding and furnishings is extremely important. Studies have also found that controlling dust reduces our exposure to household toxins, such as PBDE flame retardants that are probably in your mattress. The average household dust bunny consists of 70 percent human skin and 30 percent a mixture of dirt, fibers, pet dander, mold, bacteria, and insects like dust mites.

Your bed is the perfect ecosystem for dust mites because they thrive in warm, dark, and moist places, and they feed on

Dust Mites

- Dust mites don't bite or burrow in your skin. In fact, unless you have an allergy to them, you may not be affected at all.

- If you are allergic, symptoms include watery eyes, sneezing, itching, sinus, and respiratory problems. They are caused by dust mite feces and decaying mites.

- To fight dust mites, use a dehumidifier to dry out your bedroom and wash bedding once a week in hot water.

- Vacuum at least once a week with a filtered vacuum.

Mattress Dust

- Some experts claim that dust mite waste can double the weight of a mattress every ten years.

- Vacuum your mattress with a filtered vacuum once a month—more if you're suffering from allergies.

- Use a mattress-specific attachment or just use a flat tool so you can cover the area efficiently. Clean the attachment if necessary before using.

- Drag the attachment very slowly across the mattress in long, straight, overlapping lines. Don't forget to do the sides.

human skin. This makes them very happy to hang out in your bed all day and night where there is no shortage of food.

To reduce the amount of dust in your bedroom, it's important to stop being so hospitable to dust mites. If your room tends to be damp, use a dehumidifier. It's also a good idea to get rid of wall-to-wall carpeting, which provides a desirable home for mites and hangs on to air pollutants. Regularly vacuuming or vapor-steam-cleaning area rugs, mattresses, and curtains will also help control the problem.

Dust here

Headboards

Vacuum here

Bed Skirts and Drapery

- Bedding isn't the only dust collector in your room.

- Before changing your sheets, use a damp T-shirt rag or microfiber cloth to dust your headboard, footboard, and other visible parts of the bed frame, including legs. Use a vacuum for any upholstered parts.

- Work your rag into details or carvings where dust can build up.

- When you finish dusting, remove sheets to wash and vacuum the floor around the bed to catch any fallen dust.

- The bed skirt is another dust catcher in the bedroom.

- Bed skirts are machine-washable, but require a lot of work to remove them and put them back when they're clean.

- To keep them clean in between washings, use your vacuum's upholstery attachment and vacuum in overlapping vertical lines.

- Do the same for curtains or drapery and any other fabric or upholstery that is collecting dust in your bedroom.

WINDOWS AND GLASS

Clear your view and your air and reduce your energy bills in one simple step

With their bright blue or green coloring, it's not too surprising that conventional window cleaners pack a lot of chemicals. One of the worst is ammonia, an irritant that mixes with chlorine, a common ingredient in cleaning products, to form toxic gases. Other chemicals in glass cleaners include butyl cellosolve, a known irritant and neurotoxin and suspected teratogen, and dioxane, a carcinogen.

If you have previously used a chemical glass cleaner, these chemicals leave a coating on your glass that will streak when you wipe it with vinegar and water. Add a few squirts of castile soap to the mixture for the first few cleanings and then you can switch to vinegar and water with no streaking.

Window Frame

Dust and grime build up here

- Dust regularly with a microfiber cloth or damp T-shirt, being careful to work your rag into tight spaces. Use a cotton swab around the lock and handles.

- For a deeper clean, wash frame with mild soapy water and a soft cloth.

- Use a toothbrush for hard-to-reach places and the seam where the frame meets the glass.

- Dry the frame thoroughly with a clean towel.

Track

- The tracks of your window frame can get dirty fast and moisture can lead to a mold problem.

- When you clean your window, be sure to open the window all the way and clean this area.

- For dusty tracks, use the crevice tool on your vacuum cleaner to get into the corners and remove the dust.

- For wet grime, use a T-shirt rag and work into the corners, or use a cotton swab.

Regularly cleaning both the inside and outside of your windows can lift your mood and lower your energy bills. Cleaner windows let in more light, which can reduce the amount of energy you need to power lamps and your heating and cooling system. Maximizing your use of the natural light coming into your home for light and heat is called "daylighting," and clean windows can make a big difference.

Glass Cleaning

Tools for glass cleaning:
2 cups water and 1 cup vinegar
1 teaspoon of castile soap
Spray bottle
Newspaper
Gloves

- For clean glass without streaks combine vinegar, water, and castile soap and use newspaper as your rag. If you've already been using vinegar and water and your windows are not streaking, you do not need the castile soap.

- Wear gloves to keep the newsprint from blackening your hands.

- Spray the cleaner on the newspaper instead of the window to keep it off the frame.

- Wash the window in a circular motion.

Mirror

Dust builds up here and here

- Use a damp T-shirt or microfiber cloth to dust mirror and frame, being careful to wipe the front and the sides. Work the cloth into any grooves or seams.

- To wash the frame, use mild soapy water to slightly dampen your cloth or sponge.

- Rinse with a clean, damp, but soapless, sponge. Dry with a clean towel.

- To wash the mirror, spray your glass cleaner mixture on your paper towel or clean T-shirt rag to protect the frame.

GREENER CLOTHING STORAGE
Reduce, reduce, and ventilate

If you see small holes in your sweaters or even catch moths fluttering out of view when you turn on the closet light, don't reach for the mothballs. Mothballs can contain naphthalene or paradichlorobenzene, both classified by the EPA as suspected carcinogens. Naphthalene may also damage the liver, destroy red blood cells, and cause brain damage in children.

Mothballs certainly don't make your closet smell very clean or natural. Your clothes keep that sour mothball smell for months after you've used them because they are designed to disintegrate and permeate the air around the clothing to keep the moths away. But that also means we easily inhale these chemicals every time we walk into the closet or open a drawer or storage container where we've used them. Plus they look edible and children may try to eat these toxic time bombs.

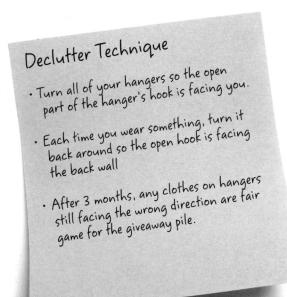

Declutter Technique

• Turn all of your hangers so the open part of the hanger's hook is facing you.

• Each time you wear something, turn it back around so the open hook is facing the back wall

• After 3 months, any clothes on hangers still facing the wrong direction are fair game for the giveaway pile.

Clean Dresser

• Like closets, dresser drawers can easily become overfilled and need to be decluttered once in a while.

• A drawer that is well organized and not overstuffed will save you time, but it will also reduce wrinkles and be less inviting for pests.

• At the beginning of each season, remove the contents of your drawers and vacuum the drawers.

• Wipe down with a sponge and leave out to air-dry before replacing your clothes.

There are much safer choices and proactive steps to take to keep your clothes clean and pest-free. Clothes moths like dark, moist places, and they are particularly drawn to clothing adorned with oils from your skin or from food or other organic spills. They don't drink water so they need the moisture to survive.

Cleaning out your closet and dresser will increase ventilation and reduce moisture and thereby discourage moths. Since moths do the most damage to clothing that isn't disturbed very often, getting rid of these items may make a big difference. Before you store clothing, be sure to launder or at least iron it, as both techniques will kill all stages of the moth life cycle.

Paring down your wardrobe will also make it much easier to vacuum and clean around your clothes so you can minimize the food supply—including fibers and lint—that the moths eat.

No-Pest Clothes

- Cedar drawer liners, closet hangers, and shoe racks can help fight moth infestation.

- Look for aromatic eastern red cedar, which has oil in it that can kill small moth larvae.

- This oil wears off so it's necessary to touch up with essential oil of cedar or replace the cedar every few years.

- Vacuuming in out-of-sight areas like the backs of drawers, under furniture, and on top of baseboards will also help fight clothing moths.

Off-Season Storage

- To keep your closets and dresser drawers clean and not overstuffed, consider storing your off-season clothing in a cedar chest.

- As the weather changes, take the opportunity to clean, and replace past-season clothes with current-season clothes.

- If you have a moth problem, placing wool sweaters in airtight plastic bags may protect them.

- Be sure not to use mothballs, which can melt the plastic, make your clothes smell bad, and pollute your indoor air.

CLOSETS

Clearing the air with a cleaner wardrobe

Most modern closets are stuffed with synthetic and natural fiber clothing that have been treated with toxins aimed at keeping the fabric flame-proof, water-resistant, stain-proof, and wrinkle-free. But the chemicals used to achieve these conveniences are an unwelcome mix of neurotoxins, developmental toxins, and endocrine disrupters.

Dry cleaning adds another highly toxic chemical, perchlo-roethylene (PERC) to your closet air. Leaving dry-cleaned clothes in their plastic bags only prolongs your exposure to the toxin (see page 5).

If everyone chose just one organic cotton T-shirt over its nonorganic alternative, nearly fifty thousand tons of agro-chemicals would be kept from polluting our environment. Other greener options include clothing made from organic

Clean Closet

- Leaving only the clothes you wear in your closet allows for air circulation and easy cleaning.

- Easy-to-remove, natural-fiber bins keep accessories dust-free.

- Empty your closet and start with the top shelf.

- Use a damp sponge to work your way down the closet, wiping each shelf and rod to get rid of dust, dirt, cobwebs, and any insects that may be sharing your closet. Rinse sponge frequently. Vacuum the floor and replace clothes.

Shoe Rack

- Storing your shoes on the floor means more dirt in your closet and more time spent cleaning because you have to remove each pair individually.

- Instead, keep everyday shoes at the door so you aren't bringing outside dirt into your home.

- Store less frequently worn shoes and slippers on a shoe rack, an over-the-door hanging rack, or a shoe organizer that hangs from the rod.

- Simply remove organizer when it's time to clean.

72

wool, bamboo, soy, and hemp. These fibers are grown without lots of pesticides, but keep in mind that dyes can still contain heavy metals and other toxins.

Shoe care products also tend to contain toxins that can disrupt the brain and hormonal systems. But you can easily avoid these unnecessary chemicals by using the natural shoe polish recipe on this page. Keeping shoes on a designated rack or hanging bag in your closet will also limit the dust on your floor and make it easier to clean.

MAKE IT EASY

Natural shoe polish:
Apply a dime-sized amount of jojoba oil and a squirt of lemon to an old T-shirt. Rub the mix into the leather in a circular motion. Buff the shoes with a clean end of the T-shirt

Dust-Free

Vacuum here

- Dust will accumulate on the shelves around your clothes and may even be noticeable on your wool sweaters.

- Use your vacuum attachment for a quick clean around your clothes.

- For a seasonal clean, remove clothing from shelves and take the opportunity to sort and store past-season clothing.

- Dust with a cloth and wash each shelf with soap and water. Dry with a towel before replacing clothing.

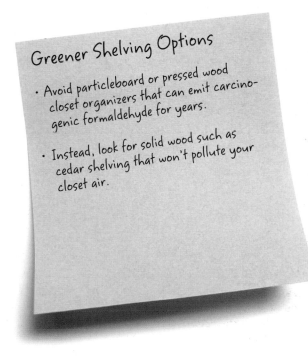

Greener Shelving Options

- Avoid particleboard or pressed wood closet organizers that can emit carcinogenic formaldehyde for years.

- Instead, look for solid wood such as cedar shelving that won't pollute your closet air.

PERSONAL CARE TOXINS
Limit your exposure through educated decision making

Personal care products really are personal. We rub them into our skin and hair, paint them on our nails and lips, and even put them in our mouths and eyes. Unfortunately, many of these products contain chemicals that are known to have adverse health and environmental effects and the industry is not required to do safety testing. Chemicals designed to preserve, mask or add scents, color, and sanitize personal care products are some of the most dangerous ingredients. Given that the typical adult is exposed to more than one hundred different chemicals a day from personal care products, the health risks are staggering.

If you compare labels you'll find certain ingredients, such as parabens and sodium lauryl sulfate, in a good number of the products you use daily. This much exposure is alarming

Fragrance

Could mess with your hormones

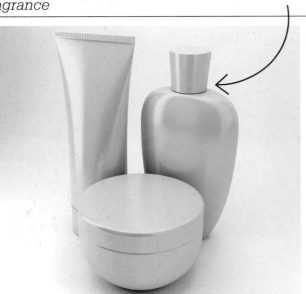

- The FDA requires personal care product labels to list all ingredients except fragrance, which can include fifty to one hundred ingredients per product.

- The Environmental Working Group has found phthalates in nearly 100 percent of the fragrances they tested.

- Phthalates are a family of chemical plasticizers that bioaccumulate in our tissues, leaving us vulnerable to long-term exposure.

- They have been shown to cause birth defects and liver cancer in lab animals and are suspected of disrupting the reproductive development of young boys.

Preservatives

The most common family of preservatives:
Methylparaben
Propylparaben
Ethylparaben
Butylparaben

- Parabens mimic estrogen. They are potential hormone disrupters and are linked to breast cancer. Yet 99 percent of personal care products contain them.

- Another, bronopol, can break down to produce carcinogenic formaldehyde or react with other chemicals to form carcinogenic nitrosamines.

- Carcinogenic formaldehyde is a preservative in eye makeup and other cosmetics.

- Although a known neurotoxin, mercury is still permitted as a preservative in eye makeup. The preservative form of mercury is called thimerosal.

74

because many of these products are designed to penetrate deep into the skin. As a result, scientists are finding that we store these chemicals in our tissues and fat. Parabens, in particular, have been found in breast cancer tissue suggesting a strong link between exposure and cancer.

Chemicals that create (or mask) a product's scent are typically listed as simply "fragrance," but can include phthalates (see page 2), which make the scents last longer but are strongly suspected carcinogens and can interfere with the hormonal system.

Some personal care products also include triclosan and other antibacterial chemicals, contributing to the rise in resistant bacteria and contaminating our waterways.

Luckily there are products available that do not contain these chemicals. The basic information below will help you read labels and make healthy decisions the next time you purchase one of these products. For specific information about the brands and products you use, the best resource is the Environmental Working Group's Skin Deep project (see resource section).

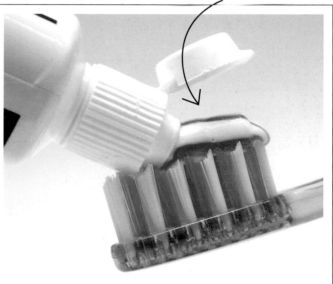

Color

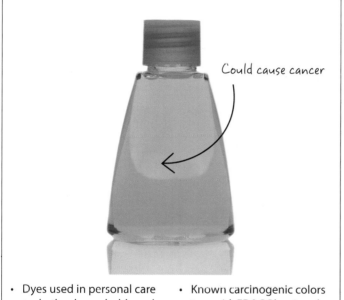

Could cause cancer

- Dyes used in personal care and other household products may contain heavy metals, such as neurotoxic lead acetate and carcinogenic arsenic.

- Colors labeled FD&C or D&C with a number often contain dyes that are allergens, irritants, and carcinogens.

- Known carcinogenic colors to avoid: FD&C Blue 1 and FD&C Green 3.

- Colors that may contain impurities that are carcinogenic: D&C Red 33, FD&C Yellow 5, FD&C yellow 6.

Antibacterials

Pesticides for your mouth

- Personal care product manufacturers have jumped on the antibacterial bandwagon adding pesticides to products.

- Yet these products are designed to be applied directly to our skin, mouth, and eyes.

- As in cleaning products, triclosan is a common

pesticide found in personal care products. Triclosan is an environmental pollutant and found in most of the nation's waterways.

- Triclosan is registered as a pesticide with the EPA, but many experts challenge whether it is effective or safe as an antibacterial.

PERSONAL CARE

75

MORE PERSONAL CARE TOXINS
How to avoid past and present dangers

Surprisingly, some of the world's most dangerous and banned chemicals have been turning up in personal care products. Some of these are chemicals that have been banned in other industries. Many have been tried, convicted, and banned in cosmetics by the E.U. Some are so new they haven't been tested yet.

Lead and mercury may be off our radar because other industries have banned them (lead from paint, mercury from thermometers). But these ingredients are still alive and well in the personal care industry.

Some petroleum by-products are already kept out of cosmetics in the E.U., but they are common in the U.S. Besides

Placenta

- Human and cow placenta are added to some products because of their ability to condition skin and hair.

- Although placenta is a naturally occurring substance that is even healthy and vital to fetuses, it is quite dangerous in personal care products.

- Placenta contains estrogen, which is absorbed by the skin.

- Recent studies report that the added hormone is enough to spur breast growth in toddlers.

Glycol Ethers

May be toxic to your reproductive sy...

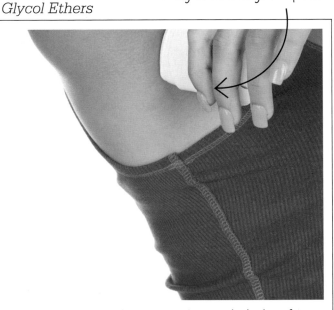

- Glycol ethers are synthetic solvents used in deodorant, nail products, perfumes, and other cosmetics.

- They irritate skin, eye, nose, and throat, and can cause anemia as well as damage to the reproductive system.

- Keep on the lookout for labels that list EGPE, EGME, EGEE, DEGBE, PGME, DPGME, and glycol ethers that have "methyl" as part of their name in the ingredients.

- Skip the product and find a greener option.

76

the fact that they include possible carcinogens and immunotoxins, research shows that they also can be contaminated with 1,4-dioxane, a known carcinogen. According to the Environmental Working Group's (EWG) testing, 22 percent of all cosmetic products are contaminated with this chemical.

Nanoparticles are a new trend in cosmetics and especially sun care. The particles are so small they easily enter the optic nerve and go to the brain and red blood cells. While they don't have to be listed on labels, EWG found them in one-third of the products they tested.

ZOOM

Many mascaras rate as high as eight out of ten on the EWG hazard scale. Along with carcinogens, mutagens, and allergens, mascaras can contain neurotoxins like thimerosal, a form of mercury. Because the eye is an extremely sensitive body part and offers a direct line to the brain, finding a nontoxic alternative is worth the effort.

Petroleum By-Products

Petroleum Distillates

Naphtha

Petrolatum

2-Nitro-P-Phenylenediamine (PPD)

- Petroleum-based chemicals in personal care products are often contaminated with toxic impurities, such as carcinogenic 1,4-dioxane.

- Petroleum distillates and naphtha are found in most cleaning products and in many personal care products.

- These are neurotoxins and endocrine disrupters that accumulate in our bodies.

- PPD is found in hair dyes and can irritate the skin and respiratory system. It is a mutagen and suspected carcinogen that has already been banned in Europe.

Nanoparticles

- The Environmental Working Group found nanoparticles in ⅓ of all personal care products.

- Nanoparticles enable minerals that may be safe on the surface of the skin to penetrate the skin and possibly enter the brain.

- Because they do not behave the same as larger molecules of the same substance, experts believe more testing must be done to know they are safe.

- Common nanoparticles that you may see on a label: Nano zinc oxide, fullersomes, fullerene (C60 hydroxide), microspheres, nanosomes, buckeye bullets, and micronized minerals.

LABELS TO LOOK FOR

Chasing arrows, leaping bunnies, and other labels (oh my!) can distinguish natural products

Although we've been trained to think we need fancy chemicals to smell and look better, have softer skin and less wrinkles, there are plenty of natural ingredients that achieve the same or better results. Knowing which natural ingredients work and what else to look for on the label will make shopping for green care products a toxin-free breeze.

A typical green personal care product will come in biodegradable or recyclable packaging and feature inviting claims like "paraben-free" or "no animal testing." It will also be covered with an array of good-looking symbols like chasing arrows and cute bunnies.

Because there is as yet no regulatory body for green claims,

CLEAN HOME, GREEN HOME

Greener Cleansers

- These are some of the mildest and safest cleanser ingredients:

- Amphoteric 2, 6, or 20, cocamido betaine, cocamidopropyl betaine, sorbitan laurate, sorbitan palmitate, sorbitan stearate.

- Even better, choose cleansers that grow in nature and are not the product of a laboratory.

- Look for these natural cleanser ingredients: alfalfa extract, flaxseed, honeysuckle oil, oatmeal, quillaya bark, yucca root.

Safer Preservatives
- grapefruit seed extract
- phenoxyethanol
- potassium sorbate
- vitamin A (retinyl or retinoic acid)
- vitamin C (ascorbic acid)
- vitamin E (tocopherol)
- citric acid
- pycnogenol

we need to weigh the claims with what we know about the brand and what other information we find on the label. Buy products that are *fragrance-free, cruelty free,* and *hypoallergenic,* but understand that the claims have not been legally defined.

For example, some products that claim to be "fragrance-free" actually contain fragrance that counteract the chemical smells already in the product. You smell nothing, but the toxins are still there. This does not mean you shouldn't buy products that make claims; it just means you need to look at other parts of the label before you buy.

Natural Moisturizers

- Lucky for us nature is over-flowing with great ingredients to moisturize our skin and hair.

- Look for these moisturizing ingredients: Aloe vera, avocado, beeswax, bluebottle (cornflower), candelilla wax, cocoa butter, jojoba oil, macadamia nut oil, pyc-nogenol from pine trees, rice bran oil, shea butter, sunflower oil, sweet almond oil, vitamins A, C, and E.

- Look for products that contain these ingredients and have as few other ingredients as possible.

Better Organics

- The USDA Organic logo certifies that the product contains ingredients that have been grown, processed, and certified free of synthetic pesticides and fertilizers.

- However, the requirements for care products are not as strict as they are for food.

- If a care product contains at least one ingredient that is organic, then the whole product gets the label.

- Look to see how many of the ingredients are actually organic before spending the extra money.

NATURAL HOME SPA
Be a natural beauty with these easy do-it-yourself recipes

Your skin is your biggest organ and will greedily absorb whatever you choose to lather and slather over it. A great way to be extra sure that you are putting only the most natural ingredients on and in your body is to use just natural ingredients that come right out of your own garden, refrigerator, and cupboard. The recipes here don't require a lot of time or extra shopping for exotic ingredients, and they work really well. If you master these recipes, you'll be off experimenting with others in no time. See the resource section for where to find them.

The basic ingredients for skin care recipes are herbs, vegetables and fruits, fruit and nut oils, distilled water, apple ci-

Easy Thyme/Fennel Cleanser

- 2 sprigs fresh thyme, crumbled (or ½ T dried thyme); 2 teaspoons fennel seeds; crushed; ½ cup boiling water; Juice of half a lemon

- Mix thyme and fennel seed in a bowl and cover with boiling water. Add lemon juice and steep for fifteen minutes. Strain infusion and store liquid in a jar in the refrigerator. Use a cotton ball to dab cleanser on your face. Then rinse.

- Fennel seeds are gentle cleaners and tone the skin by reducing swelling and soothing any irritation. Thyme works as a natural astringent.

Deep Cleansing Mask

- Avocado mask to exfoliate and moisturize: 1 avocado, juice of half a lemon; Skin tightening mask: 2 egg whites

- For best results, steam your face first: Boil a pot of water and fresh herbs. Place the pot on a table. With your hair tied back and a towel draped over your head, lean your face over the pot for five minutes. Blot dry. Mash avocado with lemon juice and apply evenly to face and neck. Leave on for 20 minutes, then rinse with cold water. Or, beat egg whites until just stiff. Apply to face and leave on 20 minutes. Rinse with cold water.

der vinegar, honey, and other bee products. From there the possibilities are endless. These recipes are focused on exfoliation to support you in your efforts to detox your surroundings. Exfoliation sloughs off the dead layer of skin cells, which helps your skin do a better job of regulating and eliminating whatever toxins are in your body. The lemon juice in both the cleanser and mask is an alpha hydroxy acid (AHA), which works to break up the dead skin for thorough exfoliation. Yogurt and apple cider vinegar are also AHAs. The sea salt rub is for whole body exfoliation.

PERSONAL CARE

Sea Salt Exfoliator

- 2 cups fine sea salt; 4 cups grapeseed or almond oil; Up to 10 drops essential oil (optional)

- Mix ingredients in a recycled, clean glass jar with a top. Shake vigorously. Wet body in the shower and apply salt mixture with your hand or a bristle bath brush to scrub. Use circular motions and move from your feet up to your shoulders. Use a long handled brush to get your back. Rinse well, but it's okay to leave the oil on as it will naturally moisturize your skin.

Exfoliating Tools

- Exfoliate with only a loofah—no product or recipe is needed.

- Stand in the tub or shower without turning the water on. Rub the loofah all over your body to slough off dead skin cells.

- Shower as usual. Store your loofah in a dry place and replace regularly because bacteria can build up.

- Sea sponges also exfoliate and are natural, but they are very slow growing and are already at risk due to water pollution as well as overharvesting.

NO-POLISH NAILS

Have sophisticated nails without the toxins found in polish

If you've ever been in an enclosed space like an airplane or an office where someone decided they needed to touch up their manicure, you already know how toxic nail care products must be. In unventilated areas, the fumes can cause almost instant headaches or make us feel sick to our stomachs.

In the past, polishes on the market that were less toxic just didn't measure up, but now a new breed of higher-quality, less toxic nail polishes are appearing. Unfortunately, nail polish removers are not keeping pace and most can expose you to irritants and more. Unless you're willing to let the polish chip its way off your nails, you might want to skip having colorful nails. If you must use polish, choose a brand that lists all

Shape

- For best results, make sure your nails are completely dry.

- Place the nail file at an angle under the outer edge of your nail.

- Do not seesaw—file the nail in only one direction toward the center on each side of the nail until you've achieved your desired squared-off or rounded shape.

- If you notice uneven results or that the grains on the file are broken or uneven, replace it.

Soak

- Apple cider vinegar is an alpha-hydroxy acid (AHA) that works to dislodge dead skin cells.

- By soaking your hand in the vinegar you will help remove the dead skin of your cuticles and make them much softer.

- Wash your hands first and then soak in vinegar for 5–10 minutes.

- This will also soften your nails and prepare them for the rest of this technique.

of its ingredients proudly. Claims should also be very specific, such as "formaldehyde and toluene free." Be wary of any polish that claims to be organic, as this isn't a product category that is eligible for certification. If you can forgo the flash of polish, pamper youself with this nontoxic method for shiny nails that is healthier for you and the environment.

Nail care ingredients to avoid:
Toluene: A central nervous system depressant that can cause headaches and nausea. Xylene: An irritant that can cause dermatitis on the skin and is a blood toxin in lab animals. Dibutyl phthalate (DBP): A plasticizer linked to reproductive mutation and cancer. Formaldehyde: A known carcinogen. Acetone: A respiratory irritant that is toxic if ingested, acetone also dries out nails and makes them fragile. Ethyl acetate: A respiratory and eye irritant that has anesthetic effects.

Cuticles

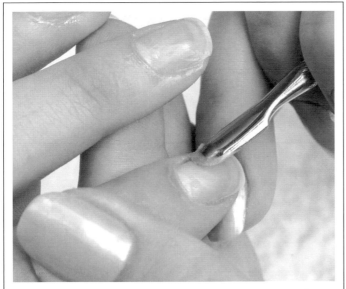

- Push the cuticles back from your nails using a manicure stick.

- If they are still not soft enough, apply a nut oil, like almond, or a dab of lotion and rub it in.

- You can cut your cuticles, but it's best to soften them and push them back.

- Cut cuticles can get infected and may grow back thicker.

Smooth and Shine

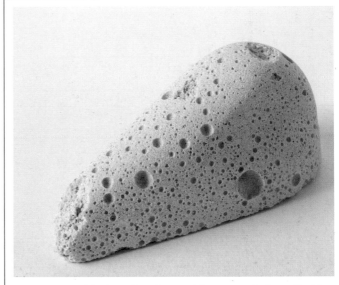

- A manicure block is a handy tool because it has different sides to file, sand, and polish nails.

- First, sand the tops of your nails using the "remove ridges" side of your tool, or a fine pumice stone.

- Then smooth the nail with the smoothing file or a buffing chamois.

- For extra soft hands and beautiful nails, use the avocado mask (see page 80) on your hands and follow with a nontoxic moisturizer.

OTHER PERSONAL CARE PRODUCTS
Essential products that are good for both you and the environment

Many personal care products are designed to keep us in health and good hygiene. They protect our skin from the sun, our teeth from cavities, and help to manage body odor and menstrual cycles. Because we use these products on our skin and in our most intimate of body parts, they have direct access to our blood, tissues, and organs.

There are a million new cases of skin cancer diagnosed each year, so sunscreen is not something we want to abandon. Look for products that are fragrance-, color-, and paraben-free. Sunscreens containing minerals like titanium dioxide and zinc oxide are good choices because they physically block UV rays instead of penetrating the skin. Avoid products that contain these minerals in skin-penetrating nanoparticle form (see page 77).

Sun Care

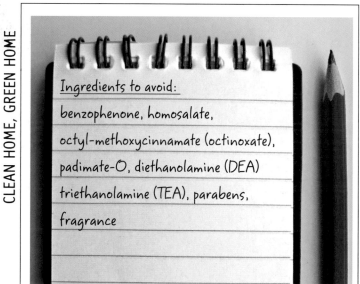

Ingredients to avoid:

benzophenone, homosalate,

octyl-methoxycinnamate (octinoxate),

padimate-O, diethanolamine (DEA)

triethanolamine (TEA), parabens,

fragrance

- These ingredients include irritants, allergens, suspected endocrine disrupters, and carcinogens and should be avoided when picking sun-care products.

- SPF measures how long it will take you to burn. SPF 10 means it will take 10 times longer than usual to burn.

- But SPF represents only the product's ability to protect against UVB rays, not UVA rays, which also burn and contribute to wrinkles and cancer.

- Look for a broad spectrum sunblock that will guard against A and B UV rays.

Deodorants and Antiperspirants

- Antiperspirants prohibit sweat by using astringents like aluminum to close pores. Deodorants cut the odor by reducing smelly bacteria.

- Washing under your arm more frequently and choosing clothing that breathes and wicks away moisture can help eliminate the need for these products.

- Otherwise look for these safer ingredients: Annatto, beeswax, candelilla wax, carmine, carrageenan, cornstarch, kaolin, pycnogenol (from pine trees), shea butter, as well as jojoba, rice bran, sunflower, and sweet almond oil; and vitamins A, C, and E.

Deodorants and antiperspirants containing aluminum have long been rumored to cause Alzheimer's. Yet the Alzheimer's Association, along with the EPA, the World Health Organization (WHO), and the U.S. National Institutes of Health (NIH) agree that there is no conclusive evidence to support this. There are, however, carcinogens and a whole host of irritants to motivate us to seek nontoxic products.

Toothpastes can also keep us healthy, but they are filled with synthetics, including preservatives, artificial sweeteners, colors, and flavorings. The debate continues over whether fluoride should be added to dental products and municipal water systems to fight cavities. The Food and Drug Administration and the American Dental Association still say "yes," but many natural caregivers highlight studies that link fluoride to reproductive disorders, bone cancer, and poor kidney health. At this point, fluoride is a matter of personal choice. See the resource section to begin your research.

Considering that women use up to 11,000 feminine products in their lifetime, they are particularly vulnerable to whatever chemicals the manufacturers put in them. Look for unbleached, certified organic cotton products that are better for your health and for the environment.

Oral Care

Ingredients to avoid in toothpaste:

sodium lauryl sulfates (SLS)

parabens

artificial colors and sweeteners

Ingredients to avoid in mouthwashes:

SLS	FD&C Yellow 5
FD&C Blue 1	FD&C Yellow 6
FD&C Green 3	

- Look for oral care products that are free of artificial colors and flavors, including artificial sweeteners.

- Some natural toothpastes are available in fluoride-free versions (see page 86).

- Look for floss products that don't contain perfluoro- chemicals (PFCs) and do contain vegetable waxes and essential oil flavoring.

- To close the recycling loop, look for toothbrush brands that use 100 percent recycled plastics or that reduce waste with replaceable heads.

Menstrual Products

- Tampons and pads are generally conventionally grown cotton products bleached white, which means they have a high cost to the environment in pesticide use and organochlorine pollution.

- One of the many toxic by-products of bleaching is the carcinogenic and reproductive toxin dioxin.

- Buying products that are made from unbleached organic cotton products is better for the environment and your health.

- Look for products that say "chlorine-free" and "organic."

- Other options to reduce waste are reusable menstrual cups and washable pads.

BABY PERSONAL CARE
Smart choices keep babies healthy

Despite the cute pictures and marketing lullabies on the labels, baby personal care products are just as toxic as adult products. As babies can absorb proportionally more contaminants in the air and through the skin than adults, it's even more important to shop smart.

In general avoid products with fragrance, dyes, harsh preservatives, and antibacterial agents. Choose the mildest products available and resist the urge to over-clean your kids. Most experts recommend washing newborns (after the umbilical cord falls off) in warm water alone. Babies only need to be washed every two to three days or else soaps can dry out their skin. As they get older a plant-based castile or glycerin soap is really all they need to get clean.

For oral care, toothpaste does not need the artificial sweet-

Baby Wash

Also look for phthalate-free baby toys

Teeth

No artificial sweeteners, no artificial flavors, no artificial colors

- Using baby wash implies milder ingredients, but they contain many of the same toxic chemicals that adult products contain.

- Look for surfactants that are milder than SLS, like cocamidopropyl betaine or cocamidopropyl hydroxy-sultaine.

- Check for washes that proudly list all of their ingredients on the label.

- Double-check by reading about the product online at Environmental Working Group's Skin Deep Web site (see resource section).

- Toothpastes can give some carcinogenic artificial flavors and colors direct access to our kids' bodies.

- Fluoride is a controversial chemical in toothpaste. In moderation it can reduce tooth decay by 60 percent.

- Yet when there is overexposure, it is a suspected neurotoxin and linked to reproductive disorders, cancer, and poor kidney health.

- Check to see if your water is already treated with fluoride and, if it is, consider reducing exposure with fluoride-free toothpaste.

ener saccharin or carcinogenic coloring to clean a child's teeth. Many nontoxic toothpastes use appealing natural flavorings of everything from cinnamon to raspberry.

As for sun care, babies under six months should not use any sunscreen. Instead floppy sun hats and long sleeves and pants are just the right SPF. For older babies, sunscreen is important on sunny days at the beach, but covering up is still more effective and nontoxic than sunscreen.

To wash a baby, first fill a baby tub with 2 to 3 inches of warm water. Support the neck and head, and pour water over your baby by squeezing a washcloth or using a small cup. Use a wet washcloth to gently wipe from head to toe and rinse. Wrap your baby in an organic towel and hug dry!

Sun Care

- Most experts recommend not putting sunscreen on babies under 6 months old.

- Sunscreens can contain toxins and are too harsh for baby's skin.

- Covering up with hats and long sleeves is the least-toxic sun-care option available.

- However, when it is time for sunscreen, look for mineral-based products, such as zinc and titanium dioxide, and make sure they are not in nanoparticle form (see page 77).

Chemicals to Avoid in Baby Products

2-bromo-2-nitropropane-1,3-diol
BHA
DMDM hydantoin
Oxybenzone
Triclosan
Boric acid and sodium borate
Dibutyl phthalate
Toluene

- DMDM hydantoin and 2-bromo-2-nitropropane-1,3-diol are allergens that can form carcinogens. Both are found in baby wipes, washes, and other products.

- BHA is found in diaper cream and affects children's skin pigmentation.

- Oxybenzone is found in sunscreen, bug spray, and lip balm. It's an allergen that damage skin.

- Boric acid and sodium borate found in diaper cream and baby powder are considered unsafe for infants

- Phthalates and toluene are endocrine disrupters and suspected carcinogens.

THE DIAPER QUESTION

What you need to know to choose the best diaper for your baby, lifestyle, and the environment

The not-so-funny thing about conventional disposable diapers is that they're not disposable at all. The National Association of Diaper Services estimates that 18 billion single-use diapers go into the landfill each year. These can take up to five hundred years to break down. This sounds like the makings of an environmental catastrophe.

But the damage begins in that fleeting moment between when you put the diaper on your baby and when it becomes trash. Disposables can expose your baby's skin to chlorine, plastics, glues, dyes, and worse. While many parents like the fact that disposables stay "dry" next to the baby's skin, the chemicals that create that dryness are not natural.

Disposable Diapers to Avoid

- Disposable diapers account for mountains of trash in landfills, along with groundwater and land contamination.

- Diaper bleaching also has a huge environmental impact.

- The bleaching process creates dioxin as a by-product, which is released into the air and water.

- Dioxin is highly toxic—a carcinogen and a persistent organic pollutant (POP) that has been found in our meat, fish, and dairy products, as well as our breast milk.

Greener Disposables

- While studies show that no diaper is actually biodegradable in a landfill, choosing chlorine-free diapers reduces the environmental impact of disposables.

- Diapers made from renewable resources like wood pulp and cotton that do not contain fragrances or dyes are also good choices.

- Disposable diapers wick moisture away from the baby's skin because they contain the super-absorbent gel sodium polyacrylate. However, experts still do not agree on how safe this gel is for your baby's skin.

- There are greener diaper options available both with and without this gel.

Fortunately you have choices, but there are so many greener options that it's hard to decide which is best. These options use fewer chemicals, and some really are disposable because they do biodegrade in a reasonable amount of time or they're flushable.

The green standard, cloth diapers, are making a comeback. Cloth diapers have the advantage of being washable and re-usable. While cloth diapers do have some environmental impact, especially if you use conventional cotton or when you use a diaper service, they remain the greenest choice. The key is to weigh the facts with your lifestyle and priorities to make the green choice that's right for you.

Easy wipes:
1 cup water
1 teaspoon baking soda
Combine and apply to clean soft flannel squares. Store in a sealed plastic bag until used and then wash after use. For disposable wipes, use recycled, bleach-free paper towels.

Flushable

- Like cloth, flushable diapers reduce waste because most of the diaper is reusable.

- But like disposables, flushables relieve you of having to deal with the mess.

- Remove the insert and flush it down the toilet without involving the landfill at all.

- Look for flushables that are Cradle-to-Cradle certified, telling you that all waste from the product goes back into the ecosystem in a neutral or even beneficial form.

Cloth

- Cloth diapers avoid landfills but require water, energy, and detergent for laundering either at home or through a service.

- A lot of pesticides go into growing conventional cotton for cloth diapers.

- Organic cotton cloth diapers washed at home in nontoxic laundry soap and chlorine-free bleach and line-dried are the greenest option.

- Whatever diaper option you choose must be balanced with what suits your own lifestyle needs.

BABY'S WORLD

89

EASY CLOTH DIAPER CARE
The greenest diaper option for babies

Diaper services are certainly convenient. They pick up your dirty diapers each week and drop off fresh clean ones. You don't even need to rinse them. Yet, the fossil fuels used to make deliveries and the water and detergent used to launder such mass quantities of diapers add up. Buying organic cotton diapers and laundering them at home can be the most eco-friendly option, especially if you have an efficient washer and line-drying is a possibility at least part of the year.

Cleaning cloth diapers is as easy as disposable diapering is supposed to be, if you follow manufacturers instructions to rinse diapers before sending them to the landfill. This is to avoid contamination and the spread of viruses in groundwater and land. If you're already rinsing disposables, throwing cloth diapers in the wash may not seem like such a big inconvenience.

Toxic Waste

- Reduce your consumption of plastic by skipping the diaper pail.

- To control odor, these pails use chemical-laden scented bags, deodorizing pucks, or aerosol sprays, which affect our ability to smell.

- Deodorizing pucks may emit polluting VOCs and aerosol propellants can be neurotoxic and/or carcinogenic.

- Instead, use a covered waste can that will last beyond the diapering stage. Look for nontoxic deodorizers or sprinkle baking soda. Wash frequently with borax and vinegar.

Natural Stain Removal Tricks

- Spray a nontoxic enzyme cleaner on soiled diapers before washing. (For ideas on cleaners, see the resource section.)

- Add ½ cup vinegar or lemon juice or borax to the wash cycle (as long as your detergent does not contain chlorine bleach).

- Dry diapers in the sun for natural whitening.

- Try non-chlorine, oxygen bleach for less toxic bleaching.

As with disposables, the first step in washing cloth diapers is to dispose of any solid waste in the toilet. From there some people choose to soak the soiled diapers in a pail filled with water and baking soda, and others store them in a dry, covered pail. When you have enough for a load, take diapers from a wet pail and run them through the spin cycle to get rid of the extra water. Or take diapers from the dry pail and run them through a cold cycle or a cold soak to loosen the stains. From there the steps are the same: Wash the diapers in hot with a cold rinse. Use less detergent than you would for your own clothes, about a ¼ cup. Add borax to the wash cycle to whiten, and white vinegar to the rinse cycle as a fabric softener. It's recommended that you don't wash more than twenty-four diapers at a time to prevent unnecessary wear from friction. Line-dry the diapers in the sunshine when possible for added whitening and sanitizing benefits.

Baby Detergents to Avoid

- Baby-specific detergents can get expensive because it means you'll be washing baby's clothes separately from your own.

- Separate detergents also mean extra packaging that eventually hits the waste stream.

- Plus, many baby detergents contain the same harsh irritants and environmental pollutants that adult detergents have. The best bet is finding a less-toxic option for everyone's clothes.

- Avoid "whitening enzymes." These are too strong for babies and may cause severe rashes.

Baby Detergents to Look For

Fragrance-free
Dye-free
Chlorine-free
No optical brighteners
No masking agents

- The truth is that what is best for baby is also best for you.

- Look for a detergent that is free of dyes, fragrances, and colorings that you can use for both you and your baby, so you can wash all the laundry together.

- Look for detergents that list all of their ingredients on the label.

- You'll still want to do the dirty diapers separately to minimize wear and maximize cleanliness.

TOYS
Wood and organic cotton are the best bets for safe toys

Plastic toys have been a big hit with parents because they are easy to clean and come in bright colors that kids love. But, plastics contain chemicals that may be endangering our children.

Teething rings, dolls, polymer clay, and other toys made with #3 plastic or PVC can expose kids to lead and other heavy metals as well as phthalates, which studies show can cause reproductive and sexual development problems in children even with limited exposure. And exposure is not limited for most children. Phthalates are in everything from baby washes and laundry detergent to shower curtain liners and practically everything with fragrance.

Plastics aren't the only danger in toys. Choking remains the top cause of toy-related infant death and injuries and is the

Washable Toys

- Stick to simple toys that don't involve plastics.

- Look for soft toys made from organic and renewable resources that use only natural dyes and are age-appropriate.

- Organic cotton and hemp toys are soft and washable, which means they start off clean and can stay clean for your child.

- Be sure to wash toys at least once a month in unscented laundry detergent. Add vinegar to the rinse cycle to make sure they come out soft.

Wood Toys

- Choose wood toys that are solid wood rather than plywood or particleboard that can offgas formaldehyde and other toxins.

- Wood that looks layered is most likely pressed wood.

- Look for finishes that use natural oils or beeswax.

- If the label doesn't tell you what the paint or finish is, call the manufacturer for details.

basis for recalling tons of toys. These toys are found to have unsafe construction or inappropriate age designations. Lead content is another reason toys get recalled. To keep up with all these recalls, it's important to check the U.S. Consumer Products Safety Commission Web site often, where you can search by company or product category (refer to the resource section).

To simplify your life, remember that less is more—kids don't need mountains of toys with unsafe paint and parts. Elimi-nate PVC toys and reduce plastics as much as possible in your nursery and home. Luckily other options exist, such as wood and organic cotton or hemp toys. Choose products that are easy to clean and free of heavy dyes and small pieces that can break off. Your child will have hours of fun without the risk of long-term damage.

Questions to Ask about Toys:

- How long will the toy hold the child's interest?

- Will it last for generations?

- Does the label assure you that the paint and finishes are toxin-free and safe?

- Is it imported or antique, which may mean lead paint?

- Does it smell toxic or perfumed?

- Is it made of PVC/vinyl plastic?

- Is the packaging wasteful?

- Can you get a version made locally?

Cleaner Bath Toys

- Bacteria and mildew can be a problem with bath toys—especially popular ones that tend to stay pretty wet.

- Cleaning them once a month helps reduce this problem.

- Put them in a big bowl, tub, or bucket and add ½ cup vinegar for each gallon of water.

- Let them soak for ten minutes. Then rub them with a sponge to get any dirt or grime off and let them dry completely.

NURSERY
A healthy environment means a healthy baby

To reduce your baby's exposure to toxins in the nursery, focus on making changes to those elements that can have the most impact on air quality: furniture, mattresses, linens, and cleaning chemicals. For example, spending a bit more for hardwood furniture instead of pressed or laminated wood or particleboard will reduce formaldehyde exposure. Even better, choose pieces that were treated with low-VOC paints or coatings, or buy unfinished wood and low-VOC products to finish them yourself. Recycling is also a great option because older furniture has already offgassed most of its chemicals.

The average baby spends about ten to fourteen hours a day either sleeping or playing in his or her crib. That's a lot of time spent breathing on or just above the mattress. Yet most mattresses have PVC surfaces to make them waterproof (see

Crib

- Avoid non-hardwood cribs, which can offgas carcinogenic formaldehyde for years.

- Look for finishes that are no-VOC or that you can finish yourself.

- Forest Stewardship Council–certified products tell you the wood came from an environmentally and socially responsible source.

- A hand-me-down or used crib that is only a few years old is another green choice, but check the U.S. Consumer Product Safety Commission Web site to make sure it was not recalled and that it meets the latest standards in crib safety.

Mattress

- Avoid cribs and mattresses covered in vinyl, infused with toxic fire retardants like PBDEs and "antibacterial" pesticides, and stuffed with petroleum-based polyurethane foam.

- Look for organic cotton, wool, or natural latex fillings. Wool is a natural fire retardant.

- Food-grade polyethylene makes a safer waterproof cover; less-toxic fireproofing options are also available.

- Another option is a used conventional crib mattress that has had a chance to offgas, but still offers firm support for your child.

page 36), with toxic phthalates making up about 30 percent of this surface's weight. The outer surface is also treated with toxic flame retardants, and the filling for most mattresses is polyurethane foam with all kinds of chemical additives, many of which are well-known toxins. Plus, this foam is highly flammable so it is also treated with PBDE.

Organic, nontoxic crib mattresses are readily available on the Internet, and some even have earth-friendly waterproof covers so you don't have to sacrifice any of the convenience of a regular mattress. Look for brands that have been certified by the third party certifier Greenguard to be extra sure you know what you're getting. You will spend a little more upfront, but the payoff is huge for the long-term health of your baby.

Once you have the basic components in place, organic cotton bedding and consistent green-cleaning practices will ensure a healthy, soothing environment for your baby.

Bedding

- Waterproof mattress pads made of wool and organic cotton are good options to top off your nontoxic mattress.

- Regular cotton sheets are hard on the environment because of pesticide use in growing the cotton and pollution from bleaching it.

- Sheets are often treated with formulas that contain formaldehyde to prevent wrinkling, as well as harsh dyes and even antibacterial toxins.

- Look for organic cotton or bamboo sheets that are not treated with synthetic dyes or anti-wrinkle formulas.

Nursery Easy Clean

- Cleaning the nursery should not add toxins and dirty the air your child is breathing.

- Wash the bedding every week and as needed if there are stains or smells.

- Vacuum the floor and any upholstery weekly to minimize dust and dust mite exposure.

- Castile soap, warm water, and a sponge will do the job for everything from crib and changing table surfaces to baseboards and windowsills. Use vinegar and water for the windows.

BODY TOXINS

Limit your toxins to get cleaner, healthier nourishment for your baby

There is no question that breast milk is still the healthiest food for babies. However, recent studies have revealed that we are all carrying stores of persistent toxins around with us in our bodies that get into breast milk. Dangerous chemicals, including DDT and PBDEs, and heavy metals, like lead and mercury, are among the chemicals found most often in breast milk worldwide.

While many chemicals simply pass through our bodies, others build up over time in our fat stores. They're in breast milk because it's full of fat. The good and bad news is that breastfeeding rids the mother's body of at least some of these chemicals, but they go directly to the baby. If a woman breastfeeds multiple children, each one will get cleaner milk than the last. By limiting the toxins you bring into your home,

Cleaner Breast Milk

- A drastic change of diet will not completely eliminate the stores of toxins we harbor in our tissues, but it can make a difference.

- Eat less animal fats and limit your intake of bigger fish that tend to contain more mercury (see page 48).

- Increase the amount of organic foods you eat to reduce your exposure to chemical pesticides and fertilizers.

- Eating more organic fruits and vegetables and whole grains is healthier in general.

Bottles

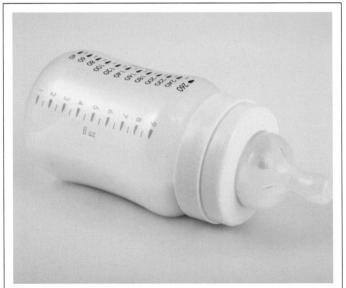

- Glass bottles are making a comeback because they don't leach any toxic chemicals and they come from a renewable resource.

- While these bottles are tough, children should not walk around with them unsupervised or sleep with their bottles.

- Other green options include BPA-free plastic bottles.

- These are generally opaque and made from safer plastics, like polypropylene (#5 plastic) or polyethylene (#1, #2, or #4).

you're already on the right track to cleaner breast milk.

Once the baby graduates to bottles and sippy cups, new concerns arise. Most plastic bottles are polycarbonate plastic (#7) and contain Bisphenol-A (BPA), which can cause long-term problems with normal hormonal functioning and development. BPA-free plastic as well as classic glass bottles are available for babies, and BPA-free and steel sippy cups are great options for toddlers.

Nipples

- Synthetic rubber nipples can be contaminated with carcinogenic nitrosamines, which can be ingested along with the contents of the bottle.

- Rubber nipples tend to be amber-colored and don't last that long.

- Look for longer-lasting and safer natural rubber or clear silicone nipples.

- Whenever you see a crack or tear in a nipple or in a bottle, it's time to recycle and replace it. Cracks can be havens for bacteria and, in glass bottles, lead to breakage.

Sippy Cups

- Avoid sippy cups made from polycarbonate plastic #7.

- If you want plastic, look for cups made from polypropylene or polyethylene plastic.

- Steel or aluminum sippy cups don't leach chemicals into your child's drink. They can weigh as little as 3.5 oz. and are small enough to fit small hands.

- Make sure the spout is made from safer plastics and look for reputable brands, as some knockoffs have been found to contain lead in their paint.

BABY'S WORLD

WASHING
Reduce your environmental impact without sacrificing clean clothes

The simple act of washing your clothes can have a far-reaching impact on the environment. After the toilet, the washing machine wastes the most water and is one of the biggest energy consumers in the home. Once the water leaves your home and enters the treatment plant and beyond, it takes with it the chemicals from your laundry detergent. Conventional detergents may clean the spot out of that sweater, but they can pollute air and waterways near and far.

Unlike soap, detergents are synthetic and most are petroleum-based. They contain surfactants that enable the product to penetrate stains and wash them away. Many detergents use surfactants that belong to the chemical class alkylphenol ethoxylates (APEs), which are known to be toxic to the immune system and suspected to interfere with the

Greener Washing

- Switch to an EPA-certified ENERGY STAR washer and reduce your energy and water consumption by over 40 percent.

- Only do full loads or adjust the water level according to the load size.

- Wash in cold and save even more energy—90 percent of the energy used to wash clothes is spent heating the water. Switching from hot to warm can cut your energy use by half.

- Run the washer at off-peak energy hours.

What to Avoid

Alkylphenol ethoxylates (APEs)
Linear alkylate sulfonate (LAS)
Diethanolamine (DEA)
Triethanolamine (TEA)
Chlorine
Fragrance
Dyes

- APEs are highly toxic surfactants with long-term impact (see page 4). LAS is corrosive and can cause major damage to skin, respiratory system, and eyes.

- DEA and TEA are used to cut grease but can react with some preservatives, to create carcinogenic nitrosamines (see page 4).

- Chlorine is an irritant that takes a toll on our environment and is responsible for a high proportion of household poisonings.

- Fragrance usually hides a long list of chemicals, including phthalates. Dyes are unnecessary and can be carcinogenic.

hormonal system. APEs are a major contaminant in U.S. waterways and are suspected of disrupting the reproduction and threatening the survival of fish. Because they do not readily biodegrade, APEs and other petroleum-based surfactants do a lot of damage to marine life and to the soil and plant life around the water.

To reduce your environmental impact, buy an ENERGY STAR–certified model that saves energy and water when it's time to replace your washer. Look for detergents that are plant-based, biodegradable, and free of fragrance and dyes.

Easy laundry soap:
$1/8$ cup castile soap
½ cup washing soda (to cut grease)
½ cup borax (to remove stains)
Optional: Add ¼ cup vinegar to rinse cycle to soften fabrics and water.
Combine. If your clothes don't feel clean enough, increase the castile soap until you're satisfied with the results.

What to Look For

Fragrance-free

Dye-free

Biodegradable in 3–5 days

Plant-based

Recycled container

- Look for products that are plant-based as opposed to petroleum-based. This means they use renewable resources and do less damage to the environment.

- Pay careful attention to the packaging. Does it come in bulk? Is it recyclable, and is it a product made from recycled materials?

- Look for concentrated formulas that you use less of and therefore have less packaging.

- Or try the recipe above to make your own laundry soap.

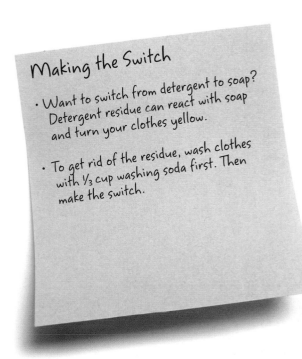

Making the Switch
- Want to switch from detergent to soap? Detergent residue can react with soap and turn your clothes yellow.

- To get rid of the residue, wash clothes with ⅓ cup washing soda first. Then make the switch.

LAUNDRY ROOM

WHITENING CLOTHES
Try some green alternatives to bleach

Bleach has been around forever. It's dirt cheap and does a great job of whitening clothing. However, it is also a registered EPA pesticide that can damage our health and the environment.

Chlorine bleach is highly caustic and can irritate skin, eyes, noses, and airways. The American Association of Poison Control Centers reports that it is the most common cause of poi-soning in children under the age of six. If you have children, this is not a product you want to keep under the sink or on the laundry room counter.

Using chlorine bleach in combination with cleaners that contain ammonia or acids, as in many toilet and oven clean-ers, can produce chloramines and chlorine gases that are

Proactive Step

- Create a system where it's easy for everyone in the household to sort their dirty clothes.

- This will make doing the laundry go a lot faster and reduce the need for bleach.

- Sort by fabric so rougher, heavier clothes are washed separately from lighter, more delicate clothes.

- This can prolong the life of your clothes and reduce the energy you use to dry them.

Natural Whitening

- Sunshine is the most natu-ral whitening and sanitizing solution available.

- For maximum whitening, first add lemon juice to the rinse cycle and wash normally.

- Then hang the clothes on a line outside to dry. Choose a sunny day when the wind is not blowing too strongly. Otherwise you may find your clothes are dirtier than when you started.

- Line drying will also save you money and the energy of using the dryer.

immediately and extremely toxic. After the bleach has done its job whitening your socks, it enters the wastewater stream and can contaminate drinking water. Specifically, it produces organochlorines that are suspected carcinogens, neurotoxins, and immunotoxins.

Adding borax to your wash and drying it in the sun may be all you need to whiten your load. If not, there are quite a few bleach alternatives on the market that are eco-friendly.

Vinegar or hydrogen peroxide goes here

Borax goes here

Non-Chlorine and Oxygen Bleach

- Non-chlorine bleaches generally use hydrogen peroxide to whiten clothes.

- Oxygen bleach generally uses sodium percarbonate, which is a combination of washing soda and hydrogen peroxide. It breaks down into oxygen, water, and soda ash, which are harmless to the environment.

- You can find these alternative bleach products in powder or liquid form.

- It's a good idea to experiment to see what works best with your water and clothes.

Other Whiteners

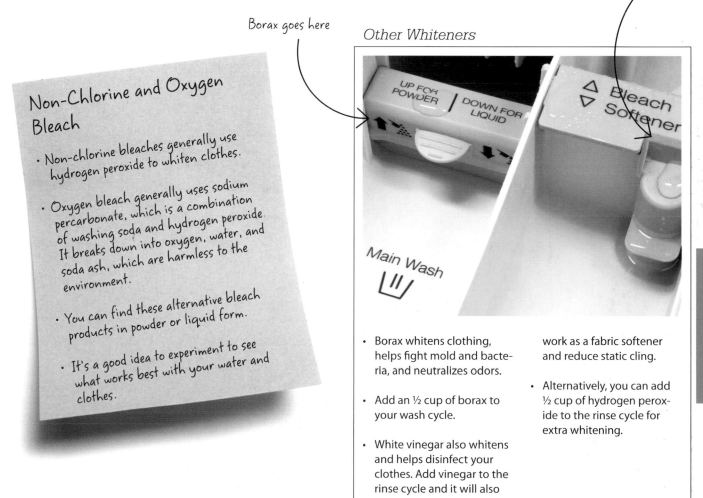

- Borax whitens clothing, helps fight mold and bacteria, and neutralizes odors.

- Add an ½ cup of borax to your wash cycle.

- White vinegar also whitens and helps disinfect your clothes. Add vinegar to the rinse cycle and it will also work as a fabric softener and reduce static cling.

- Alternatively, you can add ½ cup of hydrogen peroxide to the rinse cycle for extra whitening.

DRY-CLEANING ALTERNATIVES
Clean even your most delicate garments without polluting the air

Dry cleaning is not good for the environment or your health. The main culprit is the chemical perchloroethylene, or PERC, used by 90 percent of all dry cleaners. The EPA classifies PERC as a hazardous air pollutant, and the International Agency for Research on Cancer classifies it as a probable carcinogen. In fact, places like New York City are slowly phasing out the use of PERC in dry cleaners in residential buildings because of

reports of tenants getting sick from it. But what do you do if your favorite sweater says DRY CLEAN ONLY?

There are several greener alternatives beginning to sprout up, especially if you live in a progressive area or a major metropolis. One promising option is wet cleaning, which uses computer-controlled machines and nontoxic, biodegradable detergents to wash and dry garments. Wet cleaners then fin-

Dry Cleaning

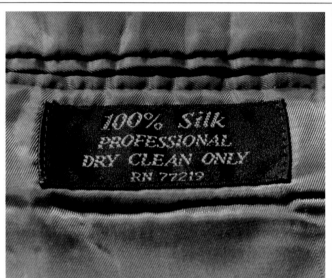

- Clothing manufacturers sometimes put this label on clothes that can also be hand washed.

- You can hand-wash unlined cotton, silk, linen, wool, or even cashmere items that are not embroidered.

- Angora sweaters, as well as lined and tailored clothing, should be taken to a professional wet cleaner or very rarely dry cleaned.

- In the future, avoid buying clothes with these labels unless you are sure you can wash them by hand.

Hand-Washing Alternative

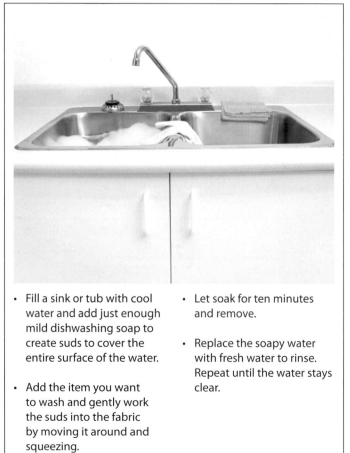

- Fill a sink or tub with cool water and add just enough mild dishwashing soap to create suds to cover the entire surface of the water.

- Add the item you want to wash and gently work the suds into the fabric by moving it around and squeezing.

- Let soak for ten minutes and remove.

- Replace the soapy water with fresh water to rinse. Repeat until the water stays clear.

ish by ironing or steam-pressing the garment. There is no air or water pollution, and you're not bringing home a bag full of carcinogens.

Home dry-cleaning kits are another PERC-free option. However, they do contain toxins that are very similar to those you want to watch out for in your laundry detergent. Kit manufacturers tend not to come clean with their actual chemical ingredients on the labels, claiming it's proprietary information. However, we do know most contain detergent with petroleum-based surfactants in their stain-removal prod-

ucts and mega amounts of fragrance, which usually means phthalates, in the sheets that go in the dryer with your garments. All of that and the fact that they are designed to be disposable make these not a great choice for your health or the environment.

Many products that claim to need dry cleaning actually do just fine with hand-washing. As you experiment with these techniques, keep in mind that if you ignore the manufacturer's dry-cleaning recommendation, don't expect the store or manufacturer to be sympathetic if it backfires.

Drying

- Squeeze item carefully to release excess water.

- Lay it out on a clean, dry, neutral-colored towel and arrange it in its proper shape. Pull gently if needed.

- Roll the towel and item up as you press down to squeeze the water out.

- Repeat with a dry towel and spread the item out on another dry towel to air-dry or hang from a line if the fabric won't stretch.

Wool and Silk

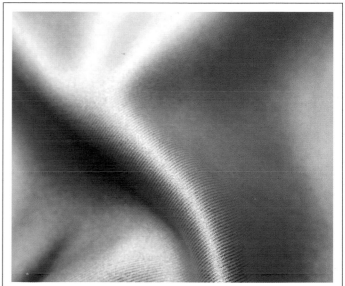

- To avoid shrinking wool, use cold water and press out water instead of rolling in a towel.

- For colored silk, test an inside seam for color fastness by wetting it and then dabbing it with a white towel.

- Wash colorfast silk in tepid water and add ¼ cup vinegar to your first rinse water to get rid of any residue. Then rinse with clear water.

- Hang silk on a padded hanger to dry.

DOWN COMFORTER
Skip the dry cleaner and safely wash your down

Down comforters are another place you typically find DRY CLEAN ONLY labels. The fear is that washing might destroy the down clusters and wash away the natural oils that protect them. Yet the ducks and geese that originally owned the feathers had no trouble getting wet and drying without losing their fluff.

The truth is that down comforters will do just fine without dry cleaning, if you know what to do. Whether you dry-clean, wet-clean, or hand-wash, the real issues are cleaning too often, with too harsh a detergent, and with too much agitation.

Professional wet cleaning is a good way to go, but, if you have a big enough space to wash it, you can save money

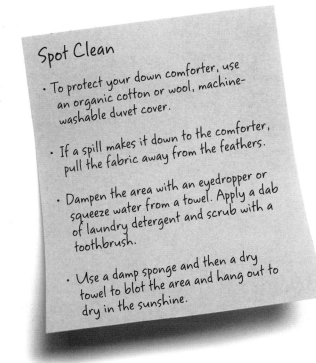

Spot Clean

• To protect your down comforter, use an organic cotton or wool, machine-washable duvet cover.

• If a spill makes it down to the comforter, pull the fabric away from the feathers.

• Dampen the area with an eyedropper or squeeze water from a towel. Apply a dab of laundry detergent and scrub with a toothbrush.

• Use a damp sponge and then a dry towel to blot the area and hang out to dry in the sunshine.

Washing Down

• To wash your down comforter in the washer, you need to have a large front loading washer. The central agitator in top-loading washers can damage the comforter.

• Use warm water and a small amount of very mild laundry detergent.

• Run the rinse cycle twice to ensure all of the detergent is out of the comforter.

• If you don't have a front loader, take it to a laundromat or wash by hand in the bathtub.

by doing it at home. Since most household washers are not designed for such large, heavy pieces, hand-washing in a large tub will yield the best results for your comforter and your washer.

Hang your comforter in the sun a few hours a month (see page 100) to increase the time between cleanings. If you do that consistently and spot-clean when necessary, you may only need to wash your comforter every couple of years.

(see page 100)

If you're drying your comforter in your dryer, throw in a couple of tennis balls. This will save you the trouble of pulling the comforter out of the dryer to refluff periodically. The tennis balls do the fluffing work for you.

Drying Down

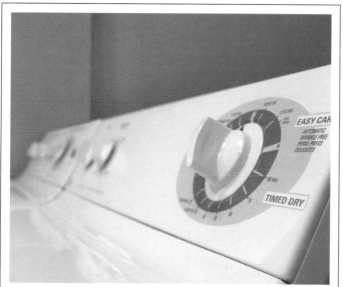

- Run the comforter through the washing machine's spin cycle a second time to remove excess water.

- As you remove it, squeeze out any remaining water without wringing or twisting the comforter.

- If you use your dryer, you'll need to dry the comforter for a few hours on low heat.

- Remove periodically to fluff and add dry towels to help absorb the moisture.

Line Drying

- The best way to dry down is in the sunshine.

- Because a wet comforter is heavy, use plenty of clothespins to hold it on the line.

- If you have parallel lines, it may work better to securely attach two sides, creating a

kind of hammock, to reduce the amount of weight on one line.

- Periodically remove the comforter and shake it. Then reattach to completely dry.

STAIN REMOVAL
Start mild for effective, nontoxic stain removal

Conventional stain removers are petroleum-based and contain many of the same harsh chemicals as detergents. What's more, in their quest to treat all stains equally, they are often ineffective. The general rule for effective and nontoxic stain removal is to treat the stain as soon as you can and start as mild as possible.

The first step is to scrape or absorb by dabbing (not rubbing) any part of the stain that hasn't yet penetrated the fabric. A knife or cloth works well, depending on the substance. For greasy stains try cornstarch to absorb the oil. For older stains, apply glycerin to loosen the stain for easier removal.

Next, hold a colorfast towel behind the stain to absorb it

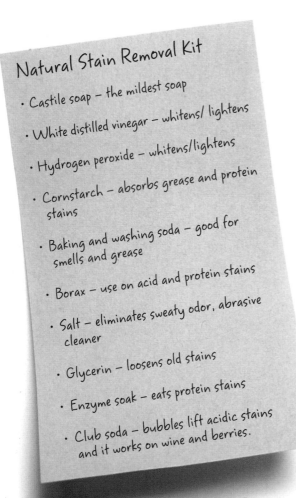

Natural Stain Removal Kit

- Castile soap – the mildest soap
- White distilled vinegar – whitens/ lightens
- Hydrogen peroxide – whitens/lightens
- Cornstarch – absorbs grease and protein stains
- Baking and washing soda – good for smells and grease
- Borax – use on acid and protein stains
- Salt – eliminates sweaty odor, abrasive cleaner
- Glycerin – loosens old stains
- Enzyme soak – eats protein stains
- Club soda – bubbles lift acidic stains and it works on wine and berries.

Common Stains

- Mustard – Flush with white vinegar. Wash with dish soap and cold water.

- Tomato sauce – Scrape off solids. Dab with diluted dish soap and soak in cool water.

- Soy sauce – Apply diluted dish soap and use a toothbrush to work it into the fabric. Flush with cold water. Do the same with vinegar if the stain persists.

- Sweat – Soak garment for an hour in enough water to cover and ¼–½ cup of salt. Wash as normal and line dry in the sunshine. The lower temperature and the sun's bleaching power prevent the sweat from yellowing the garment.

and use another towel to dab ice-cold water on the front of the stain. If that doesn't do it, the next step is to continue to hold the towel behind the stain and apply an ice cube to the front of the stain. For many stains, this is all it takes. If there is only a faint stain left on a white garment, apply white vinegar with a cotton swab. The vinegar is a whitener and may take care of it.

If that's not enough, you'll need to try less-mild solutions, but pretest the fabric in an inconspicuous place to make sure your chosen technique won't ruin the fabric.

Beverage Stains

- For coffee, tea, or wine stains, boil water in a teakettle.

- Have someone hold the stained fabric taut over a sink.

- Stand on a chair and slowly pour boiling water from 2–3 feet above the fabric until the stain starts to lighten and disappear.

- Alternatively, rinse with club soda and blot the stain up with a clean light-colored towel.

Kid Stains

- Grass – Use an enzyme spray and wash as usual.

- Blood – Place stained clothing in a sink with cold water and $\frac{1}{8}$ cup salt. Soak for an hour. For tough stains, try soaking area in hydrogen peroxide. Scrub with detergent. Wash as usual.

- Chocolate/ice cream stains – Scrape off any unabsorbed food. Wet area with water and mild dish soap. Scrub with a toothbrush.

- For tough chocolate or ice cream stains, spray with an enzyme cleaner. Launder as usual.

LAUNDRY ROOM

107

MACHINE AND NATURAL DRYING

Dry garments smartly to conserve energy—and cost

The EPA excludes clothes dryers from its ENERGY STAR certification program because they simply consume too much energy. In fact, they are the second-biggest energy drain after the refrigerator (which is constantly running) in the average household. But you can save energy with your clothes dryer by making a few smart choices.

Some dryer features can help you save energy. These include controls that automatically shut off the machine when the clothes are dry and set a start-time in the future to run during off-peak hours when energy is cheaper. Try shortening the drying time to prevent over-drying your clothes and run only full loads during off-peak hours.

Greener Machine Drying

- Another energy-saving step includes drying heavy clothes separately from lighter clothing, which take far less time to dry.

- Do consecutive loads to make use of the hot air that's already in your dryer from the previous load.

- Clean the lint filter often and make sure the outside dryer vent closes tightly.

- If the vent does not close tightly, fix or replace it so you can keep the cooler outside air from leaking in.

Fabric Softeners to Avoid

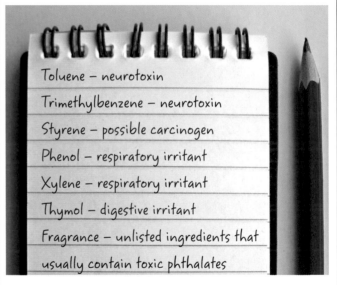

Toluene – neurotoxin
Trimethylbenzene – neurotoxin
Styrene – possible carcinogen
Phenol – respiratory irritant
Xylene – respiratory irritant
Thymol – digestive irritant
Fragrance – unlisted ingredients that
usually contain toxic phthalates

- Wash natural-fiber clothing, like cotton and linen, separately from synthetics. Synthetics are prone to static, but natural clothing by itself is not.

- Add vinegar to the rinse cycle (see sidebar above) to eliminate static and soften your clothes. Baking soda in

the wash cycle also softens clothes.

- For fragrance, add a few drops of your oil of choice to the rinse cycle.

- Or put it on a washcloth and throw it into the dryer with your clothes.

Drying your clothes presents you with another also choice—whether to use dryer sheets. They are a big contributor to the mountains of items building up in our landfills. They can contain neurotoxins, respiratory irritants, and skin irritants, which are transferred to your clothes. Look for less-toxic options or try out this recipe for easy fabric softening.

Hanging your clothes out to dry in the sunshine can also save money and energy. Line-drying one load of laundry cuts 3.35 pounds in carbon dioxide emissions, which adds up to over a thousand pounds in a year.

Fresh-Air Drying

- To build a line, run a rope between your fence and your house or between two poles.

- Seven to 8 feet off the ground is a good height, but adjust depending on what's comfortable for you.

- For small spaces, use a multilevel drying rack because you can fit more clothes and still have air circulation between them.

- Pay attention to the weather when you're line-drying. Windy days can kick up dirt and dust.

Wrinkle-Free Shirts and Pants

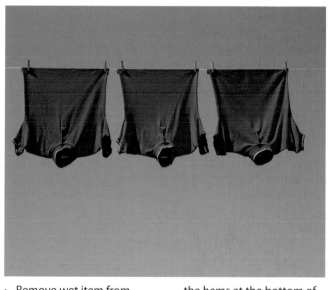

- Remove wet item from washer and shake out wrinkles and excess water.

- Arrange shirt as if you were going to lay it out flat. Attach bottom of shirt securely to line.

- Fold pants along the desired vertical crease. Attach the hems at the bottom of the pants to the line with clothespins

- For brightly colored clothing, turn the article inside out before hanging so it won't fade in the sun.

LEAVE THE DIRT AT THE DOOR

Take a proactive step to reduce your cleaning burden for the entire house

The simplest way to keep dirt out of your home is to leave shoes at the door. Shoes can track in everything from mud and pet waste to pesticides, lead, and tar. Although wearing shoes in the house doesn't seem like a big deal, an EPA study showed that pesticide-carrying shoes are a major source of exposure for children. This is because children are more apt to be closer to the floor for longer periods of time and to constantly put their hands in their mouths. Even if you don't use pesticides in your yard or have lead content in your soil, you really don't know where everyone's shoes have been and what they're tracking into your home.

Creating a designated space to store shoes and contain

Provide the Tools

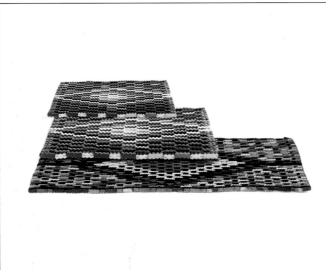

- A textured recycled rubber or rope mat will get the dirt off and helps close the recycling loop.

- Placing a shoe scraper on the step or porch next to your door will help with particularly muddy shoes that have deep grooves in the soles.

- Make your own scraper by placing an old rectangular, stiff-bristled broom head alongside your doormat.

- Screw both into an appropriate-sized board for stability.

Make It a Rule

- For a shoes-off system to work, it has to be a habit with household members and a clear request for guests.

- Create or buy a sign and display it prominently so guests are clear on the rule.

- Once everyone gets used to it, it will just come naturally and your home will stay cleaner longer.

the dirt will mean less exposure for your family. It will also support you in your efforts to reduce the amount of cleaning products you need to use and the amount of time you need to spend cleaning. Don't forget to apply this same rule to the people delivering items to your home or performing a service. They should come equipped with their own shoe protectors, but you may need to prompt them to put them on. If not, and they aren't lifting heavy objects, ask them to remove their shoes just like everyone else. If this is a frequent occurrence, it's a good idea to buy your own stash of protectors at the hardware store.

It may seem awkward at first to ask guests to remove their shoes, but, as long as you make it a rule and don't cave to every complaint, they'll get used to it. And with the right setup, you can make it an easy and even inviting thing to do.

Shoe Storage

- Provide a space that is clean and easy for people to remove their shoes.

- Stacking shelves have room for more shoes without taking up too much space.

- These shelves will get dirty, so be sure to wash them as part of your regular entryway cleaning routine.

- Remove the shoes and vacuum the shelves or use a dustpan and brush. Then wipe clean with all purpose cleaner and a rag.

A Cozy Touch

- Fill a basket with inexpensive, washable, and comfortable slippers and place it by the front door.

- Make sure you have a basic range of sizes—small, medium, and large.

- When guests enter and remove their shoes, they can grab a pair of slippers and no one will ever notice the hole in their sock.

- Remember to wash these slippers frequently, especially in the summer when guests might not be wearing socks.

HIGH-IMPACT MUDROOMS
Let your mudroom keep your whole house clean

It's easy to put off cleaning when it seems like there just isn't enough time in the day. It's not that you don't really have the time to, say, wipe down the kitchen counter, but if it means first sorting the mail, recycling the newspaper, putting away sunglasses, keys, and the dog's leash, you just might not have time. The more you can do to keep these things off the coun-

ter, the better chance you'll have of keeping it clean.

If you're lucky enough to have a spacious mudroom, using the space wisely will help control clutter throughout your home. Create specific spaces in the room to place shoes, keys, mail, pet gear, and outdoor clothing. The kitchen counter and table, as well as the back of the couch, the floor, and

Cleaning Station

- Put up a wall-mounted rack for long-handled brooms and mops. Mops will dry better and your cleaning tools won't be sitting in a dusty corner.

- It's also easier to clean the floor without having to move them around.

- Store cleaners in a cupboard or closet near the brooms and mops.

- Keep the basics together in a carrying container so it's easy to transport everything you need with you as you clean your home.

Gardening Station

- Store gardening tools where they are most convenient to the garden.

- Place pots, watering cans, and any larger objects on shelves; spread them out enough so you can see what you have without wasting space.

- Use bins or empty pots to hold gardening gloves and other soft goods as well as any smaller tools that don't hang.

- Put up hooks for small garden tools that do hang, so you can see them easily.

the stairs can then stay clear. It may also save you hours of searching for the dog's leash, your keys, or your umbrella. Best of all, designated stations that offer a place for everything make the usually arduous task of cleaning the mudroom much easier. Bins can be removed easily for dusting or washing shelves and counters.

If you don't have a designated mudroom, setting up a corner of an entryway or hallway will help you control daily clutter from spreading throughout your home. Small bookshelves or shelves hung in specific locations will help with this process.

Pet Station

- Place food in a storage bin that closes tightly so it won't tempt unwanted rodents or pests and will stay fresh longer.

- Set up a feeding station so it's convenient to the food.

- Have a separate bin for leashes and extra collars and a bag or basket for waste bags you'll need when you go for walks.

- A cookie jar for treats and bones and a bin for toys will complete the station.

Small-Space Mudroom Necessities

- A mat or shelf for shoes

- Hooks for coats with mats below to catch drips

- Hooks or a bin for keys

- Slots or baskets for mail

- Baskets for seasonal gear like hats and gloves

- A container for umbrellas

ENTRYWAYS AND MUDROOMS
Follow some routine tasks for dirt control

If you tend to do most of your cleaning right before guests arrive, you probably aren't focusing too much on your mudroom. It is, after all, the mudroom. Yet mudrooms and entryways work best at controlling dirt when they are cleaned regularly. If not, whatever dirt you're trying to contain builds up, spreads out, and gets tracked into the rest of the house anyway.

Main entryways create the first impression on your guests. Routine cleaning should include dusting and occasionally polishing any furniture you have there as well as weekly vacuuming and occasional mopping, depending on your floor.

Even if guests never enter through the mudroom, it should also be dusted and vacuumed or swept on a fairly regular basis to keep the dirt down to a minimum. That's why orga-

Easy Prep

- Place shoes on sheet or tarp that you can drag outside. Clean muddy shoes and hose down mats. Vacuum and wash shoe shelves.

- Remove all bins and baskets from shelves or counters so you can wash the shelves. Empty bins and wipe down or vacuum.

- Wash throw rugs.

- Sweep and wash the floor.

Maintenance

- Remove coats from hooks and inspect hooks for rust and sturdiness.

- Tighten loose screws so hooks can handle the multiple coats that often get piled on them.

- Try to remove minor rust stains by applying a paste of borax and lemon juice. Let dry and rinse off.

- If the rust is beyond cleaning, replace the hook. The rust will stain jackets and tote handles that hang there.

nization is key. A pile of shoes in the corner makes for a lot of prep work when you need to wash the floor. Shoes neatly arranged on a recycled rubber utility mat are easy and quick to move. The less prep required, the more often you'll clean and the more effective the space will be in containing dirt so it won't get tracked into your home.

But even if you don't have time to remove shoe storage or bins on the floor, vacuum or sweep around them to control the dirt as much as you can. Then, schedule a periodic deep clean based on how dirty your mudroom gets. If you have kids, plan on spending some time dusting and washing shelves and moving shoes, mats, and bins out for a thorough floor cleaning every month or two. Better yet, delegate the job to your kids. Having the responsibility of cleaning the mudroom might just give them the encouragement they need to keep it clean on a daily basis.

Containing Dirt: Tools for the Mudroom

- Recycled rubber utility mats

- Washable throw rugs

- An extra door mat between mudroom and home

- Regular cleaning

Seasonal Clutter Control

- Schedule one mudroom deep-cleaning session at the beginning of each season.

- Check bins and baskets for past-season gear and replace with current season necessities.

- For the winter to spring transition, hats and gloves can be stored out of the way to make room for rain hats and umbrellas or sun visors as you head into spring.

- Remove heavy coats and replace with windbreakers and raincoats.

HALLWAY DECOR AND STAIRS
Keep art and stairs dust-free for easy cleaning

Hallways and stairs can be neglected spaces when it comes to cleaning. After all, most of us don't linger long in the hallway or on stairs. Instead, we use them as a means to get from one room to another. We may not notice dusty buildup on pictures or stairs, or fingerprints that can lessen the appearance of hallway decor and may even ruin valuable art if left unattended.

Regular cleaning can be less frequent for these places than the kitchen, bathroom, or living areas. Depending on your family, once a month may keep it looking neat and clean. Start at the top for both and remove any spiderwebs accumulating in the corners of the ceiling or steps. Dust lamps to keep them clean and in good condition. Dust furniture and railings periodically dust and wash the baseboards where

Framed Photos

Plexiglas

- If your photos or art are behind Plexiglas instead of glass, wipe them with a damp cloth only.

- Even a soft dry cloth can scratch Plexiglas.

- Dust accumulates in tight spaces. If your frame is delicate or has some chipped paint or detailed carving, dust gently with a clean paintbrush.

- Use a T-shirt rag or microfiber cloth to dust the sides and front of the frame and glass.

- Dust the surfaces that immediately border the glass. Use a cotton swab if you can't get your cloth into a space.

- Dust the back of the frame.

dirt can accumulate. Dampen an old, clean T-shirt with warm soapy water and wipe them down. Vacuum against the direction of traffic on carpets to slow the wearing process. Vacuum both bare and carpeted stairs.

Aside from these routine cleaning tasks, the most important job in the hallway may be caring for art and photos that line the walls. Keep these emotionally or financially valuable pieces clean and dust-free to prolong their life and keep them looking their best. But dusting art is not the same as

dusting an end table. Too much pressure or the wrong tool can cause damage like paint flaking. Photographs may seem straightforward, but harsh cleaning solutions or even water can ruin them.

Dust Control

Dust builds up here.

- As in any room, start your dusting at the top. That means use a vacuum attachment or long-handled broom to get at any cobwebs on the ceiling.

- Next dust any photos or other wall hangings.

- Then, tackle the railing. Dust the top and sides with a just-damp T-shirt, wool sock, or dry microfiber cloth.

- Dust each baluster or post separately and work your cloth into any carved area or detail that may harbor dust.

Handheld Vacuuming

Use attachment or handheld to get in here

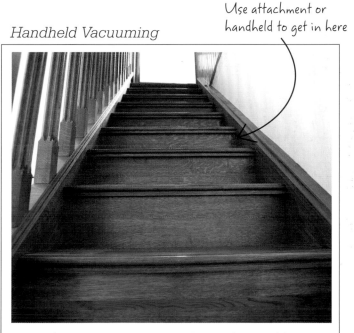

- For a shorter staircase, a handheld vacuum may be the easiest tool to use.

- Make sure the dust canister is empty before starting this task so you'll have more suction power to do the job.

- Start at the top of the staircase and slowly drag the handheld in strips from back to front on the stair tread.

- Line up the vacuum opening with the sides and then the back of the stair and slowly vacuum.

ENTRYWAYS

CEILING FANS
Dust buildup reduces air quality and shortens the life of your fan

Ceiling fans improve ventilation in your home and help fight against global warming by reducing your need to run your A/C or heater. But a ceiling fan gets dusty fast and, when you do turn it on, it can reduce air quality by throwing dust around the room. Dust buildup can also harm the fan because the extra weight of the dust knocks the fan off bal-ance, causing unequal pressure on the motor bearings. The fan may begin to squeak and will start to wear out.

The first step in cleaning your ceiling fan is to clean the ceiling and walls around the fan. Dust may have mixed with grease from the fan's motor, and this shows up in surrounding areas as dark grime. This is especially a problem for kitchen

Routine Clean

Dust here.

Deeper Clean

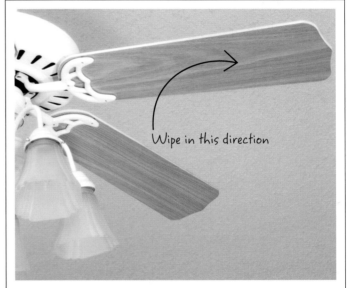

Wipe in this direction

- If you haven't dusted your fan for a while, start with the Deeper Clean step.

- Routine cleaning will work when there is much less dust to pick up.

- Use a long-handled duster to access the tops of each blade.

- Be sure that the duster is microfiber or lamb's wool so the dust actually sticks to it instead of creating a dust storm in your living room.

- Be sure the fan is turned off and position a sturdy ladder under it.

- Do not use a feather duster or dry cloth for this job or you will scatter the dust everywhere.

- Instead, bring a few cloths and all-purpose cleaner up the ladder with you.

- Spray the cleaner on the cloth, not the fan, to protect the motor. Wipe each blade from the center of the fan out. Change cloths as needed.

ceiling fans because cooking grease can add to the grime. Try using all-purpose cleaner (see page 31) to cut the grease and clean this up.

When the surrounding areas are clean, turn your attention to the blades. It's a good idea to test each one to make sure they are securely attached and immediately fix any loose blades. Inspect any other parts of the fan, including pull strings and the light fixture if you have one.

To get the most climate-saving power for your buck, change the fan's direction by season. In warm weather, run the fan counterclockwise to make you feel cooler and reduce your need for A/C. In the winter, reverse the blade direction to make the room warmer by pulling the cooler air up and redistributing the warmer air that hovers near the ceiling.

Base and Light

- Use a clean cloth, dampened with all-purpose cleaner (see page 31) to wipe around the base of the fan.

- Work the cloth into tight spaces where the blades attach and in the light fixture.

- Wipe down the glass shade or shades of the light fixture. If possible, remove and carefully bring the shade down with you. Wash and dry the shade at the kitchen sink.

- Use a dry cloth without solution to dust the lightbulbs individually. Removing the dust will increase your light quality.

Inspection

- Check the blades - Lightly lift up and press down on each blade.

- Check the light fixture - Examine bulbs for cracks and make sure each bulb and shade is screwed in completely.

- Check your energy use - Replace standard bulbs with energy-saving compact fluorescent lightbulbs.

- Check the "on" switch - Pull lightly on the string to be sure it's secure.

BOOKS
Keep your books dust-, mold-, and pest-free

In well-ventilated and dry living areas or offices, book collections can be cozy and inspiring. However, if the room tends to be damp and humid, you may have to deal with mold and silverfish that love to nestle up with the likes of Shakespeare, Emily Dickinson, and even Suze Orman and Harry Potter. Running a dehumidifier may do the trick to fend off pests, but if the mold problem is already widespread, you may have to consult a mold remediator and start getting your books at the library.

Silverfish pose a much easier problem to solve. Since they feed on the glue in book bindings, as well as the paper, it's a good idea to get rid of any unruly stacks of magazines or

Coffee-Table Books

Dust accumulates here

- Coffee-table books should be dusted every time you clean the living room. Do not use a solution for this job or you risk damaging the books.

- First use a dry microfiber cloth to dust the areas that are visible where the most dust can accumulate.

- Then pick up each book and run the cloth over the spines, the backs, and the pages.

- Dust underneath the books and replace.

Spine Smudges

Look for smudges here

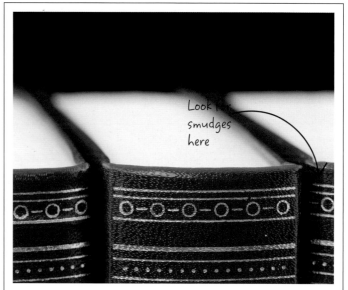

- When people peruse your bookshelves, they can leave oil from their fingers (or lunches) on the spines of glossy books.

- Dampen a towel or clean T-shirt rag with lukewarm water. Do not use soap or detergent.

- Wipe the length of the spine until the smudge disappears.

- Dry immediately with a dry cloth.

newspapers you have lying around. In her book *Home Enlightenment,* Annie Berthold Bond suggests two more direct methods for ridding your books of silverfish. The first is to wrap a jar in grippy masking tape and place it uncapped on the shelf alongside your books. Overnight the bugs will climb up and fall in, making it easy to flush them down the toilet the next morning. Another technique is to microwave the book for 30–60 seconds and shake out the dead insects into the garbage. Do not use this technique with fragile, older books or books with gilded edges or any metallic elements that could cause a fire in the microwave.

To keep your book collections clean and pest-free, remember that while you are collecting books, the books are collecting dust. Using the right vacuum attachment can make regular dusting easy and fast. That, and an occasional deep cleaning for which you actually take the books off the shelves, will keep your books in good order and your home less dusty.

Quick Clean Bookshelf

Vacuum here

- First, remove any small objects that could be sucked up by the vacuum.

- Use the small brush attachment to gently dust the tops of books and spines as they are lined up vertically or the sides and spines for horizontal stacks.

- This can also be done for other sturdy objects like bookends that share the shelves.

- Next, use the crevice tool to dust any open spaces on the shelves around the book.

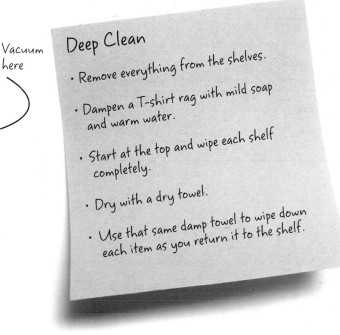

Deep Clean

- Remove everything from the shelves.

- Dampen a T-shirt rag with mild soap and warm water.

- Start at the top and wipe each shelf completely.

- Dry with a dry towel.

- Use that same damp towel to wipe down each item as you return it to the shelf.

UPHOLSTERY

Fight dust mites and stains without using toxins

While there is an impressive range of products devoted to getting your upholstery clean, a little green knowledge can completely eliminate your need for a special cleaner. It's a good thing, too, because conventional upholstery cleaners can contain the same carcinogenic chemical used by dry cleaners (perchloroethylene), as well as irritants, neurotoxins, and suspected teratogens like butyl cellosolve.

When cleaning, think about what makes upholstery dirty. The most visible issues are spots and stains. As with other fabrics, the faster you treat stains, the better chance you have of removing them.

Stain removal is easier if your cushion covers can be removed, soaked, and washed. Look for furniture that has this feature when you are in the market for a new couch or chair.

Upholstery

- For routine dust removal and cleaning, vacuuming works best.

- Attach your upholstery brush tool and vacuum the seats, back, and armrest of your sofa or chair.

- Vacuum throw pillows and behind back cushions as well.

- Switch to the crevice tool for tight spaces like in between the cushions. Flip cushions to minimize wear on any one side.

Cushions

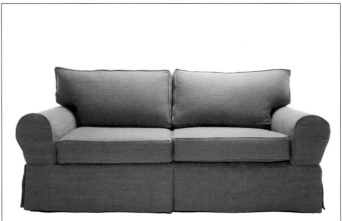

- If you notice your cushions looking a little dingy or stained, look for zippers.

- Unzip and remove the cover. Soak any stains in mild dishwashing soap and water or choose another stain-removal technique (see pages 106–107).

- Look inside for care instructions and wash accordingly.

- Pay particular attention to the drying instructions because a shrunken cushion cover will not do you much good at all.

Upholstery also gets dirty because it is a natural magnet for the dust that is on every surface in your home. No matter how sophisticated the science, an upholstery cleaner won't be able to do much about dust. Instead, make the most of your vacuum attachments to remove dust and control dust mites in your furniture. Alternatively, vapor steam cleaners work really well on upholstery.

Leather furniture needs a little extra care and protection. Try this easy leather cleaner to keep your leather furniture clean and conditioned.

MAKE IT EASY

Leather cleaner
½ cup jojoba oil
⅛ cup distilled white vinegar
Rub into leather with a soft cloth for cleaning and conditioning. Do not use on suede.

Emergency Clean

- Scrape off any unabsorbed spill with a knife.
- Grab a white cloth and press it firmly into the spot.
- Repeat until you've absorbed everything you can.
- Scrub with castile soap and water.
- For oily spills, sprinkle cornstarch on the spot.
- Let sit. Then scrape off with a knife.

Leather

- Dust regularly with the dust brush attachment on the vacuum or with a microfiber cloth.
- For spills, dampen a white cloth with warm water and blot the spot until you've absorbed everything you can. Do not scrub.
- To clean, make sure the furniture is dusted and test the leather cleaner recipe (see above) on an inconspicuous spot.
- Dip a soft cloth into the mixture and apply small amounts at a time to your furniture with circular movements. Remove any extra cleaner with a dry rag.

123

LAMPS
Lighting the way to cleaner air and lower energy bills

Like ceiling fans, and even because of ceiling fans, a lamp can harbor loads of dust that reduce the amount of light it gives off and cause unnecessary wear. Dusty lamps can also decrease indoor air quality because the dust gets released back into the air every time someone disturbs the lamp or turns it on or off.

It's important to dust the lamp base and lightbulb regularly, but don't forget the shade. Microfiber cloths work well, but so can pantyhose if you happen to have some around. Slide your hand inside the hose and wipe the shade clean. For deeper cleaning, some fabric shades can be fully submerged in water and others, such as those made from parchment, need another approach.

Keeping lightbulbs and shades clean can help maintain

Dust Control

Dust gets in here

- Fluted shades or other types of shades that do not have flat, even surfaces can get very dusty in hard-to-reach places.

- Turn off the lamp and remove the shade. Take it outside or hold it over a sink or garbage can as you wipe each valley with a clean paintbrush, soft brush, or feather duster.

- Apply only the slightest pressure as you brush each valley and eliminate the dust.

- Dust the lightbulb with a microfiber cloth.

Washable Shades

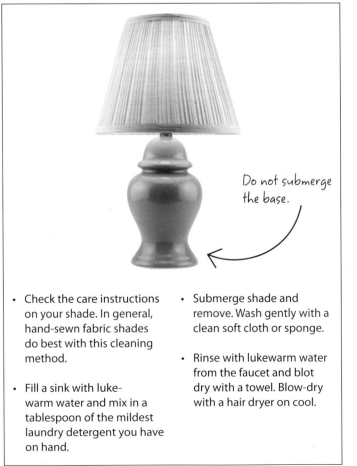

Do not submerge the base.

- Check the care instructions on your shade. In general, hand-sewn fabric shades do best with this cleaning method.

- Fill a sink with luke-warm water and mix in a tablespoon of the mildest laundry detergent you have on hand.

- Submerge shade and remove. Wash gently with a clean soft cloth or sponge.

- Rinse with lukewarm water from the faucet and blot dry with a towel. Blow-dry with a hair dryer on cool.

the quality of light coming from that lamp. But choosing the right lightbulb is crucial for setting the mood you want in the room, as well as for managing your energy bills and reducing your carbon emissions. Since the EPA estimates that 20 percent of household energy use comes from lighting, choosing an energy-efficient compact fluorescent lightbulb is a great idea. These bulbs have come a long way from their glaring-white-light ancestry, and they are also becoming even more efficient. One bulb can last up to eleven years.

GREEN ● LIGHT

When choosing a lightbulb, look for ENERGY STAR–certified compact fluorescent lightbulbs to get the most energy-efficient bulbs available. Keep in mind that CFLs generate more light with less wattage, so here's how to know if you're buying the right wattage for your space: 15-watt CFL = 60-watt incandescent bulb; 20-watt CFL = 75-watt incandescent bulb; 26–29-watt CFL = 100-watt incandescent bulb.

Non-Washable Shades

- Parchment or paper shades cannot be washed. Instead, dust frequently to keep them from showing dirt.

- Use a paintbrush or soft brush to dust all the way around the shade. Pay special attention to seams and details where dust can stick.

- A hair dryer on a cool setting can also do this job, although the dust will scatter.

- To remove marks, try a pencil eraser. Apply very light pressure to avoid leaving an eraser mark.

Bases

- Lamp bases should be dusted regularly with a microfiber cloth, just damp t-shirt rag, or wool sock.

- Pay special attention to seams and detailed areas where dust can collect.

- Run your cloth down the cord to remove dust there as well.

- For fingerprints and other dirty residue on the base, spray all-purpose cleaner (see page 31) or castile soap and water on the cloth and wipe clean.

FIREPLACES
Keeping the fireplace clean minimizes its impact on indoor and outdoor air quality

The debate over whether a wood or gas fireplace is greener continues to rage on, with gas usually winning. Wood seems like the obvious green choice since it is a renewable resource and smells so natural and pleasant. However, according to the American Lung Association, wood fires are the biggest contributor to "particulate matter air pollution" coming from our homes. Health experts say that the more we breathe in these particles, the more we risk developing health problems that range from asthma and bronchitis to lung and heart disease.

Part of the problem here is improper use such as burning garbage in the fireplace as well as neglecting routine main-

Wood

- For occasional fireplace use, clean out your firebox (the area where you actually build the fire) after each fire to reduce the amount of ash that gets blown into your air.

- Be sure the fire is completely out and coals are cold. Sweep out firebox into a metal bucket with a lid.

- Take bucket outside and away from the house. Let it sit one day to eliminate any fire hazard.

- Sprinkle the ashes around non-edible vegetation like roses or other flowers as a no-cost mulch.

Gas Insert

- Gas fireplaces are much easier to clean than wood because there is no soot or ash to remove.

- Just wash the interior and exterior glass with vinegar and water glass cleaner (see page 51) and newspaper.

- Wipe down the exterior of the fireplace with all-purpose cleaner (see page 31). Vacuum the surrounds free of dust.

- Have your gas fireplace inspected once a year.

tenance and cleaning. If you prefer wood, there are a number of things you can do to make your fireplace green.

A woodstove insert that keeps the fire burning at a higher temperature emits fewer emissions than lower-temperature fires. Purchasing a woodstove built after 1980 means that it is compliant with EPA standards and pollutes less than older stoves. Burning wet or soft wood (like pine) creates more smoke, so always burn dry, seasoned, harder woods and avoid painted or treated wood. Regular cleaning of the fireplace is crucial to reducing both indoor and outdoor pollution.

· · · · · · · · · · · · GREEN ● LIGHT · · · · · · · · · · · · · ·

To reduce pollution and ensure the safety of your fireplace, set up an annual visit by the chimney sweep. He or she will remove creosote buildup that can increase pollution and cause chimney fires. The chimney sweep also looks for damage to the flue and other fireplace components that could cause indoor pollution or fire hazards in your home.

Surrounds

Use the crevice tool to vacuum here

- Soot creates stains, so clean the fireplace surrounds regularly.

- A wet/dry vacuum is best for this dirty job. If you use your regular vacuum, clean the attachments thoroughly before putting it away.

- Vacuum the area in front of the fireplace and in the cracks and corners. Use the brush attachment on the vertical surface of the fireplace.

- Clean the glass with vinegar and water glass cleaner (see page 51) and newspaper and the frame with all-purpose cleaner and a rag or towel.

Fireplace Tools

Vacuum under here

- These tools are meant to get dirty, but to keep the dirt from spreading, periodically take them outside for cleaning.

- Vacuum or sweep the area where they sit near your fireplace.

- Wipe off each tool with a rag and all-purpose cleaner (see page 31). Use vinegar and water for shiny handles.

- Take the broom and sweep the grass to remove any ash that has collected between its fibers.

WINDOW COVERINGS
Keep window cover cleaning to a minimum

Drapes are another household essential that are often labeled "Dry Clean Only." To avoid coming in contact with carcinogenic Perc and other toxic chemicals (see page 102), consider hand-washing the fabric (if it can withstand this). If you don't want to risk it, locate an eco-friendly wet cleaner to have your drapes professionally cleaned once a year. Or use a vapor steam cleaner, which may eliminate the need to ever take them off the rod for cleaning.

Use a vacuum cleaner with a hose extension and an upholstery attachment to prolong the time between cleanings and control the dust. For natural wood and fiber shades, vacuuming is also an easy method to control dust. Alternatively,

Dust-Free Drapes

Vacuum in this direction

Washing Curtains

Detail here

- As an alternative to toxic dry cleaning, vacuum your drapes at least once a month.

- Use the upholstery tool and set the suction on your vacuum to low.

- Spread the curtains out flat across the window.

- Vacuum from the rod at the top to the hem at the bottom in long slow lines. Overlap lines so you don't miss any dust.

- For washable curtains, unscrew the ends of the rods and slide the curtain off. Remove rings or other attaching devices.

- Follow the directions on the label of your curtains, but as a general guideline, wash your curtains on the gentle cycle.

- To avoid ironing, shake out wet curtains and put them in the dryer on low for 10 minutes.

- They will still be damp. Remove and hang outside to dry.

blinds can be dusted with a microfiber or recycled flannel cloth and sponged clean using mild castile soap and water.

Besides enhancing your décor and creating privacy, your drapes and other window coverings can help make your home more energy efficient. Heavy and insulated drapes reduce drafts. Blinds and shades reduce the amount of heat coming into the home during prime sunlight hours.

If you're in the market for new window coverings, find natural fabrics and fiber options that also help conserve energy. Matchstick-style bamboo shades are one green choice, but they do nothing to conserve energy. Look for shades made out of bamboo that also have an insulated lining or insulated curtains. If you're feeling crafty, buy insulation panels to sew into your own curtains.

If your main problem is heat in the summer, Forest Stewardship Council certified wood blinds are a good choice because the wood comes from consciously-managed forests. Wood blinds are easy to clean and will help you regulate how much heat and light comes into your home.

Shades

- Lower the shade to have as much of the fabric as possible visible.

- Use the upholstery brush on your vacuum and set the suction to low.

- Vacuum across the very top of the shade.

- Dust either from top to bottom or side to side, whichever more closely follows the weave or detail on the shade. This way you'll remove the most dust possible.

- Overlap strokes to avoid missing spots.

Blinds

Vacuum or wash horizontally

- Lower the blind all the way and flatten the slats. Use your vacuum brush attachment with the suction set to low.

- Start at the top and vacuum across the top panel. Work your way down, vacuuming each slat from side to side. If possible, flip the slats and repeat.

- If there are vertical fabric strips, finish the job by vacuuming those from top to bottom.

- Once or twice a year, use a rag or towel dampened with mild soap and water and wipe down each slat individually.

129

DESKS AND PHONES
An organized desk makes cleaning quick and easy

When you're in the middle of a project or have multiple family members using a desk, it's easy for mountains of clutter to pile up. The more clutter, the bigger the project it will be to actually clean the desk, and the dirtier the space will become. Contrary to the familiar image of the messy professor, dusty office air is not good brain nourishment for creating your best

work. And if anyone is using the computer as their lunch- or snack-time companion, crumbs and spills are added to the dirty mix.

Dust, crumbs, and spills can encourage pests and also ruin your electronics, so it's important to get this area set up for easy, regular cleaning. Creating clearly marked places for every

Paper Clutter Control

BILLS

PENDING

TO FILE

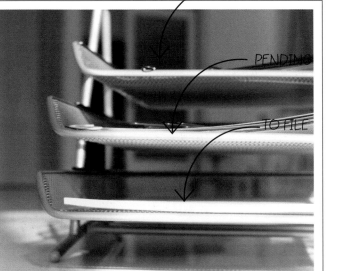

Desk Organizer

- To manage paper clutter, label three separate bins BILLS, PENDING and TO FILE.

- Write the due date on the outside of the envelope for each bill and arrange in chronological order.

- Place paperwork and mail that needs action in PENDING

and finished business in TO FILE.

- Pick one day a week that you go through each bin. For example, pay bills on Monday, take action on pending matters on Wednesday, and file on Friday.

- Skip the plastic desk organizer set, and look for containers around your home.

- Use a mason jar or jam jar, washed and stripped of label, to hold your pens and pencils.

- A plate or small tray can hold smaller objects, like a dish of paper clips, a calculator, and a stapler.

- These items will be easy to remove when it's time to clean your desk and can easily be emptied and washed periodically.

form of clutter as well as reducing the amount of clutter coming into the space will set you on track for a cleaner office.

Once you've got your system in place you'll find that it's much easier to clear off your desk each evening or after each use so you can start fresh the next time. From there, you can dust your desk weekly and wash as needed.

Drawer Organizer

- To keep your drawers neat and easy to dust and clean, use an organizer.

- You can use an office specific organizer or an old flatware organizer that fits the drawer.

- Separate the items that you use regularly, like pens and staplers, so they are visible and easy to grab.

- To clean the drawer, remove the organizer. Dust or vacuum inside and then wipe down with warm soapy water. Dry and replace the organizer.

Cleaning the Phone

Use cotton swab here

- Unplug the phone and dampen a clean cloth with warm sudsy water.

- Wipe the base of the telephone and headset.

- Use cotton swabs dipped in vinegar (but just damp) to get into dirty tight spaces like between the buttons.

Be careful not to let any liquid drip into the phone.

- To disinfect, dampen a cloth with vinegar and wipe the handset. Do the same with your headset if you use one.

COMPUTERS
Dust and dirt can ruin computers—here's how to keep them clean

The more a computer runs, the more heat it generates. And the more heat, the more risk of damage to the machine. The computer also generates static, which draws in dust from the surrounding area, and that dust acts as an insulator, causing the computer to run even hotter. Dust, along with temperature extremes, humidity, smoke, and air pollution, can substantially shorten your computer's life span.

The first step in computer care is to position the computer in a well-ventilated area so the cool air flows in and the hot air can flow out. Clutter around the computer obstructs this airflow and adds to the dust that gets on and in your computer. It's important to keep the whole area as dust-free as possible.

While there are chemical products designed specifically

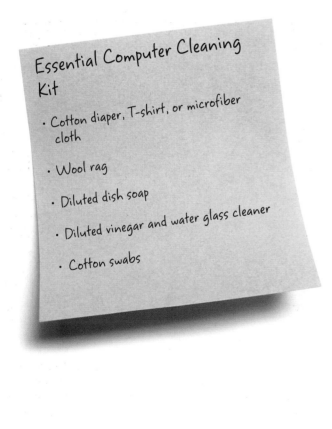

Essential Computer Cleaning Kit

- Cotton diaper, T-shirt, or microfiber cloth
- Wool rag
- Diluted dish soap
- Diluted vinegar and water glass cleaner
- Cotton swabs

Monitor Screen

- Flat-screened monitors have LCD or plasma screens. To clean, turn the monitor off and wait until it has cooled completely.

- Use a dry cotton diaper or microfiber cloth to remove dust from the screen. Do not press too hard or you could damage the screen.

- For a CRT monitor, dampen the cloth with plain water. It should be just damp but not wet.

- Wipe down the monitor screen, and then polish with a dry cloth.

for computer cleaning, they are unnecessary, and nontoxic methods can work just fine. Don't use a vacuum when cleaning out dust from a computer. Vacuums generate static that can damage the computer's components. Check your computer manual before cleaning to make sure there aren't special instructions you need to follow. Otherwise, regular dusting along with occasional cleaning with the mildest solutions possible will keep your computer clean and green and functioning for many years.

Monitor Frame

- Dampen a cloth with diluted dish soap and fold over so it fits entirely into your hand with no trailing ends.

- Wipe down just the frame without touching the screen with this solution. If

you do, dry with a clean dry cloth immediately.

- Turn the monitor around and wipe down the back of it as well.

- Use cotton swabs to get into tight spaces.

Other Equipment

- Use the same cloth you used for the monitor frame, but fold it to a clean surface.

- Spray cloth with diluted dish soap so it's just barely damp.

- Wipe down the casing of your CPU, printer, scanner,

fax, and other equipment. Use cotton swabs for vents and between buttons.

- Use diluted glass cleaner on your fax and printer screen, but just dust your scanner screen with a dry cloth.

MORE COMPUTERS
Keyboards and mouse devices are magnets for dirt and crumbs

In a family with kids or someone working full-time from home, the best intentions, and even the strictest rules, may not stop the occasional computer-front meal. Crumbs can join dust in the crevices between computer keys and in the seams of your mouse. Both need to be cleaned regularly but delicately, and neither object makes that job easy. While compressed-air cleaners seem like a good idea in theory for ridding dust from a keyboard or a mouse, they pose several unseen risks to both your health and the environment.

When you take a closer look at these products you'll notice that that's not air you're blasting into your breathing space. It's actually a mixture of greenhouse gases like tetrafluoro-

Laptop Keyboard

Dust accumulates here

- Your computer should be off and unplugged.

- Check your manual to see if your keys are removable. If they are, remove them.

- Wipe the area under the keys with a cloth just moistened with distilled water.

- Allow to completely dry before replacing the keys.

- Wipe the casing and keys with a cloth that is dampened with diluted dish soap. Make sure it is dry before plugging it in.

Detached Keyboard

- Unplug keyboard from the computer.

- Take it outside or hold it over a garbage can. Hold it upside down and shake gently. This will loosen the dust stuck under the keys.

- Repeat until you don't see any more dust coming out.

- Dampen a cloth with diluted dish soap and wipe down keys and keyboard casing.

134

ethane, a form of HFCs that work as a refrigerant like CFCs, or freon, before their use was severely restricted. If inhaled in high concentrations, these gases can lead to heart trouble, unconsciousness, or even death. When you spray them on the keyboard you inhale this gas. But there is another big danger to consider if you have children. Recently, teenagers have been using these products as a way to get high. It's called "dusting," and kids are dying from either heart attacks or asphyxiation as the gas replaces the air in their lungs.

There are safer and more environmentally sound ways to clean your keyboard, and, it turns out, they're not that difficult.

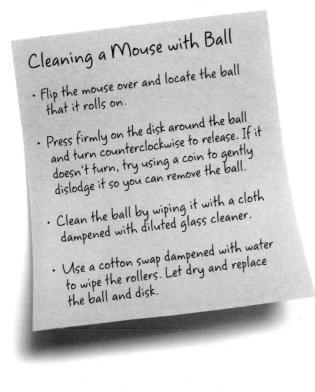

Cleaning a Mouse with Ball

- Flip the mouse over and locate the ball that it rolls on.

- Press firmly on the disk around the ball and turn counterclockwise to release. If it doesn't turn, try using a coin to gently dislodge it so you can remove the ball.

- Clean the ball by wiping it with a cloth dampened with diluted glass cleaner.

- Use a cotton swap dampened with water to wipe the rollers. Let dry and replace the ball and disk.

Cleaning an Optical Mouse

- For newer mouse products that don't have a roller ball:

- Disconnect the mouse from computer.

- Dampen a microfiber cloth with diluted glass cleaner.

- Clean the entire mouse except the optical center, which can be easily damaged by any lint or solution.

- Let dry completely before reconnecting to the computer.

ELECTRONICS AND OTHER MEDIA
Keep components out of the landfill with regular cleaning and maintenance

Cleaning and maintaining your electronics and other media has become a serious environmental issue. Electronic waste accounts for 2 percent of the contents in U.S. landfills, and 70 percent of that e-waste is toxic, with heavy metals like lead and mercury, flame retardants, plastics, and more. As with your computer, dust and dirt are attracted to these machines and create a natural insulation, making them run even hotter, which can cause more wear and tear.

Cleaning these electronics is important, but cleaning them the wrong way can cause damage. For example, with flat-screen TVs and monitors, it's important not to touch the screen because the pressure can cause the pixels to burn out.

Flat-Screen TV

Look for dust here.

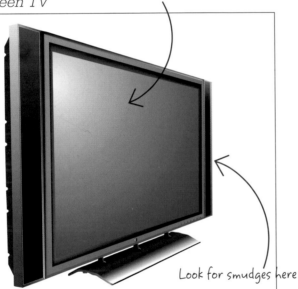

Look for smudges here.

- Never use a glass cleaner or detergent on LCD or plasma screens, and apply only minimal pressure while cleaning.

- There are special cleaners you can buy for these types of screens, but they are generally unnecessary.

- Use a dry microfiber cloth to dust and a clean soft flannel rag to polish the screen.

- Use a just-damp cloth with diluted dish soap on the frame, base, and back of the television.

Speakers

- Refer to your manual for specific cleaning instructions.

- Generally, dusting with a microfiber or lamb's wool duster is the most important step toward clean speakers.

- Dampen a cloth with diluted dish soap and wipe down all plastic or wood surfaces. Use a cotton swab to get into tight places.

- Some speakers have removable cloth covers that can be rinsed in the sink. Be sure to let them dry all the way before replacing.

Spray a cleaner on the screen, and you'll regret it every time you try to view something through the cloudy surface.

Another consideration here is upgrading your technology when it's not really necessary. Every year the new latest and greatest product hits the market, making your current model seem woefully inadequate. Yet, constantly upgrading computers, MP3 players, and cell phones means you're contributing heavily to the e-waste stream. One simple solution is to resist these upgrades and keep your current equipment running for the long term.

But sometimes upgrading is actually good for the environment. With 1.8 billion CDs sold annually worldwide, you can imagine the number of discs and plastic cases that end up in landfills. Going digital with an MP3 player can lessen your contribution to this waste in the long run.

If it really is time to upgrade, first check with the manufacturer of your old equipment to see if it recycles the products or check Earth 911 for alternative recycling programs (see the resource section). Also, if your old machine is not too old, you may be able to sell or donate it.

Media

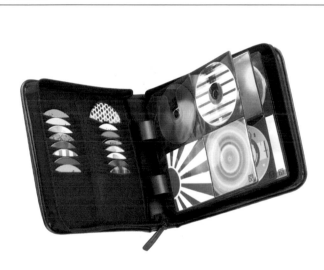

- Store CDs and DVDs away from direct sunlight.

- Use your dust brush attachment to vacuum the tops, sides, and shelf area around your media as you would your books (see page 121).

- To clean the disc, use a cotton T-shirt rag and wipe from the center to the edge all the way around. If necessary, use vinegar and water glass cleaner (see page 51).

- Once or twice a year, remove all media from shelves and dust and wash the shelves.

CD Waste

- Jewel cases are not easily recyclable. Consider going digital by purchasing an MP3 player.

- Be sure to buy a player that will last from a manufacturer with a take-back recycling program.

- E-waste contains toxic chemicals and fills up our landfills.

MANAGING OFFICE WASTE
How to create a practically no-waste office

A home office or computer nook generates a lot of waste with botched print jobs as well as junk mail and depleted office supplies. It's important to set up the office to encourage and simplify recycling. By creating designated and clearly labeled spaces for things like reusable printer paper or scrap paper for phone messages, it's easy to minimize office waste.

When you're ready to buy new paper, look for the "PCW" label ("Postconsumer Waste recycled"). This is different than just "recycled" paper because PCW is made from paper that was actually used by consumers and then recycled. Otherwise, you may be buying paper that is just made from paper scraps left over from making new paper.

Reuse

- Not all of the documents printed from your computer need to be on pristine paper.

- Use unwanted documents that are only printed on one side to print new documents.

- Place used paper, printed side down in a clearly marked bin and load the printer with it.

- Get yourself and anyone else who uses your computer in the habit of using this paper first and only grabbing new paper when it's absolutely necessary.

Recycle

- If you print a lot, buy printer cartridges where you can also recycle them.

- Some major office supply stores offer programs where you can send back empty cartridges and receive money off your next purchase or an even exchange for a new cartridge.

- Another green choice is refilling ink cartridges.

- However, some printers won't recognize a refilled cartridge that it already recognized as empty. Test this on your printer before refilling more than one cartridge.

Dead batteries need special treatment. They contain hazardous materials like cadmium, lead, and potassium hydroxide that can affect the reproductive system, kidney, liver, and brain functions, as well as pollute the environment. Regular household alkaline batteries contain 97 percent less mercury than ten years ago, but they are still dangerous if not handled properly. In many places, it's harder to find a way to recycle these single-use batteries than it is rechargeable NiCd or NiMH batteries. If your area doesn't recycle, dispose of your household batteries as hazardous waste.

Rechargeable batteries are more eco-friendly because they can last for 10 years and 500–1,000 charge cycles. When it is time to recycle them, look for a collection site near you by visiting the Rechargeable Battery Recycling Corporation (RBRC) Web site (see the resource section). To extend their life, remove batteries from devices when they're not in use.

Safe Storage

- Certain office supplies contain toxins that are emitted into the air you breathe as you work.

- These include ink and toner cartridges, non-water-based permanent marker, adhesives, correction fluid, and some craft supplies.

- If you have these supplies, store them in a closed cabinet.

- As you begin to run out of each item, look for replacement products that are less toxic like water-based markers.

Disposing of E-Waste

- Recent models: Consider donating it or selling it to someone who could use it.

- Try online auction sites or call your local school district or library.

- Outdated models: Contact the manufacturer to find out if they have a program to recycle their old computers.

- Need help? See the resources section to find a recycling option near you.

VACUUMING

Follow these green strategies for more effective floor care

Experts recommend that homes with allergy sufferers need daily vacuuming to reduce dust, pollen and other particulate matter that trigger symptoms. But even homes without allergy sufferers need vacuuming once or twice a week to control dust and improve indoor air quality.

How you vacuum is as important as how often you vacuum.

If the vacuum bag or canister is full, the machine will have less sucking power. Vacuum too fast and you can miss a lot of the dust and debris embedded in the carpet fibers or in the seams of hardwood. If you vacuum without moving the furniture, the room will look better, but you'll miss tons of dust that builds up behind the furniture. Moving furniture is also

Vacuum Inspection and Maintenance Checklist

Before every use: Empty bag if more than three-quarters full; Cut strings or hair wrapped around the brush roll.

After every use: Use the crevice tool attachment to vacuum clean the brush attachments and roll brush under the vacuum. Wipe down the casing with a damp rag to remove dust and debris.

- To keep your vacuum in top shape there are a few more things you should do every month:

- Clean and lubricate the bearings on the brush roll.

- Check the belt and wipe it clean with a dry rag.

- Check the filter. Some filters can be easily removed, rinsed, and replaced. Follow your vacuum's specific instructions.

High-Traffic Areas

- High-traffic carpeted areas show wear quickly because there is only one path of travel.

- To combat this wear and tear, vacuum against the flow of traffic. This will make the fibers stand up in a different direction so they don't stay matted down.

- These areas also tend to get dirtier faster because of so much use.

- Vacuum at least twice a week in these areas and your carpet will last longer.

a good strategy for combating the tendency of carpeting to permanently flatten out under the weight of furniture. For hard floors, make sure you can shut off the vacuum's roller brush, otherwise you'll be scattering the dust away from the vacuum instead of picking it up.

Given that U.S. consumers buy 18 million vacuums a year, it's important to make your vacuum last as long as possible. Routine inspection and maintenance are key to optimal performance and a long life.

The most common thing to break on a vacuum is usually the belt. You know it's broken because the roller brush is no longer spinning, but you might be able to catch it before that happens. If the machine is hard to push or smells like burnt rubber, it could mean that the belt is slipping. Refer to your manual and try adjusting the belt; but you may need to replace it to get it operating smoothly again. As long as replacement belts for your machine are available, this can be a cheap and easy thing to fix yourself.

Strategy

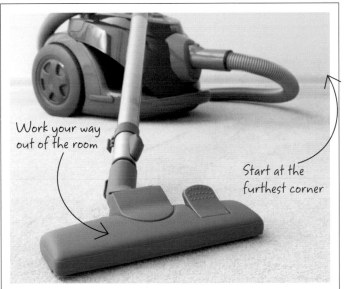

Work your way out of the room

Start at the furthest corner

- Dust the room before vacuuming so you pick up anything that has fallen to the floor.

- Start at the furthest corner away from the door. Vacuum yourself out of the room—that way you won't leave footprints on your newly vacuumed carpet.

- Move furniture as you go. This keeps the carpet under the furniture from getting matted and controls the dust buildup in areas that don't get used often.

Long Overlapping Strokes

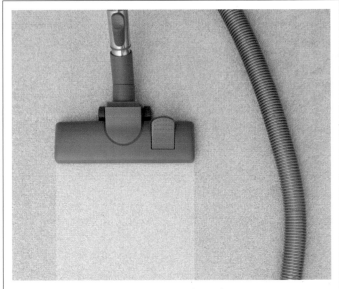

- Survey the floor and pick up any plant leaves, pins, or paper clips that could cause damage to your vacuum.

- To vacuum, pull back in a long slow stroke.

- Push the vacuum forward right next to where you pulled it and overlap the

line. This is easy to see on carpeting, but try to overlap lines on hard floors as well.

- The key is to go slowly and pay attention to your lines so you don't miss any spots.

CARPETS AND AREA RUGS
Spot-clean and shop smart for cleaner carpets

Most wall-to-wall carpeting is petroleum-based and may contribute VOCs, formaldehyde, and xylene to your indoor air pollution. Carpeting also traps dust and provides an appealing home for dust mites. If you have the choice, opt for other types of flooring and use natural fiber area rugs wherever you want to tread on softer ground. If you need to get rid of a carpet, look for recycling programs in your area by visiting the Carpet America Recovery Effort (CARE) Web site. Then help close the loop by buying rugs made out of recycled materials and that bear the Carpet and Rug Institute Green Label Plus logo (see Web sites) for certified low-VOC products.

To keep your carpet free of toxins, avoid conventional carpet cleaning solutions. Carpet-protective treatments, cleaners, and deodorizers are loaded with fragrances and other toxins such

Carpet Cleaner: What to Avoid

Eyes: corrosive, severe irritation. May cause chemical burns with permanent corneal injury & sensitization. Skin: severe irritation.

- Watch for this ingredient on the label: Perchloroethylene,

- PERC is a known human carcinogen and suspected neurotoxin, which can also make you sick with nausea, dizziness, fatigue, and produce long-term kidney and liver damage.

- Other ingredients to avoid: napthalene (neurotoxic and suspected carcinogen), butyl cellosolve (neurotoxin), propylene glycol methyl ether (irritant), aliphatic petroleum solvent (neurotoxic), isopropyl alcohol (carcinogenic), fragrance.

- Can include 1,4-dioxane (carcinogenic), ethanol, and ammonia.

Carpet Cleaner: What to Look For

Ingredients:
Hydrogen peroxide (the active stain removal agent)
Biodegradable surfactants (soil removal)
Citrus oil (for grease removal)
Food-grade, nontoxic oxygen stabilizers (to help the hydrogen peroxide last longer)
Water

- Look for products that provide a complete ingredient list.

- Choose plant-derived ingredients and look for specifics on how long it takes to biodegrade.

- The more words you recognize in the ingredients list the better.

- Look for packaging that is made from recycled materials and is recyclable.

as perchloroethylene that are known or suspected carcinogens and can cause immediate irritation as well as long-term organ and nervous system damage. Regular vacuuming, deodorizing, and nontoxic spot treatment will reduce your need to have the carpets cleaned. When it is time for cleaning, it's a great idea to rent a steam cleaner. To keep it green, rinse the machine to rid it of any toxic residue, and use your own choice of mild detergent to clean.

Carpet deodorizer:
Liberally sprinkle baking soda on carpet or rug and leave overnight. If your vacuum is temperamental, sweep baking soda and then vacuum. Otherwise, just vacuum.

Dust, dirt, soot, animal dander, mold, fungi, and VOCs build up here

Routine Cleaning

- Carpets can be home to a lot of different allergens and unwanted guests. A filtered vacuum cleaner and baking soda are your best defense.

- First, vacuum the carpet thoroughly to get up as much dirt as possible.

- Next, sprinkle baking soda to thinly cover the carpet. Leave on overnight.

- If your vacuum is temperamental, sweep baking soda and then vacuum. Otherwise, just vacuum, and you'll have a clean and deodorized carpet.

Spot Cleaning

- Coffee, wine, tomato, fruit juice, and other acid stains are extremely common but they shouldn't mean the end of your carpeting.

- All you need is a bottle of club soda and a clean white towel.

- First, pour ¼ to ½ cup of club soda on the stain and blot with a clean white towel.

- Repeat until the stain is gone.

FLOORS

MOPPING
One job where less is more

We've been trained to use sudsy products every time we clean the floors, but the truth is, you're better off dry or damp-mopping and vacuuming more and washing less. This is especially true for wood and bamboo floors that wear better when they stay dry. Using a dry microfiber or damp sponge mop instead of a broom for sweeping keeps the dust on the mop instead of scattering it into the air.

Microfiber mops are made from polyester and nylon, and thus are petroleum-based, but their usefulness in cutting the need for cleaners and their long life make them a good choice for floor care. They work by trapping or "hooking" dirt in their fibers in the same way that pieces of Velcro fasten to-

Dust Mop

Slide off here for washing

- Use a dry microfiber or dampened looped cotton dust mop.

- Start in the far corner of the room and mop in long strokes that overlap as you work your way out of the room.

- Avoid picking the mop up off the floor and scattering the dirt you just picked up; use the swivel function instead.

- When the head is saturated with dirt, remove head cover and throw in the washer. Replace with a clean head cover and continue.

Damp Mop

Squeeze here for a drier mop

- For larger spaces, damp mopping with a squeezable sponge mop may be easier.

- Fill a bucket with clean, plain water. Dip sponge head and squeeze as much water out as possible.

- Mop in overlapping strokes from the furthest corner of the room out.

- Rinse and squeeze your mop every few strokes to ensure you aren't spreading the dirt around.

gether. Microfiber mops are designed to trap the dirt without needing any solutions or moisture. Using microfiber is ideal for dry-mopping in smaller spaces. As soon as the mop is filled with dirt, you can just throw it in the washer and reuse it later. For larger spaces you need multiple mop heads so you can keep working after the first one fills up with dirt.

Damp mopping is also a great alternative for larger spaces. Damp mopping can be done with any type of mop head, but one of the greener options is a cellulose sponge head made from wood pulp. The key is to have an effective system to thoroughly wring the mop out after every dip in the bucket so you don't soak the area you're cleaning. It's also important to change the water in your bucket when it looks murky so you aren't just reapplying the dust to the floor. Damp mopping absorbs the dust without detergent and leaves the floor looking great.

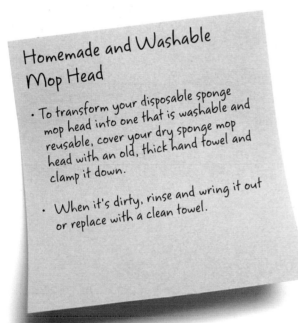

Homemade and Washable Mop Head

• To transform your disposable sponge mop head into one that is washable and reusable, cover your dry sponge mop head with an old, thick hand towel and clamp it down.

• When it's dirty, rinse and wring it out or replace with a clean towel.

Wet-Mopping Strategy

• Vacuum or sweep the room. Then fill a bucket with warm water (tepid if floors are waxed) and a tablespoon or two of cleaning solution or castile soap (see page 31).

• Work your way out of the room from the furthest corner, moving the bucket to unwashed floor as you go.

• Work across the room in overlapping back-and-forth strokes.

• Rinse and squeeze mop head every few minutes. Replace water in the bucket when it looks dirty.

WOOD, CORK, OR BAMBOO FLOORS
The drier the better for clean wood floors

To give your wood, cork, or bamboo flooring a long life, it's crucial that you know the appropriate care for your specific product, so check with the manufacturer to be extra sure. That said, the most important thing to know about any wood floor is that water can cause major damage. Clean up any spills as quickly and thoroughly as possible and use area rugs wherever you have wood flooring near a sink or other water source.

In general, vacuuming and dry- or damp-mopping are the best way to do regular cleaning for all types of wood floors. Spot cleaning with a damp cloth and mild dish soap is much better than wet mopping, which risks dulling the finish or ruining the floor. Oil soaps are also not a great idea because

CLEAN HOME, GREEN HOME

What to Avoid

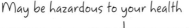
May be hazardous to your health

- Most floor polish and cleaners contain skin and eye irritants as well as carcinogenic formaldehyde.

- Petroleum distillates, another common ingredient, can be toxic to the nervous and digestive systems.

- To eliminate the need

for such harsh cleaners, vacuum regularly with a machine that lets you turn off the rotating brush so you don't scatter the dirt.

- Mop or sweep up spills as soon as they happen so crumbs don't get ground in and liquids don't damage the wood.

What to Look for

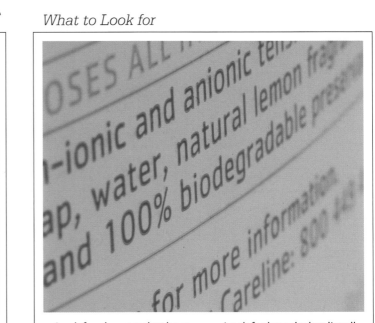

- Look for cleaners that have more plant- and mineral-based ingredients than synthetic—the more you can pronounce the better.

- Choose products that are either fragrance free or scented with natural essential oils.

- Look for brands that list all of their ingredients on the label.

- Or try the simple recipe (see sidebar right) and do it yourself.

they can leave behind a residue that damages the floor.

Even floors with wax seals do not completely block out water. For occasional deep cleaning of sealed floors, you can damp-mop using the solution on this page. The vinegar cuts grease but also helps the solution evaporate quickly so the floor is not affected.

Unsealed as well as varnished or shellacked floors all do better with a damp mop and a solution of just equal parts vinegar and water.

Strategy

- Although your floor looks smooth and impenetrable, the grains of the wood and the seams between the boards create perfect hiding places for dirt.

- Follow the direction of the grain when you vacuum, sweep, or mop to be sure that you get as much of this dust as possible.

- Sealed wood floors can be cleaned with the damp-mop solution (above).

- Waxed wood floors should be cleaned with a sponge mop only slightly dampened with clean tepid water.

Drier Mopping

- Wood, cork, and bamboo floors will look better longer if you don't get them wet.

- Instead of using a bucket to wash the floors, put the wood floor solution (above) in a spray bottle.

- Squirt an area of about 3 feet by 3 feet in front of you and mop. Continue that way across your whole floor.

- Only use what you need to reduce the risk of getting your floors too wet.

FLOORS

OTHER FLOORS
Start mild for long-lasting flooring

You could probably buy a special cleaner for every floor surface there is, but you'd be wasting a lot of money and introducing a lot of toxic chemicals into your home. Many of these products contain mineral spirits and petroleum-based solvents, which are both eye, skin, and respiratory irritants and known neurotoxins. Petroleum-based solvents can also contain small quantities of benzene, a known carcinogen.

As with wood floors, less wet-mopping and more vacuuming and dry- and damp-mopping is best, especially for the most natural types of flooring like natural linoleum and cork. It's also important to start out with as mild a solution as possible, and often vinegar and water does the trick. Then if you have blemishes, stains, or spots, you can target those directly with castile soap and water.

Ceramic Tile and Slate/Grout

- Vacuum or sweep often to remove dust. Damp- or dust-mopping is good for cleaning. Wet-mop with a sponge mop, warm water, and a few squirts of castile soap.

- For grimy residue, spray diluted vinegar on the floor, and avoid getting the vinegar into grout. Too much can etch glazed surfaces.

- For neutral-colored grout, spray a 50/50 solution of hydrogen peroxide and water on the stain every fifteen minutes until you see it lighten. For stubborn stains, create a paste of baking soda and hydrogen peroxide. Let it bubble and then apply.

Concrete

- Vacuum or sweep often to control dust and catch debris before it damages the seal on concrete.

- Catch spills immediately. Mop up and dry with a clean towel.

- Damp and dry mopping are your best choices for cleaning concrete floors.

- Spot clean if you see dirt or spots with castile soap and water.

If you're in the market for new flooring, consider natural linoleum. It's an ideal flooring choice because it's a renewable resource, low-maintenance, and durable. To keep your linoleum floor as green and clean as possible, be sure to use low-VOC sealants that don't contain formaldehyde. Concrete linoleum also comes from renewable resources and is a good choice for green homes.

Marble

- Be sure your vacuum wheels are clean and the vacuum itself will not scratch your flooring. Vacuum often to remove dirt and grime that can damage the marble.

- Damp mopping with just plain water is your best cleaning solution.

- For tough spots, use castile soap and water, and dry the area when you've finished.

- Do not use acid cleaners like vinegar on marble because they will etch the stone.

Other Linoleum

- Sheet vinyl floors can be wet-mopped. Mix 3–4 squirts of castile soap in warm water or 3 cups of vinegar in a bucket of water.

- Squeeze mop slightly. Wash once with a wet mop. Then go over same area with a fully squeezed mop to dry.

- For vinyl floor tiles, stick to damp-mopping to avoid swelling and cupping that could happen if you get them too wet.

- To shine dull spots, make a paste of cornstarch and water. Apply with a rag and rub into the floor. Remove paste with a damp cloth and buff with a dry cloth.

VENTILATION

Cleaning the air in your home can be as simple as opening the right windows

Your indoor air quality can be four times worse than the air just outside your home. In fact, the EPA ranks indoor air pollution in the top-five biggest threats to our health. Part of the problem is that in our efforts to build more energy-efficient homes, we've done everything we can to seal ourselves inside. In the past, indoor air quality (IAQ) concerns centered on cigarette smoke, radon, lead, and asbestos. But more recent studies show that pollution sources include household products like cleaners, pesticides, and air fresheners, as well as furnishings and building materials. Sealed houses mean these chemicals stay put and pollute the air we breathe. This may be why reported cases of allergies in the U.S. have

Ventilation Strategy

- Breezes and temperature differences inside and outside your home move air in and out of your home.

- Cross-ventilate using two windows directly opposite each other to clean the air in one room. Experiment with more complex airflow patterns to cover a larger space.

- Open a small window on the shady side of your home and a large window or door on the sunnier side. Keep all windows between these two shut.

- The air will enter through the small window and ventilate a larger space on its way to the larger opening.

Fans

- Use circulating fans to increase the effectiveness of window ventilation.

- Place a fan in front of your open shady window so its back is facing the window and the fan is blowing into your room.

- Place another fan, this one blowing out of your house, in front of the larger window or door where the air exits your home. This can also be effective when the intake window is on the ground floor and the outlet is on a higher floor.

doubled in the past thirty years, and asthma has gone up by almost 75 percent in the same period.

By following the suggestions in this book, you can improve your IAQ. Another easy step is to develop a strategy for increased and effective ventilation in your home. Simply opening a few windows can help, but being strategic about which windows you open will give you better results. Cross-ventilation is key, and can be even more beneficial when coordinated with fans that help guide the indoor air circulation and effectively clean the air.

Whole-House Exhaust Attic Fans

- Whole-house fans consist of a series of ducts and vents.

- The exhaust fan pulls air through the house so there is a constant exchange of air between inside and outside.

- An attic fan draws up and blows hot air out of your home.

- The movement of air draws cooler air into your home through open windows on the lower floors.

Other Exhaust Fans

- Exhaust fans are important in humid rooms such as the bathroom, laundry, and kitchen.

- These fans will help clear out moisture and warm air generated by your appliances and shower and effectively cool the room.

- Exhaust fans are key to fighting mold and mildew, which can't survive without excess moisture.

- Turn the fan on when you're using the appliances or shower and leave running for 20 minutes after. Open windows to speed up the drying process.

INDOOR AIR QUALITY

PLANTS
Make use of the most natural air cleaner available

Common houseplants are a simple, attractive, and effective way to clean the air in your home. Three cleansing plants per 100 feet of space in your home or office can improve your indoor air quality (IAQ), and they add to the natural look and feel of your home. While there are some pollutants that plants cannot absorb, such as asbestos or soot, they do ab-sorb many of the chemicals from common household products. In fact, if you have a specific concern like formaldehyde from particleboard furniture or toluene and xylene from paints and adhesives, you can choose the plants that are particularly good at eliminating those chemicals.

Researchers found that as these plants absorbed carbon

Aloe Vera

- Aloe is one of the most effective plants for the removal of low-level concentration formaldehyde.

- Place aloe anywhere you think formaldehyde is a problem, such as near very new pressed wood or particleboard furniture, latex paint or wallpaper, or just finished wood flooring (see page 156).

- Aloe will do best in or near a window that gets full sun.

- For each watering, soak the plant with water but allow enough time between waterings for it to dry out.

Peace Lily

- Peace lilies help remove formaldehyde, benzene, and carbon monoxide from the air.

- They also remove "bioeffluents," which are the gases, including ethyl alcohol and acetone, as well as odors, bacteria, and viruses that we exhale.

- Keep peace lilies away from direct sunlight to avoid burning their leaves.

- Water at least once a week. Check the soil and water before it dries out completely.

dioxide in the process of photosynthesis, they also absorbed other chemicals and rendered them harmless in the process. As the roots and microbes in the soil also play a role in air cleaning, cutting the bottom leaves that touch the soil help to make the plants even more effective.

Plants absorb both light and pollutants through the pores in their leaves, so it's important to keep them dust-free. Clean your plants regularly by wiping the leaves with a microfiber or damp cloth to remove dust.

Philodendrons

- Philodendrons are one of the best plants for removing formaldehyde from the air at high concentrations.

- Both vines and large floor plants are effective. It's a good idea to put one anywhere you have particleboard or pressed wood furniture, cabinets, or other formaldehyde sources

- Keep the plant out of direct sunlight.

- Let the soil dry out between waterings and don't soak it.

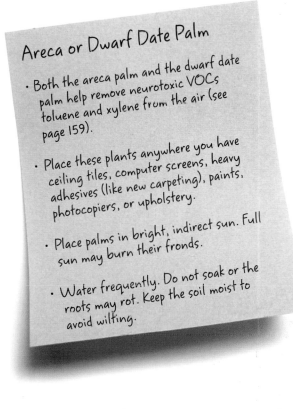

Areca or Dwarf Date Palm

- Both the areca palm and the dwarf date palm help remove neurotoxic VOCs toluene and xylene from the air (see page 159).

- Place these plants anywhere you have ceiling tiles, computer screens, heavy adhesives (like new carpeting), paints, photocopiers, or upholstery.

- Place palms in bright, indirect sun. Full sun may burn their fronds.

- Water frequently. Do not soak or the roots may rot. Keep the soil moist to avoid wilting.

INDOOR AIR QUALITY

153

FILTERS
Maintaining and replacing filters is key to having clean air

You probably have a number of air filters in your home. They are in your furnace, air conditioner, and vacuum. Be sure to follow the manufacturer's instructions for cleaning and replacing the filters. A dirty filter in any of these machines will not help your indoor air quality (IAQ) and may even make it worse. HEPA (or High Efficiency Particulate Air) filters are the most well known and remove 99 percent of the particulate matter in the air. However, because they are not designed to handle such large volumes of air, they are not effective for central heating and cooling systems. There are other types of filters, such as media filters for your heating-ventilation-air conditioning system, that can clean the air just as well.

Room Air Purifiers

- Most portable air purifiers only clean the air in small spaces.

- For best results, place the purifier near an appliance or window that brings pollution into the home.

- It's important to clean and replace filters according to your manual's instructions.

- To clean: At least once a month, wipe down the purifier, including the slatted vents, with a cloth moistened with warm soapy water. Wipe a second time with just water and dry.

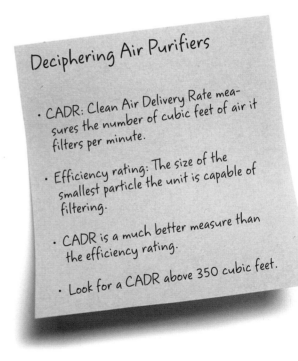

Deciphering Air Purifiers

- CADR: Clean Air Delivery Rate measures the number of cubic feet of air it filters per minute.

- Efficiency rating: The size of the smallest particle the unit is capable of filtering.

- CADR is a much better measure than the efficiency rating.

- Look for a CADR above 350 cubic feet.

During heating season, check your furnace filter and possibly replace it every month. The same is true for your air-conditioning during cooling season. These filters can collect dirt and pollen, but if they're too dirty, they're ineffective.

The filter on your vacuum should also be inspected regularly. For vacuums that have filters designed to last the life of the vacuum, wash the filter every six months. For others these filters should be replaced every six months. Look for a vaccum with a washable filter to avoid any unrecyclable waste.

Air purifiers can also help clean, but not all are created equally. Whichever type you have will work better with routine filter inspection and replacement when necessary. HEPA filters in air purifiers require the same simple care as they do for vacuums. Carbon filters, on the other hand, should be inspected and probably changed every month. Electrostatic filters don't need to be replaced every month, but some manufacturers recommend cleaning them regularly.

Furnace Filters

- In cooler weather, much of the air circulating in your home passes through your furnace filter.

- The state and quality of this filter makes a big difference to your indoor air quality. If you have allergies, pets, or use your fireplace often, look for special allergen filters.

- Furnaces can have flat mechanical filters or pleated electronic or charged-media filters.

- Generally, pleated filters are much more effective in cleaning the air.

Furnace Filter Maintenance

- If your furnace filter is dirty, so is your air, which is why filters should be cleaned or replaced monthly during heating season.

- Plastic or metal filters can be rinsed with a hose. Fiberglass filters need to be replaced each month.

- In most furnaces, the filter will be between the furnace and the return-air duct. It will slide out easily.

- Clean, properly adjusted furnace filters will save you 5 percent on your heating bill.

SPECIAL AIR QUALITY CONCERNS

How to identify and eradicate the most threatening pollution problems in your home

Carbon monoxide, radon, lead, and mold can make your home unsafe, but they can also be detected and remediated before they become a problem. The key is being proactive and knowing the signs.

Carbon monoxide can cause severe health problems before you can actually smell it in your home. At low levels, carbon monoxide poisoning is easily mistaken for the flu. As the level rises, health effects become severe, ranging from angina, reduced vision, and neurological effects to death. The likely poisoning suspects are combustion appliances or equipment including nonelectric, poorly vented space heaters, gas fireplaces, car exhaust, and gas appliances.

Carbon Monoxide

- Install at least one carbon monoxide sensor on each floor of your home. One of these should be near bedrooms.

- Place the sensor further than 15 feet away from kitchen and heating appliances and not in humid places like the bathroom.

- For safety, use single-use batteries that hold their charge longer than rechargeables. Replace the batteries twice a year and the whole sensor every two years.

- Schedule routine inspections of your gas appliances and fireplace.

Radon

- Every home should get a home radon test at the hardware store.

- Alternatively, you can find a certified tester by calling your state radon office.

- If your radon level is high, you'll need a state-certified radon contractor who will help you fix the problem.

- Typically, this involves filling in cracks and installing a special exhaust system that draws the radon from under the foundation and releases it out the roof so you aren't breathing it in your home.

Even sneakier and more difficult to detect than carbon monoxide is radon. A dangerously high radon level indoors is the second-leading cause of lung cancer. Radon gas is produced when uranium in the soil breaks down, and it enters the home through cracks in concrete, drains, and sumps.

Lead can pollute air and drinking water, contaminate soil, and linger in dust. But the most dangerous threat is from old lead-based paint that is chipped, sanded, or scraped. If your home was built before 1978 you may have lead in your home, and, before the 1960s, you can assume you do. Lead affects fetuses and children more severely than adults and can result in developmental impairments from behavioral problems to lower IQs.

Most mold is visible in damp places like showers or under leaky sinks, but some mold is hidden. It can grow behind wallpaper or other places that you don't usually see. Mold can severely affect those who are allergic or who have asthma, but it can act as an eye, skin, and respiratory irritant to anyone. Some molds can also produce "mycotoxins" that can cause liver and nervous system damage, affect the endocrine system, and cause cancer.

Lead

- Pre-1978 chipping paint is the clearest sign that you should get the paint chips tested for lead.

- You can also have your drinking water and your children tested for lead.

- If you do have lead paint, have it professionally removed. Do not do this yourself.

- For cleanup, the EPA recommends any all-purpose cleaner for the job.

Mold

- Mold likes damp, dark environments and may grow in places that you don't normally see, like air ducts.

- Musky smells or mold growing on the visible parts of air ducts or insulation are signs of a larger mold problem.

- Also, mold can set off unexplained allergic reactions.

- If you suspect mold, find a reputable inspector who will send samples to a lab for testing. As with all mold, focus first on eliminating the moisture.

VOCS
Low- or no- VOC is the way to go

Volatile Organic Compounds or VOCs are chemicals that leach out of sealants, paints, wood preservatives, particleboard, carpets, moth repellents, air fresheners, dry-cleaned clothing, cleaners, and other products. Health effects include eye and respiratory irritation, headaches, dizziness, trouble seeing, and memory problems. Some VOCs are suspected of affecting the nervous and respiratory systems and causing cancer.

There are a few ways you can limit your exposure. First, reduce the amount of VOC-emitting products you bring into your home. Avoid dry cleaning and switch to green and no-VOC cleaners, air fresheners, paint, and sealing products.

Fortunately, several companies specialize in these no-VOC products, which are regularly available at some of the big DIY retail stores. If you already have carpeting and particleboard

Formaldehyde

Symptoms of formaldehyde exposure:

Joint pain	dizziness
depression	loss of sleep
headaches	
chest pains	
ear infections	
chronic fatigue	

- Formaldehyde is a known human carcinogen, according to the International Agency for Research on Cancer.

- It is also a suspected neurotoxin and a sensitizer that can cause asthma.

- To reduce exposure, look for formaldehyde-free alternatives.

- Store products that contain formaldehyde where you won't breathe their fumes. Increase the ventilation when you use them. Use aloe and philodendron plants to help clean the air.

Hidden Sources of Formaldehyde

- Here are some secret spots where formaldehyde hides: Sheets, clothes, mattresses, nail polish hardeners, latex paint, particleboard, fiberboard, pressed wood, wallpaper, permanent-press clothes and draperies, glue, sealants, insulation, baby wash, pet shampoo, furniture polish.

in your home, apply nontoxic sealants to seal in the VOCs and keep them out of your air space.

If you do need to use or already have products that emit VOCs, focus on ventilation and proper disposal when you're finished with them. If you are storing any of these products, make sure they are stored properly and well out of the way of normal home traffic.

Toluene

- Toluene is a common solvent found in many household products.

- These include nail products, engine cleaner, auto paint, rust remover, adhesive, bathroom cleaner, house paint, metal polish, caulking, wood finish, paint thinner, and lawn products.

- Symptoms of toluene overexposure: headaches, fatigue, eye, nose, and throat irritation.

- Long-term effects: Liver and kidney damage, damage to fetuses.

Xylene

- Xylene is also a very common solvent that is a severe eye irritant and a skin irritant.

- Xylene is found in floor wax, automotive products including cleaners and paints, home paints, varnishes, and sealants, markers, herbicides, and other yard products.

- It is a strong neurotoxin that can cause memory loss, and high exposure can cause loss of consciousness or death.

- Xylene can also cause damage to liver and kidneys as well as birth defects.

INDOOR AIR QUALITY

AIR FRESHENERS
To truly freshen the air, go natural

Despite the name, air fresheners don't actually freshen the air. Instead, most of these products work either to neutralize our sense of smell or mask one odor with a different one. Given what we know about synthetic fragrance (see page 2), it's no surprise that products that are almost completely made up of fragrance can pollute our indoor air. These fragrances are generally petroleum-based and can contain neurotoxic phthalates as well as suspected carcinogenic naphthalene and neurotoxic xylene. It's also not surprising that fragrance is a huge allergy and asthma trigger for many people.

But air fresheners can be dangerous in another way. Your nose is one of your best tools for knowing what's going on in

What to Look For

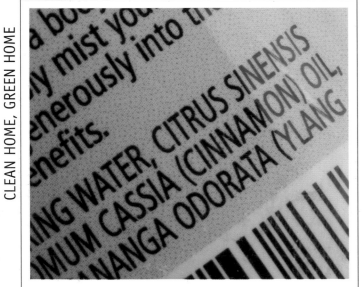

- A green air freshener comes in a recyclable and recycled pump sprayer rather than an aerosol can or other more plastic-intensive dispenser.

- It is completely plant-derived and biodegradable.

- Its fragrance comes only from natural (not synthetic) essential oils.

- Natural essential oil scented soy or beeswax candles also make great air fresheners.

Essential Oil Benefits

- Citrus – Soothes tension and depression.

- Frankincense – Boosts mental activity.

- Lavender – Helps with sleep, stress reduction, depression and tension.

- Lemongrass – relaxes and helps eliminate headaches.

- Peppermint – clears sinuses, good bug and rodent repellent.

- Rosemary – boosts memory and energy level.

- Pine – Reduces anxiety and stress. Helps with respiratory problems.

- Sage – Soothes the brain and wakes you up. Also aids with cleansing the body of toxins.

your home, and foul odors are a great alarm system, letting you know that something serious may be present. When you mask odors, you take away your ability to find the source and take care of the larger issue through cleaning, ventilating, and fixing any problems that contribute to the smell.

If you do want scent, essential oils can help your home smell fresh and also change your mood, soothe your nerves, or make you feel more alert.

· · · · · · · · · · GREEN ● LIGHT · · · · · · · · · · ·

You've identified a foul smell in your home, found the cause, and strategized how to eliminate it. But it may take a while to get the smell out. In the meantime, place an open container of baking soda or zeolite in the smelly room to absorb the odor.

Make Your Own

- Choose the appropriate oil for your mood or desired mood.

- Add 5–10 drops of the oil to a small spray bottle.

- Add 2 cups of water and shake well.

- Spray into the air or on sheets and pillows as needed.

Easy Diffuser

- Take two or three cotton balls (preferably organic) and soak them in your preferred essential oil.

- Place cotton balls wherever air can pass through them and carry the scent into the home.

- Possibilities include vacuum cleaner bags, wall vents, air conditioner units, dehumidifiers or humidifiers, air purifiers.

- Do not place them on or near any heat source that would make them a fire hazard.

INDOOR AIR QUALITY

BATHING YOUR PET
Keep it simple and plant-based for a healthy pooch

Every year, pet lovers spend tens of billions of dollars on dogs and cats, buying everything from chaise lounge–style doggy beds to rhinestone-studded collars. A better way to focus our efforts and money is on reducing their exposure to toxins. Like children, pets' smaller size, closeness to the ground, and desire to sniff everything make them more vulnerable to tox-

ins, such as pesticides, than full-sized adult humans. On top of that, dog and cat bathing products contain similar or worse toxins than adult products. Many contain harsh detergents as well as antibacterial chemicals. Pay particular attention if a product designed for your pet has a label advising you to wash your hands after use.

What to Look For

- Green pet shampoos contain plant-derived ingredients, nontoxic preservatives, and natural oil fragrances.

- Look for recycled containers that are also recyclable and don't have excess packaging. Some come in bar

form, which further reduces packaging.

- Choose products that proudly declare all of their ingredients.

- Look for something that is 100 percent biodegradable.

Dog Bathing Prep

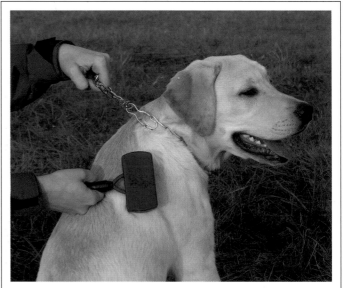

- Bathe your dog every three months unless really dirty.

- Bathing too often can reduce the natural oils in the dog's coat and lead to itchy, flaking skin.

- To save your drain, start by taking the dog outside to brush thoroughly.

- Then, line the tub with a bath mat or towel so the dog doesn't slip, and fill the tub with 3–4 inches of lukewarm water.

Reducing toxins on your pet is important, especially if you and your kids enjoy stroking, hugging, and cuddling the animal. Bathing every three months (as recommended by the ASPCA), using a mild, nontoxic shampoo, can help wash off any chemicals they've come into contact with that can put them—and you—at risk. If you bathe them more frequently or use harsh detergents or strong chemicals, you risk removing the natural protective oils on the animal's fur and drying out their skin.

· · · · · · · · · · YELLOW ● LIGHT · · · · · · · · · ·

Essential oils can make Fido smell sweeter, but they can also be dangerous if not used correctly. Apply only a dab of oil behind the animal's ears where they can't lick it and don't apply oil near eyes or other mucous membranes. Don't mix oils unless you know for sure they're safe.

Dog Bath

- Use a spray hose or pitcher to wet the dog.

- Use quarter-size squirts of shampoo and massage it into the fur. Add more shampoo as needed but don't overdo. Avoid eyes, nose, and ears.

- Rinse from head to tail. This needs to be very thorough. Leaving shampoo on the dog will result in dry itchy skin.

- Dry with a big fluffy towel, and let the dog shake off outside.

Safe Eyes

- To prevent soap from getting in your dog's eyes, try this: Create a half circle of suds around the back of the dog's head. This will create a barrier to detour soapy water from dripping into the dog's face.

PETS

PET BEDS
Control pet dander at the source

Providing your dog or cat with a comfy, safe place to sleep can help keep him off the couch and other furniture. That means you also reduce your cleaning burden and need for cleaning products. But it's important to regularly clean the bedding itself, which can get dirty fast with accumulated dander and dirt that can spread to the rest of the house if allowed to build up. Dirty bedding can also harbor pests like fleas and dust mites. There are about a million choices when it comes to pet bedding, but one key consideration is that it's easy to clean. Look for beds with durable, washable covers that can be unzipped and thrown in the washer. Shaking the bed outside periodically can lengthen the amount of

Beds

- Conventional pet beds are often filled with petroleum-based polyurethane foam, which is flammable and can contain formaldehyde and PBDE flame retardants.

- In animal studies, PBDE causes damage to the thyroid and reproductive systems, and suppresses the immune system.

- Other beds are filled with polyester fiberfill "polyfill," or PET plastic, which contains carcinogenic dioxane.

- Look for bedding that is filled and covered with natural fibers like hemp, wool, and organic cotton. Other natural fillings include kapok, buckwheat, and recycled soda bottles.

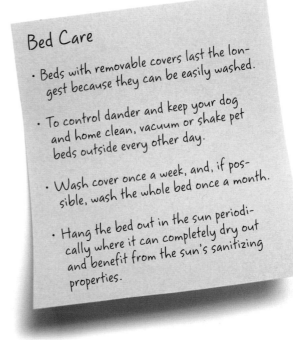

Bed Care

- Beds with removable covers last the longest because they can be easily washed.

- To control dander and keep your dog and home clean, vacuum or shake pet beds outside every other day.

- Wash cover once a week, and, if possible, wash the whole bed once a month.

- Hang the bed out in the sun periodically where it can completely dry out and benefit from the sun's sanitizing properties.

time between washings. Crates can and should be regularly hosed off and washed with mild castile soap.

The same considerations apply to pet bedding as to human bedding (see pages 62–63), and it's a good idea to avoid products that are treated with toxic flame retardants or antibacterial chemicals. Look for natural fillers, like buckwheat. Some natural bedding materials make your job easier. For example, cedar chips are a popular filling because they deter fleas and naturally absorb odors.

Blankets and Mats

- Blankets and mats for your pets can help preserve your car, furniture, and home, and save you some cleaning time.

- Look for fitted blankets for the car that can't be balled up when your pet decides to nest.

- Spread out blankets on furniture wherever your pets tend to luxuriate.

- Shake the blankets out every other day and wash them once a week.

Crates and Houses

- Wash crate and house bedding with the rest of your pet's blankets and bed covers once a week.

- Wash the structure once a month.

- For plastic, hose it down first. Then, scrub with hot soapy water and rinse.

Let dry in the sun before replacing clean bedding.

- For wicker, use a wet, soapy sponge to wipe down the entire structure. Follow with a wet, plain water sponge and towel-dry. Let it dry fully in the sun.

TOYS, ETC.
Look for earth-friendly pet accessories

For some dogs or cats, stuffed toys—no matter how tough or expensive—are disposable items. They are fun for a while, but then the moment comes when, without warning, the toy gets ripped to shreds in a matter of minutes. Of course, this is wasteful, gets expensive, and may make you want to skip the toys all together. Yet, toys can be crucial to help your pet fight boredom and behave. Be wary when picking out the right toy for Fido; some toys have been known to contain carcinogens, neurotoxins, and endocrine disrupters.

If your pet likes to rip open his toys, filled soft toys are a bad idea in general because the fillings and squeakers are unsafe. Some fillings can include things like nutshells or poly-

Scratch Posts

- Carpet-covered scratch posts emit toxic VOCs, which worsen the more your cat scratches.

- The carpet also becomes a sticking place for dander, dust, and other allergens.

- Vacuum this post once a week. For a deeper and deodorizing clean, get it out of the cat's reach and sprinkle with baking soda. Leave it on overnight and vacuum in the morning.

- For rope scratching posts, the vacuum will also work. For deeper clean, wipe the rope down with a soapy sponge followed by a plain water sponge and let dry in the sun.

Toys

- In choosing safe toys, it's important to determine whether your pet tends to destroy every toy or keep them around for years.

- For the chewers, look for nontoxic recycled plastic toys that can be washed in the sink.

- For non-chewers, look for stuffed toys that are washable and made with recycled materials, organic cotton, or hemp.

- All toys should be washed frequently, especially if they move between outdoors and indoors.

styrene beads, which are hazardous if your pet ingests them. No stuffing is truly digestible and, as with children, choking is a big hazard, especially with stuffed squeaking toys, small chips, and ropes.

Since the purpose of toys is to entertain your dog or cat, the best toys are the most interactive ones. Tug or fetch toys are great, but you can also help your pet play hide-and-seek with any toy.

Choose materials that are nontoxic, recyclable, and easy to clean. Cats will scratch on rope as easily as they will on toxic carpeted posts, and dogs will go fetch recycled denim or hemp as fast as they will the plastic ball.

Collars and Leashes

- Many collars and leashes are made from petroleum-based nylon and other synthetic materials.

- Look for natural fiber products that are sustainable. Hemp makes an excellent choice because it is tough and naturally antibacterial.

- Collars and leashes should not go in the laundry because plastic and metal parts can damage the machine or melt in the dryer.

- Instead, soak and scrub these items with mild dish soap and warm water. Dry in the sun before returning them to your animal.

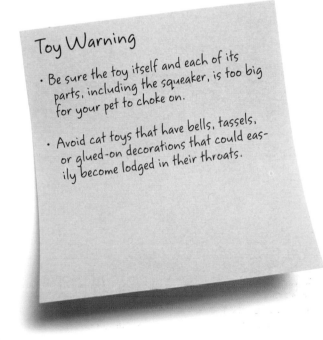

Toy Warning

- Be sure the toy itself and each of its parts, including the squeaker, is too big for your pet to choke on.

- Avoid cat toys that have bells, tassels, or glued-on decorations that could easily become lodged in their throats.

PET WASTE MANAGEMENT
Greener alternatives for cleaning up after your pet without hurting the earth or your community

Dogs and cats contribute 10 million tons of waste in the U.S. annually. And most of that clearly biodegradable matter is preserved forever in neat plastic bags in landfills. But there are greener options available.

Biodegradable bags are a step in the right direction because both the bag and the waste will break down in the short term. But the problem remains that pet waste is a threat to our soil and water supplies. That's because it's full of bacteria, parasites, and pathogens that can spread to other animals and to humans. Children playing in the dirt—or eating it as they tend to do—are particularly vulnerable.

Cat waste is of particular concern because of toxoplasmo-

Bags

- Biodegradable waste bags and cat bin liners offer a greener alternative to preserving waste in regular plastic bags that don't break down.

- They work best if you empty the bag in the toilet and then compost the bag.

- For non-composters, a better option is to reuse any plastic bag that comes into your home rather than buying new products just for this purpose.

Natural, Nontoxic Litter

- Most kitty litter is made of clay that is strip-mined at a high environmental cost.

- Kitty litter can also contain chemicals to make it clump and to mask smells. These are toxic to your cat, who breathes them and may ingest them in her morning grooming session.

- Other options include renewable, fragrance-free, chemical-free, and naturally clumping wheat-, pine-, kenaf-, or corn-based litter.

- Dump the waste clumps into the toilet and compost the litter or use as mulch in a non-vegetable garden.

sis, which is caused by a parasite. Ingestion can be fatal for kids under two years old. Pregnant women and people with weakened immune systems are warned against handling kitty litter.

The litter itself also takes a toll on the environment, as most of the clay it contains is strip-mined, which is the most environmentally costly form of mining there is. Currently there are several options on the market that use recycled newspapers or other materials to help close the recycling loop. These are generally nontoxic and a great choice for litter.

Cleaner Litter

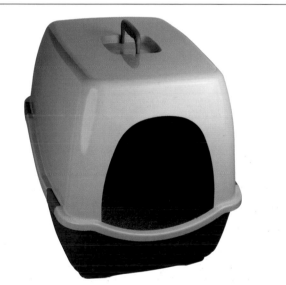

- If you are not composting it, look for litter made from recycled materials like newspaper.

- For a clean litter box, remove solid waste once a day or every other day as needed.

- Wash the litter box completely once a month. Use warm soapy water and finish with a disinfecting spray of diluted vinegar.

- Let dry and don't fill with litter until the vinegar smell has dissipated. That way your cat won't trade the box for your area rug in disgust.

· · · · · · · · · · YELLOW ● LIGHT · · · · · · · · · ·

Most scientists and the EPA warn against composting pet waste. Household composters do not get hot enough to kill dangerous bacteria like E. coli, which may be found in pet waste. Separate pet waste composters are available, but these should be used with caution and the compost should never be used on the garden.

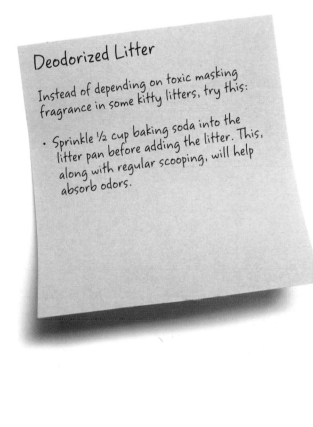

Deodorized Litter

Instead of depending on toxic masking fragrance in some kitty litters, try this:

- Sprinkle ½ cup baking soda into the litter pan before adding the litter. This, along with regular scooping, will help absorb odors.

PETS

HOME IMPACT

How to minimize your pet's impact on your home

There's a reason why they call potty training your puppy "house breaking." The damage can range from hard-to-remove spots on rugs to ruined sofas. But even full-grown dogs and cats leave their mark on our homes on a daily basis. Of course, there is a product for everything, including pet stains, but they are not likely to make it into our green cleaning kit. Like other carpet cleaning products, these pet stain cleaners can contain the dry cleaning solvent PERC (see page 102) as well as mildewcides, disinfectants, and toxic surfactants.

Dander is another pet waste that needs to be controlled. It consists of flakes of your pet's skin and can accumulate and trigger allergies and reduce indoor air quality. If your dog

Dander and Fur

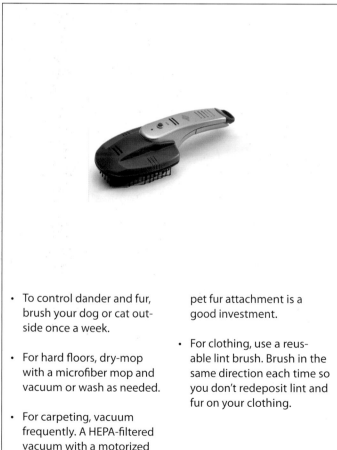

- To control dander and fur, brush your dog or cat outside once a week.

- For hard floors, dry-mop with a microfiber mop and vacuum or wash as needed.

- For carpeting, vacuum frequently. A HEPA-filtered vacuum with a motorized

- pet fur attachment is a good investment.

- For clothing, use a reusable lint brush. Brush in the same direction each time so you don't redeposit lint and fur on your clothing.

Furniture

- To protect your furniture, lay down towels, sheets, or blankets in your pet's favorite spots.

- For cats that scratch, place a rope scratching post near the chair or sofa the cat likes to scratch.

- Vacuum upholstery each week with a pet-hair specific vacuum tool or the upholstery attachment.

- Place pet beds in sunny spots near the favored furniture to tempt the animal to lay elsewhere.

sheds a lot and you see fur, you can be reasonably sure that you also have a lot of dander. Dander is harder to spot if your dog does not shed much, but you can assume it's there. Frequent dusting and vacuuming can help reduce dander.

Pets that luxuriate on furniture can dirty and even ruin it with dirty paws, fur oils, and nail scratches. Animals can certainly be trained to stay off the furniture, but if you have a hard time enforcing this simple rule, regular cleaning and precautionary measures can minimize the impact.

Another way in which animals can negatively impact your home is by chewing or scratching furniture and rugs. While this is pretty normal for puppies and kittens, it can be corrected through training. Keep in mind that exercise and stimulation are the key to well-behaved animals. Take your chewing dog on an extra walk each day or even step it up to a run, and you may find the problem disappears.

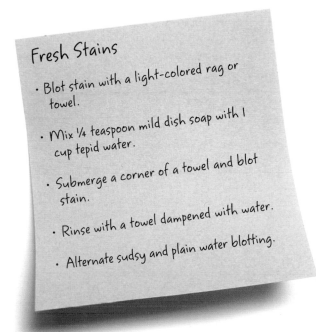

Fresh Stains

- Blot stain with a light-colored rag or towel.

- Mix ¼ teaspoon mild dish soap with 1 cup tepid water.

- Submerge a corner of a towel and blot stain.

- Rinse with a towel dampened with water.

- Alternate sudsy and plain water blotting.

Old Stains

- If you have pet stains that have been around for a while, try this:

- Apply enzymatic cleaner directly to the stain and use as directed.

- When stain is gone, sprinkle with baking soda and leave overnight to further reduce odors.

- Vacuum up the baking soda.

PETS

171

FLEAS

Flea collars aren't only toxic to the fleas

Of all the ways pets can leave their mark in our homes, fleas are perhaps the worst. They make the dog or cat miserable but can also infest rugs, furniture, clothing, and pretty much everything else. If you don't catch the infestation immediately, it's easy to feel like you've lost the war, which is why we spend so much money each year on flea and tick products to keep these pests off our pets and out of our homes.

However, in a study by the Northwest Coalition for Alternatives to Pesticides, over two-thirds of the chemicals found in flea control products are neurotoxic and can negatively impact reproductive systems. Half of the chemicals are Environmental Protection Agency–classified carcinogens or

What to Avoid

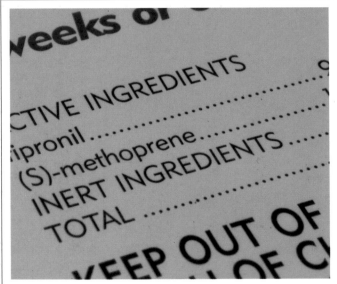

- Preventative flea treatments contain chemicals that are too toxic for us to get on our skin, yet they are meant to be absorbed by our pets.

- Pesticide use in anti-flea products is unregulated.

- Flea collars use pesticides that the pet inhales constantly while wearing the collar.

- Collar manufacturers also warn against human contact with their products, yet most people pet and scratch their dogs regardless of the collar.

Natural Flea Control

- Vacuum floors, curtains, and upholstery, and throw out the bag or clean the canister after use.

- Wash bedding and throws often.

- Switch to a cedar-filled bed for your pet.

- Introduce beneficial nematodes to your yard. These insects will kill flea larvae quickly.

- Place lavender, mint, rosemary, or cedar essential oil sachets alongside furniture cushions to repel fleas.

strongly suspected to be carcinogens, and a quarter of them are known mutagens. These products can harm many pets, and humans who apply the products and pet the animals. While we all want our homes and pets to be flea-proof, these toxins do not offer a great green alternative, and it's a good idea to avoid them.

While there are some nontoxic remedies for flea infestation, your best bet is prevention, which can be done by frequent washing of pet bedding, supplementing their diet, and knowing when flea season hits so you can be prepared.

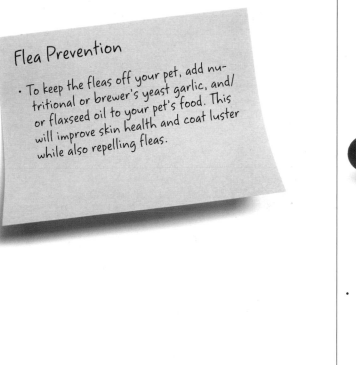

Flea Prevention

- To keep the fleas off your pet, add nutritional or brewer's yeast garlic, and/or flaxseed oil to your pet's food. This will improve skin health and coat luster while also repelling fleas.

Tools

- To get rid of fleas on pets, you will need a flea comb and bowl of warm soapy water.

- Comb your flea-infested animal daily with a flea comb.

- After each pass, dip the comb in the bowl of soapy water to ensure the fleas won't jump back on the animal.

- Comb every part of the animal, including the face.

- Regular baths can also help reduce fleas.

PETS

TOXIC PESTICIDES
Try integrated pest management for a healthier and pest-free home

If you've gone to the trouble of detoxing your cleaning, the last thing you want to do is call the exterminator. Pesticides are for killing pests, so there's no getting around the fact that they're toxic. Mild exposure to pesticides can cause eye, nose, and throat irritation, where more prolonged exposure can lead to central nervous system and kidney damage and increased risk of cancer. Spraying pesticides inside the home without ventilation can compound the already-serious dangers they pose.

Integrated Pest Management (IPM) is a green, chemical-free approach to keeping bugs out of your home or getting rid of bugs that have already taken up residence. IPM takes a

Pest Bombs or Foggers: What to Avoid

- These products cause severe irritation to eyes, skin, and respiratory systems.

- Accidents are common because the propellants are highly flammable.

- Active ingredients include pesticides like permethrin, which is a possible carcinogen and endocrine disrupter. It is also a known neurotoxin that can cause damage to kidney, liver, and reproductive systems. Tetramethrin is a carcinogen and known neurotoxin.

- Inert ingredients often include known carcinogens, such as formaldehyde, chloroethane, coal tar, and dichloroacetic acid.

Less-Toxic Pesticides

Boric acid

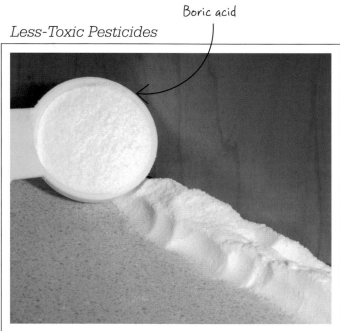

- If you are blowing or sprinkling boric acid in your home, be sure to wear a mask to prevent inhalation.

- Diatomaceous earth (DE) is an irritant when inhaled. Wear a mask when you use it.

- Silica gel is highly absorbent silicon dioxide. It won't irritate skin, but use a mask because it can cause lung damage if inhaled.

- All three are effective for crawling insects that infest homes, especially when combined with other preventative measures.

174

lot more strategizing and usually a little more time, but given the risks of pesticides, it's worth it. IPM looks at pest control from every angle to get rid of pests instead of simply pointing and spraying existing bugs, which doesn't always stop the nest from coming back.

With IPM, you can physically block bugs with window screens and by filling in cracks and holes. Use the bugs to your benefit by introducing the appropriate beneficial bug to your yard to control negative pests, such as using nema-todes to control fleas. On the inside, IPM practitioners focus on making the home inhospitable to the pest. That can mean everything from clearing clutter and removing food sources to fixing leaks and more-frequent washings of all bedding and carpeting. With IPM, use nontoxic baits or traps to catch any bugs that already made it inside.

IPM DIY Ideas

- Replace or fix screens
- Reapply caulking
- Reduce clutter and clean cupboards
- Store pet food and garbage in sealed containers
- Vacuum and clean often
- Move wood stacks away from home

IPM: Questions to Ask Before You Start

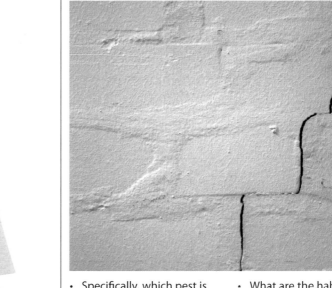

- Specifically, which pest is bothering you?

- What level of damage or danger is there with this insect? A minor nuisance or something worthy of low-grade pesticides?

- What are the habits of this insect? Does it come out at night or day? Does it stay hidden or parade across your floor?

- How is it getting in?

- Why is it staying?

ANTS

Locate their entry point and eliminate ants in an eco-friendly way

The worst thing about seeing an ant in your home is knowing that hundreds more are not far behind. While ants are annoying and not exactly a sign of the clean green home you've been envisioning, ants are not the end of the world. Most don't bite or cause structural damage to your home. And since we can see exactly where they are coming from, they're fairly easy to deter.

The labels of most ant-killing products warn against everything from breathing it to getting it on clothing and skin. Among other toxins, many ant control products contain permethrin, which is a strongly suspected human carcinogen. Toxic pesticides tend to backfire because they only target the

Pharaoh Ants

- These ants seek out food sources. Eliminate the food source by cleaning up crumbs or spills.

- Keep kitchen counters and cupboards clean and crumb-free. Wash your surfaces with vinegar to break the scent trail the ants leave to track each other.

- Any food that is not in the refrigerator or freezer needs to be in tightly sealed containers. Empty garbage daily.

- Store pet food in tightly sealed containers and keep pet eating areas clean.

No Entry

- Follow the ants to where they are entering your home. Seal the hole or crack to prevent further entrance.

- If you can't seal the area, create a barrier:

- Sprinkle a thick line of coffee grounds or use any combination of cayenne pepper, a citrus-oil-soaked string, lemon juice, or cinnamon to create the barrier.

- The ants won't cross, but you may have to replace the barrier every day.

5 percent of a colony that actually ventures out, and it splits a single colony into multiple colonies, which will then yield more ants.

An integrated pest management approach (see pages 174–175) focuses on deterring more ants from entering your home. For the ants that are already inside, be vigilant about eliminating food sources such as crumbs and pet food. For a green solution, spray the following nontoxic ant repellent to kill the ants.

Non-Chemical Warfare

Arsenal needs:

Dish soap or citrus oil

Spray bottle

Rag or sponge

Cornstarch

Vacuum

- For the ants that are already inside, combine a teaspoon of dish soap or citrus oil and water in a spray bottle.

- Spray it on any ants you see and wipe them up with a rag or sponge.

- Alternatively, put cornstarch in your vacuum bag or canister and vacuum them up. The cornstarch will suffocate them.

- Dispose of the bag immediately.

Carpet Strategy

- If the previous tactics don't take care of the problem, try diatomaceous earth (DE).

- Wear a mask as you sprinkle DE on your carpeting. If this is an area rug, you may want to do this outside.

- Work the dust into the carpet with a broom.

- Let sit for several hours or overnight. Vacuum thoroughly.

ROACHES
Take an integrated approach to ridding your home of roaches

If you have cockroaches you don't have to feel alone. Research shows that 78–98 percent of city dwellers have infestations that range from 900 to 330,000 roaches. This creates a huge problem, especially for children, as cockroaches produce an allergen in their waste, saliva, and bodies. This allergen can cause long-term respiratory problems. Pesticides can make it even worse. Anti-roach products can contain propoxur, a chemical that is linked to severe reproductive and hormonal damage. Another common anti-roach chemical is hydramethylnon, which the EPA lists as a possible carcinogen and reproductive toxin.

Roaches are often carried in via grocery bags and shipping materials so it can be trickier to locate their entry points. But it is important to make structural repairs that'll make these

Cockroach

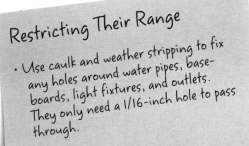

Restricting Their Range
- Use caulk and weather stripping to fix any holes around water pipes, baseboards, light fixtures, and outlets. They only need a 1/16-inch hole to pass through.

- The three most common cockroaches are German, American, and Oriental. And they share several preferences.

- They look for food and water and prefer carbohydrates.

- They feed on crumbs in your cabinets as well as the starchy glue in bookbindings and wallpaper and starch-based paints, envelope glue, and bar soap.

- Their mode of entry usually includes hitching a ride on your groceries or your mail order delivery.

pests feel less comfortable and free to roam in your home.

The next focus should be on food sources. Roaches prefer carbohydrates, including crumbs, but also paste for wallpaper, glue on envelopes and bookbindings, paper, and soap. Limiting the availability of these sources will help control the problem.

Lastly, try less-toxic pesticides like boric acid and diatomaceous earth (DE). Like any pesticide, these should be handled with care and kept out of reach from kids and animals, but they won't cause long-term health or environmental impacts.

No More Free Lunch

- Deep-clean the kitchen, including cupboards and garbage area.

- Store all nonrefrigerated food and pet food in sealed containers.

- Remove all stacks of paper, newspapers, and magazines. Store envelopes and soap in sealed containers.

- If any wallpaper is peeling, fix it immediately so the glue is inaccessible to the bugs.

Boric Acid Technique

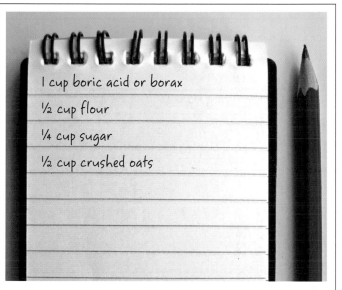

I cup boric acid or borax

½ cup flour

¼ cup sugar

½ cup crushed oats

- Combine ingredients on a piece of cardboard and position it where you have seen roach activity.

- The roaches will eat the mixture and die.

- Do not leave this mixture in places where children or pets could mistake it for a treat.

- Combining this method with the use of a duster to blow boric acid into cracks and holes can be highly effective. Wear a mask during application.

TERMITES

Knowing which type of termite you're up against is crucial to crafting your strategy

Termites in your home pose the risk of eating through and severely damaging your wood structures. Although chemical tenting (see sidebar) is usually presented as a perfectly safe and effective way of ridding the home of termites, the toxic residue it leaves behind can depress your nervous system and lead to blood and bone disorders.

The most common damage-causing varieties of these pests are dampwood, drywood, and subterranean termites. Each one requires a different management approach. The first green step for all three is to repair areas where the wood from your home is in contact with the soil. It's also a good idea, where possible, to remove and replace damaged wood.

Evidence of Termites

- Signs of termites include piles of sawdust, feces, or dead insects on your floor. If you're already seeing this, you have a serious infestation.

- To catch it sooner, regularly inspect around your home for any tunneling near the foundation or termite-eaten wood.

- Stick a knife into any wood that looks decayed. If you can easily sink it in ½-inch deep, you likely have termites.

- Look for swarms of flying termites around your home after it rains.

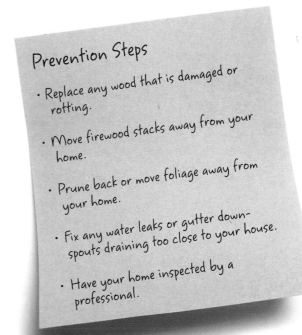

Prevention Steps

- Replace any wood that is damaged or rotting.

- Move firewood stacks away from your home.

- Prune back or move foliage away from your home.

- Fix any water leaks or gutter down-spouts draining too close to your house.

- Have your home inspected by a professional.

For subterranean and dampwood termites, moisture is another issue to address when trying to prevent or exterminate these pests. Fix leaks, point gutter downspouts away from the home, and remove shrubs or vines that are in contact with the home because they hold in moisture. While limited infestations of these pests may be addressed with nematodes or citrus oil, larger problems will most likely require the help of a specialist in integrated pest management (see page 174–175).

(see page 174–175).

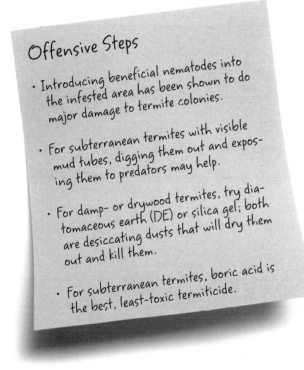

Offensive Steps

- Introducing beneficial nematodes into the infested area has been shown to do major damage to termite colonies.

- For subterranean termites with visible mud tubes, digging them out and exposing them to predators may help.

- For damp- or drywood termites, try diatomaceous earth (DE) or silica gel; both are desiccating dusts that will dry them out and kill them.

- For subterranean termites, boric acid is the best, least-toxic termiticide.

························ RED ● LIGHT ··············

Tenting involves tightly sealing the home in plastic and releasing large amounts of toxic gases like sulfuryl fluoride and methyl bromide. Although these treatments require you to leave the home for a few days, the gases do not completely disappear in that time and deaths to homeowners as well as workers have been reported.

Heat Treatment

- Like toxic "tenting," heat treatment companies cover your entire house with a tent-like tarp.

- Instead of spraying pesticides inside, they turn up the heat beyond what the termites can survive. Studies have shown this to be 90 percent effective.

- This method is not effective for subterranean termites.

- Because the heat can damage plastics and electrical equipment, there is some preparation and off-site storage that needs to happen before you do this.

FLIES

Keep a clean home to deter flies and prevent infestation

Besides being utterly annoying, a sudden influx of flies needs your prompt attention because they are expert germ carriers. House flies feed on waste and sewage as well as rotting food, which makes them prime vehicles for bacteria as serious as salmonella. Fruit flies look for garbage and decaying organic matter in your fruit bowl but also in sink and tub drains, under refrigerators, and just about anywhere else. Getting rid of flies and keeping them out is as easy as pest control gets.

The first step is to check your screens. Ill-fitting screens or screens with holes in them are open invitations to flies. Next, and even more important, find where the flies are breeding and clean it up. A good bet is to check your garbage and

Fruit Fly Deterrent

- As long as there is a supply of rotting matter in your drain, garbage, or fruit bowl, fruit fly larvae will thrive.

- To find out if the flies are coming from the drain, place a piece of plastic wrap over the drain and tape to the sink. Leave overnight and then check to see if fruit flies are stuck to it in the morning.

- Placing a basil plant near where you keep your fruit is a good deterrent for fruit flies.

Fruit Fly Trap

- For a very satisfying science project and fruit fly trap, try this: Fill a small bowl partially full with apple cider vinegar.

- Cover with plastic wrap.

- Prick holes that are large enough for the flies to get in but not too large that it's easy for them to get out. Holes should be about ½ an inch from the edge of the dish.

- Leave out overnight.

behind your garbage for any decomposing food. Keep your garbage can tightly covered and empty and wash the garbage can frequently. Pick up pet waste in the yard immediately and check your houseplants for decaying material.

With screens as barriers and thorough cleaning, all that's left to do is perfect your swatting technique, and your fly problem will be a thing of the past.

ZOOM

Studies show that when flies are ready for takeoff, they usually jump up and backwards. To swat a fly, aim your swatter about an inch and a half behind the fly and you will impress your family and friends with your Zen-like fly-swatting abilities.

Tried and True

- Flies that come in with the breeze and exit as soon as you open the screen door again are not a serious problem.

- Flies that stay and reproduce mean you have a sanitation problem.

- Empty garbage frequently and keep it in a covered container. Wash the pail once a week and clean up any other rotting organic matter like dog waste in the backyard.

- Find a good sturdy fly swatter and perfect your execution (see sidebar).

Make Your Own Flypaper

You will need:

paper bag

¼ cup corn syrup

½ cup sugar

- Cut the paper bag into 4 or 5 strips that are about 2 inches wide.

- Stir together syrup and sugar in a bowl.

- Use a knife to spread the mixture evenly onto the paper strips.

- Hang the strips but be sure you have a bowl or tray under them to catch any drips.

RODENTS

Poison can backfire—try these gentler methods to rid your home of rodents

Rats and mice are not exactly the symbols of a clean green home. If left to their own devices, they can cause damage by chewing through wiring, walls, plastic, and furniture. Considering that one pair of mice can produce up to eighty-seven babies in a year and rats can produce more than thirty-five, you need to rid your home of them as soon as possible or you'll have an even more serious problem. It may be tempting to reach for the rat poison, but don't. Rat poison is highly toxic to the rat but also to your family and pets. Poisoning rodents can make the situation worse because they tend to go into the walls to die where you can't reach them or see them—but you can certainly smell them.

House Mouse

- The common house mouse grows to about 5 inches long while rats get to be about 16 inches long.

- A rat or mouse scampering or swaggering across your floor, droppings, and gnawed food packaging, furniture, and walls are all signs of infestation.

- You may also see flickering lights because the rodents are chewing the wires or hear rustling sounds at night.

- Rat urine is hard to miss because it's quite strong and stains.

Integrated Pest Management

Seal the cracks
Eliminate hiding places
Take away the food
Cut off the water supply

- Stuff steel wool into any crack ¼-inch or larger and caulk it into place.

- De-clutter so it's harder for mice to hide, and clean out any cupboard they seem to frequent.

- Clean often and store all human and pet food in covered containers. Don't leave dishes in the sink. Cover garbage and take out often.

- Don't leave pet's water dishes out at night, and get rid of any standing water in houseplant trays, etc.

Mice and rats like living with you simply because you provide food and hiding places, so the key to getting rid of them is to stop providing both. A mouse only needs a dime-sized hole and a rat only a half inch to get into your house and walls, so make sure you stop up any that you see. Eliminate their food source by tightly covering garbage and keeping your kitchen counters and floors extremely clean. Using all-purpose cleaner with peppermint oil (see page 31) deters mice who find it distasteful.

Trapping is the final stage in the war against rodents and should do the job without chemicals. Start with the most humane traps available and progress from there. Use as many traps as you can and make sure you buy the right size traps for your pest, as rats are significantly bigger than mice. Peanut butter, fruit, bacon, and gumdrops are all attractive bait choices.

Live Trap

- Some live traps do not need to be baited.

- For the others, use peanut butter or gumdrops to lure the mice in.

- When you catch a mouse, put on some gloves and take it at least one mile away from your home so it doesn't find its way back.

- Release the mouse, and reuse the trap to catch the rest of the mice.

Snap Trap

- Snap traps are the next most humane traps after live traps because they usually result in a quick and easy death.

- Choose traps that are the right size for your rodent and place them out of the way of children and pets.

- Bait 2 or 3 traps at once. Do not set the traps for the first few nights to accustom the rodent to this new food source.

- Use gloves to avoid getting your own smell on the trap.

REDEFINING GARBAGE
Compost and recycle everything you can to reduce garbage

The EPA calculates that the average American produces 4.6 pounds of garbage per day or, as a nation, 251 million tons a year. Lucky for the planet, the definition of "garbage" gets a lot narrower in a green house. Living according to the order of the three Rs—reduce, reuse, recycle—means that products that are unnecessary or wasteful, such as disposable shower wipes and temporary, disposable food storage containers, are not purchased in the first place, so the amount of possible waste is reduced. Products like computers or baby gear are donated for reuse. And anything and everything that can be is recycled, either by setting it out on the curb or, for food waste, composting it in the garden. When trash day comes,

Cleaner Waste Management

- Keeping garbage under the sink is common, but the combination of a juicy food source and increased moisture can attract pests.

- More ideal is to create a pull-out system in a separate cabinet that is just for waste. Use covered cans or keep the cabinet door closed to deter pests.

- Place the garbage in front and recycling in back to keep the recycling free of drips and misplaced trash.

- Alternatively, use a lidded garbage can that is easy to clean.

Keeping It Clean

- Depending on your household, clean out your cans once every other week.

- Empty the garbage and recycling as usual and then take the bins outside. Use a sponge, rag, or brush to scrub them with soapy water.

- Spray with straight vinegar to disinfect and leave them to dry in the sun.

- If your bag slides down and creates a mess, tie knots at the mouth of the bag to create a snugger fit.

you can tell a green house by the small size of the garbage can in comparison to the large size of the recycling bin.

To use the three Rs to redefine and limit garbage in your home, the first step is to make it easy for everyone in the home to do the right thing with anything they're ready to discard. That means having a functional and easy to clean system of separating the garbage from the recycling, composting, and donating items.

ZOOM

The "Great Pacific Garbage Patch" is a startling reminder that garbage never really goes away. It's an island consisting almost entirely of plastic that weighs about 3.5 million tons and occupies an area twice the size of Texas. It is a huge threat to Pacific marine animals and birds who mistake the plastic for food.

Green Bags

- There are a variety of green garbage bags available.

- Look for bags that are made from as much post consumer waste (PCW) recycled material as you can find, or bags made from nonpetroleum sources like corn.

- Biodegradable garbage bags usually do not biodegrade in landfill conditions.

- If a product does claim to be biodegradable in landfills, make sure they are American Society for Testing and Materials (ASTM) certified to make that claim.

Clean Idea

- To reduce your garbage, consider composting.

- Composting keeps food scraps out of the garbage and enriches your soil.

- If that's not enough, your garbage won't smell as quickly and you may not have to take it out as much.

RECYCLING

Creating the recycling habit in your home means less garbage to the landfill and less work for you

While it's true that many Americans recycle, recycling has actually been losing ground. Aluminum can recycling dropped 20 percent between 1992 and 2004, and plastic bottle recycling has been cut in half in nearly the same amount of time. In response, many programs have eliminated the need to sort the cans from the plastic and paper, making it even easier to recycle. Making it easy is also the key to stepping up your household recycling program to make it so convenient that it is done out of habit instead of by constant prodding.

If your recycling system looks too much like a garbage can, it can often be mistaken for the trash, which means either you have to do some unpleasant sorting or throw the whole

Curbside Bins

- One sign of a clean green home is that on trash day, the recycling bin overshadows the garbage bin.

- Post the list of what is and isn't recyclable so everyone knows what goes where.

- Reduce the amount of packaging you discard by buying in bulk whenever possible.

- Make buying choices based on whether the packaging is recyclable and skip products that are overpackaged.

Recycling Etiquette

- Keep food out of the recycling bin.

- Rinse out any plastic, glass, or metal food container that is recyclable.

- Do not try to recycle pizza boxes or paper napkins or plates covered in food or grease.

mess out. Instead, and to clarify what goes where, offer well-marked bins that are noticeably different from your garbage. Be sure they are large enough so that they're not overflowing by pickup day. Recycling rules require you to rinse recyclables free of food before placing them in the bins. However, this doesn't always happen and spills make this area an attractive feeding ground for pests, so choose bins that are easy to clean. Placing the bins in the pantry or just outside the garage door mean no one needs to travel far to do their part.

······· • GREEN ● LIGHT • ·············

Make amends for all the energy wastes in your home and lifestyle by buying your greenhouse gas emissions and funding climate-positive programs like wind turbine construction, solar installation, treatment plants in developing countries, and more. Check out the resource section to see a range of what's available.

In-House Bins

- Create a clearly marked recycling center that fits your space.

- If your program requires you to sort items, create separate containers for paper, plastic, and metal.

- Make sure the containers are large enough that they won't overflow, or, if space is limited, create a schedule to empty them midweek before they have a chance to overflow.

- Wash the containers with a hose and soap once a month.

Stackable Bins

- Stackable bins may fit better in small spaces or for garage recycling centers.

- Position the bins so they require the least effort to get to and won't be blocked by cars, boxes, or other items.

- To make it even easier, leave a tray on the kitchen counter for people to put recyclables during the day and then take them out to the bins after dinner each night.

- This cuts down on trips to the bins and drips from the kitchen.

RECYCLING GUIDELINES
What you need to know to recycle effectively

A successful recycling program is dependent on the proper participation of many. As soon as you know the rules of how and what to recycle, following them is easy.

These rules vary by region, so get the information directly from your local recycling company. Post them clearly next to your bins so there are no gray areas. Some recycling programs make it easy by not requiring you to sort, picking up every week, and including a wide range of plastics and other materials in the recycling bin. Other places have strict rules on sorting and are very restrictive on what actually gets recycled.

As a general guideline, be sure to rinse out all containers before putting them in the recycling bins. Don't put in paper

Plastics

- Check with your program provider for the plastics they do and do not recycle, but here are the most commonly accepted:

- #1 is found in soda and water bottles. It is reincarnated as fiberfill for dog beds, winter coats, and beanbags, among other uses.

- #2 is the sturdier plastic in shampoo, laundry, or milk bottles. These will become toys, plastic lumber and piping, and rope.

- #6 is polystyrene or Styrofoam and will become rigid foam insulation, among other things.

Paper

- Newspapers and regular paper are accepted in any recycling program.

- In some locations you need to bundle the newspaper in twine or paper bags.

- Phone books are often not accepted because the thin paper can't be recycled to make more paper—but they can be used to make new phone books as well as paper bags, cereal boxes, and paper towels.

- Contact the company who publishes the phone book to see where you can recycle it.

products or anything else that is soaked through with food or grease. If you find something that you use regularly that doesn't get recycled curbside, try to find somewhere that will recycle it. See the resources section for Web sites that will save you time in your search. However, it's important to look at the bigger picture and not drive miles to recycle a few small items.

YELLOW ●LIGHT

To support ongoing recycling efforts, know the rules and sort accordingly. Incorrectly tossing items into the recycling bin makes it more difficult for manufacturers to buy clean source material for their recycled products. What's more—recycling is usually sorted by people, not machines. Tossing sharp objects or other hazards in the bin puts those workers at risk.

Metal

- The most commonly accepted metals are aluminum and steel or "tin" cans.

- Both are closed-loop recycled because they find immediate use; an aluminum soda can may go from curbside to shelf as a new aluminum can in as little as 60 days. Steel may become material for cars and other products.

- Aluminum cans are mainly soda cans.

- Steel and tin cans are the thicker metal ones used for tuna fish, soup, and other canned food items.

Common Exceptions

- Plastic #7, #3, or anything vinyl

- Blue and brown glass

- Window glass, pyrex, lightbulbs, mirrors, drinking glasses

- Tops from glass containers

- Tops from plastic containers

- Drink boxes

- Phone books

- Food-contaminated paper, paper towels

- Shredded paper

- Aerosol cans that are not empty

EASY COMPOSTING

Composting shrinks to fit even the smallest spaces and busiest schedules

Composting is the ultimate in recycling because it reduces waste going to the landfills and even more directly benefits the environment by improving the soil. Compost-enriched soil grows healthier plants but also conserves water by reducing runoff and resisting erosion.

But if you live in an apartment or a home with no land, it may seem like composting is not an option. These days, however, there are systems to fit any lifestyle, including bins that fit under your kitchen sink and produce just enough compost to keep you and your neighbors' houseplants luxuriously green and healthy. You just need to find the system that will work best for your lifestyle and take time to learn the ropes.

Worms

- The easiest way to get started with composting is to buy a Can-O-Worms system made from recycled materials.

- These are stacking trays designed for the worms to eat their way up through the layers as you feed them non-meat kitchen scraps and shredded newspaper.

- You can keep them in your kitchen or leave them outside on a patio.

- You'll need the can, a starter bedding brick, and about 1,000 red wiggler worms.

Undersink System

- Most in-home systems consist of a bin with a tight-fitting lid and some kind of microbial additive or "starter" to digest the scraps.

- Start the bin with a layer of additive. Then add scraps and more additive and keep it up until it's full.

- There is a waiting period before you can use the compost or bury it for further decomposition.

- It's a good idea to have two bins and alternate between the two.

If you do choose under-sink composting, keeping the bin tightly covered is key to ensuring that pests don't find this treasure trove of decaying kitchen scraps. Any system will have a tight-fitting lid, but make sure you put it on correctly each time or you could compromise your compost and have a real mess on your hands. Cleaning the whole area regularly will make turning scraps to "black gold" a much more enjoyable process.

ZOOM

Given that yard and food waste make up 30 percent of U.S. waste, composting can make a big difference. According to the Lower East Side Ecology Center in New York City, if every one of the eight million New Yorkers practiced worm composting, they would reduce the city's food waste by 75 percent.

Compost Tea

Drain compost tea from here

- Compost tea is basically liquid compost that you can use as indoor or outdoor fertilizer.

- Some composters have spigots that allow you to harvest compost tea easily.

- Making compost tea requires some equipment

and science, but you can buy a compost tea brewer that makes it easy for you (see the resource section).

- Apply tea to the soil at the base of your plants to fertilize or spray on the leaves to fight fungus.

Donating Compost

- Who to ask:

- Local farmers' markets

- City waste management program

- Arboretums and botanical gardens

- Government parks and recreation departments

- Natural food stores

LARGE-SPACE COMPOSTING
Choose a sunny spot and the tools that suit your lifestyle

For families who do have yards and produce more organic waste in the form of kitchen scraps, but also more yard waste like grass clippings and leaves, composting can pay off big. The reduction in garbage is substantial, but enriching your soil with compost helps you reduce or eliminate fertilizers and pesticides because your plants and trees will be healthier and more resistant to disease.

It's important to have a sink-side canister to make it easier on everyone to stick to composting. Who wants to traipse out to the composter every time they have an apple core or banana peel? The canister should be large enough to hold a day of scraps and have a lid that seals tightly. There are can-

Sink-Side Composting

- Make it easy for the whole household to compost with a sink-side container.

- It should be big enough to fit a whole day's worth of kitchen scraps.

- Take the crock out to add to the compost pile each night after dinner.

- Look for a crock that seals tightly or use a bowl with a tight lid. Some crocks have charcoal filters to absorb smells, in case you don't get to empty it every day.

Backyard Bins

- When looking for compost bins, look for recycled plastic bins with tight fitting lids to keep pests out and spinning mechanisms.

- You will also need compost starter that you add to the bin to jump start the process.

- Effective composting is a balance of 25 percent green matter from kitchen scraps and 75 percent brown matter from yard waste.

- If the mix is off, mold and smells will become a problem.

isters made for this use, but a glass bowl with a tightly fitting top can also work.

For your backyard composter buy an easy-to-use bin and some compost starter, or build it yourself. As in small spaces, it's important to be realistic about your lifestyle so you don't commit to a compost system that's too involved. It's also a good idea to have one person in the family who is responsible for the compost. This role can rotate, but it will ensure that the task doesn't fall through the cracks.

ZOOM

Compost decomposes rapidly in temperatures of 90–135 degrees, so cold-weather composting one pile may take a year. To help, keep several piles going at once so you always have access to the rich soil that results from the breakdown. Place compost piles in the sunniest spot and choose heat-absorbing black-colored bins with insulation jackets.

25 Percent Greens: Nitrogen

- Fruit and vegetable scraps
- Eggshells
- Rice and pasta
- Teabags or Leaves
- Coffee grounds
- Houseplant clippings
- Flowers
- Outdoor plant clippings
- Hedge trimmings

75 Percent Browns: Carbon

- Leaves
- Pine needles
- Cornstalks
- Twigs and branches
- Paper egg cartons
- Fireplace ashes
- Straw
- Sawdust
- Dryer lint
- Shredded newspaper

TOXIC SPILLS IN THE HOME
Clean up toxic messes in three easy steps

Even clean green homes may have a few toxins still lurking in garages and basements that come out every once in a while for the car or the pool. Unfortunately, in the process of moving around these toxins, many inevitably end up on the kitchen counter. The counter is a way station for just about everything, but it's also a food-prep surface that should be kept as clean as possible. When antifreeze or pool chemicals leak on it, there is definite cause for concern.

If this happens, it's important to protect yourself first—even before your granite countertops, I'm afraid. Open a window for ventilation and get protection for your skin and eyes before attempting to clean up the area. It's a good idea to keep

Protect

- Keep an emergency protection kit under your sink so it's easy to grab in case of emergency.

- If a toxic chemical or pesticide spills, first open as many windows or doors as you can.

- Next, put on eye protection and rubber gloves so you minimize your own exposure to the chemical.

- Any rags you use will most likely be ruined after the cleanup, so don't grab your nicest kitchen towel.

Step 1: Contain

- To protect your floor and counters, create an absorbent boundary around the chemical.

- You need to act fast here, so flour may be the easiest option. Other options include kitty litter and sawdust.

- Next, generously pour the absorbent material over the top of the spill.

- Use a rag and a piece of cardboard to scoop up the spill. Place the rag and cardboard in a plastic bag.

a protective kit under the kitchen sink for emergencies of this type. Next, contain the spill, keeping it from spreading to the floor or other surfaces and absorbing as much as you can with flour, sawdust, kitty litter, or whatever other absorbent materials you can access quickly.

Use a detergent to clean up the area and to remove traces of the chemical from the counter. Keep in mind that the chemical and now everything you used to clean it up classify as hazardous waste and needs to be disposed of accordingly. Contain the hazardous waste in a plastic bag or covered bucket to be taken to the hazardous waste drop-off site. Lastly, open more windows and arrange fans to increase ventilation and direct any lingering gas or smells out of your house as quickly as possible.

Step 2: Clean Up

- Pour liquid dishwashing detergent or laundry detergent directly on the spill spot.

- Now, reapply absorbent material over the top of the detergent to absorb.

- Scoop up the spill with cardboard and add to the plastic bag.

- Scrub the spot with more detergent and water.

Step 3: Dispose and Ventilate

- Set up a circulating fan pointed out the window to speed up the ventilation of this area.

- Open another window opposite the first if possible, or at least not directly next to it. Set up a fan to pull the outdoor air into the room.

- Take your items to dispose outside and let them offgas away from you and your family.

- Then place them in a sealed plastic bag and dispose of as hazardous waste.

DE-CLUTTER

The first step to keeping any space clean green is to know what to keep and what to toss

For anyone who has lived in their home for more than a few years, basements and garages become holding zones for discarded objects that we no longer want in the house. Already-read books, old baby clothes, outdated computers, and long-forgotten exercise bikes, among other things, tend to get stashed here. The longer we let the clutter build up,

the more difficult the clean up. What might have been an afternoon project grows into a multi-weekend marathon.

Much of what's stored in these spaces takes little energy to donate or recycle. The books are perfect for a library used-book sale. The baby clothes and computer can be donated. And the exercise bike . . . well there has to be someone who wants it.

Electronic Waste

- Plastic casings around electronics are usually treated with toxic flame retardants, decabrominated diphenyl ethers (deca-BDEs).

- Monitors, chips, connectors, and other materials inside the electronics can contain neurotoxic lead and mercury and carcinogenic chromium and cadmium.

- These items are hazardous materials and should not be thrown in the garbage.

- But they should also not sit idle in your garage or closet.

E-Waste Resources

- The best way to get rid of your e-waste is to donate or sell your item to someone who can use it.

- If the item is too outdated, you'll want to recycle it. First check with the manufacturer for take-back programs.

- Some manufacturers do this for free and others charge a small fee for recycling.

- If there is no take-back program, check with big box stores for recycling programs, or look for city or county e-waste drop-off programs.

To help you de-clutter, first move everything out to where you can see it and group together items that are similar, such as sporting goods or car-care tools. Sort the piles according to what you will keep and what you will let go. Anything that is clearly junk and nonrecyclable should be tossed immediately. Anything that is junk and hazardous should be set aside to take to the hazardous waste center in your area. Damaged or broken items should be set aside for recycling, repairs, or disposal in a green way. Items in good condition but not needed or wanted should be set aside for donations.

Once you know what's staying and what's going, decide where the discards will go. With a little research, you can find recycling or donation programs to fit just about everything. Start with the resource section for ideas. Give yourself a deadline and stick to it.

Sporting Goods Resources

- For old but still functioning sporting equipment, check with local schools, after-school programs, charities, and churches to see if they can use them.

- You can also sell them at a garage sale.

- Or donate or resell them through a local used sporting goods store.

- Or sell or swap them through an online auction site.

Other Ideas

- Cut old T-shirts and flannels into cleaning rags.

- Cut up your old yoga mat to make a knee pad to use while gardening or a mat for your pet dishes.

- Give your packing peanuts to your local shipping store for reuse.

- Donate old books to the local library or school.

DETOX

How to dispose of or store household toxins so they're safely out of breathing range

As you're clearing out the clutter in your basement and garage, you may come across toxins like paint, paint thinner, pesticides, transmission fluid, or hazardous household cleaners. These are all items that can't just be thrown out with the garbage or dumped down the drain so their containers can be recycled. If the label tells you it's toxic, corrosive, flammable, reactive, or explosive, it's hazardous waste and should not end up in the landfill. Read the labels for information on proper disposal, but also research the hazardous waste disposal guidelines in your area.

For the most part, it's a good idea to finish up the product (or find someone who will) and then make your next pur-

General Rules for Household Hazardous Waste (HHW) Disposal

- In the trash: solid, dried paint or adhesive.

- Down the drain: water-based cleaners or products that would normally go down the drain (mix with plenty of water).

- Hazardous waste facility: fuel, motor oil, antifreeze, pesticides, polishes with petroleum distillates, non-water-based cleaners, vinyl.

Antifreeze

TOXIC HAZARD

- Antifreeze is a staple in many garages and is often stored on a shelf with other car products.

- Yet, this one product is responsible for thousands of children and animal poisonings every year.

- It tastes sweet so kids and pets will lap up puddles of it, but the sweetness comes from toxic ethylene glycol.

- Store antifreeze in a locked cabinet. Make sure it's not leaking out of your car. For your next purchase, look for a safer antifreeze (see resources) that uses less toxic propylene glycol instead.

chase a safer alternative, or find a nontoxic homemade solution. For toxins you aren't ready to let go of, make sure you store them safely where children can't reach them and no one is inhaling them.

A locked cabinet is ideal for most toxins, but it's important to keep flammable products away from corrosives. Products that have warnings about vapors and fumes should be kept in well-ventilated spaces. Keep all toxins in their original containers with the labels intact so they are never mistaken for something nontoxic. Children get poisoned every year from toxins stored in soda cans or other old food containers that make them look like something edible. Be sure the lids are on tightly and the area is dry. If you have rags that are designated to be used with a specific product, store them in sealed containers that are clearly marked with their use.

Storage

- Store hazardous products in a locked cabinet that kids can't access.

- Keep similar products on the same shelves; put pesticides on the top shelf and paint on a lower shelf.

- Make sure the lids are on as tightly as possible. If you smell the chemicals when the doors are shut, check the lids.

- Routinely check for bulging containers and dispose of them properly.

Storage Guidelines

- Follow storage instructions on the packaging.

- Store products in original containers, and keep them sealed and dry.

- Paint should be stored upside down to ensure the tightest seal possible.

- Keep flammable materials away from direct sunlight and appliances, such as furnaces and grills that could ignite them.

CLEAN BASEMENT

Seasonal cleaning can mean the difference between a healthy home and a colossal mold or pest problem

It's not as visually rewarding as a clean kitchen or bedroom and it's certainly not the kind of cleaning you would do before guests arrive, but cleaning the basement is crucial to the overall health of your home. Since it is generally one of the least-trafficked areas in the home, it's prime for all kinds of problems, from mold growth to insect or rodent infestation.

Seasonal cleaning will keep you in touch with what's going on (or growing) in your basement and help you catch it before it's too late.

Depending on how your basement is arranged, it may work best to break the space down into quadrants when cleaning. That way you can move boxes or furnishings over into

Ceiling

- Start cleaning at the ceiling to remove spiderwebs, dust, and dirt.

- Clear the area you are cleaning as best you can so you will only sprinkle debris on the floor.

- Cover anything you can't move with tarps. Place a hat or scarf on your head and use a face mask to avoid breathing in dust particles.

- Use a straw broom to sweep the ceiling. Try to get into tight spaces and above pipes. Stand on a ladder if needed.

Appliances

Dust and dirt build up here

- Move on to the next highest surface—the tops of shelves or appliances.

- Start at the top and wipe them with a damp cloth to remove dust layer.

- Then, wash with warm sudsy water. Be careful with using too much water on electrical appliances.

- Make sure the areas around appliances are clutter-free. Any boxes or bags of stored items located near an appliance could be a fire hazard.

the next quadrant and cover with a tarp while you clean. When you're finished with one quadrant you can slide the stuff back over without too much trouble. As in any room, it's a good idea to start at the top with the ceiling. Cover your head and anything else remaining in the space and use a broom to remove any spiderwebs, dust, or debris that have accumulated there.

Next, clean any appliances like hot water heaters or laundry machines. Wipe these down and inspect them for mold or any loose parts. Shelves can be dusted, wiped down, or even vacuumed. Finally, sweep and wash the floor. A typical basement floor is concrete and thus easy to clean with mild castile soap and water. A janitor's broom is an excellent tool for scrubbing.

Floor

- Remove protective tarps by wrapping up debris and taking it outside to shake.

- Use a push broom to sweep debris into piles. If you have a wet/dry vacuum, use it to suck up the piles.

- If not, use a dustpan. Do not use your household vacuum because basement debris may include larger objects that can cause damage.

- Use a clean push broom to scrub the floor with a solution of warm water and castile soap.

Routine Inspections
- While you're cleaning, check the following:

- Stored items for water damage or moisture

- Shelves for evidence of pests like mice or silverfish

- Appliances for fire safety

- The floor and walls for evidence of moisture and cracks

BASEMENT MOISTURE CONTROL
Stop the most common basement problem at its source

Basements can be both the best and worst storage area in your home. They can be spacious and out of sight to guests, yet easier to access than the attic. The catch is that most basements have a moisture problem that can turn all your stored memorabilia into a moldy mess in no time.

To solve this problem, first find the source of the moisture.

Look for leaking pipes and cracks in the walls or floor. Check around the outside of your basement as well. Are the gutter downspouts pointed at the basement? If so, redirect them with extensions to keep the water clear of the house. Clogged gutters can also be the problem, causing rainwater to overflow and fall right down to the foundation. If the surrounding

Interior Inspection

- If you notice water damage to your stored items or smell mold, inspect the floor, corners, and walls for cracks. It's a good idea to do this after a good rain.

- Concrete is porous, so it needs to be sealed periodically.

- Look for nontoxic, low-VOC sealants to waterproof your concrete.

- Consider installing storm windows to keep your basement warmer and discourage condensation.

Exterior Inspection

- Inspect the foundation of your home to see if gutter downspouts are draining too close to the house.

- If that's the case, install a splash block or extender to take the water away from the house.

- Check for clogs in the gutters, which may cause the water to overflow and pour down near your basement.

- Consider installing rain barrels to help you recycle rainwater into irrigation for your landscaping. Make sure it's a system where overflow is not an issue.

ground is sloped toward your home, drainage ditches can help keep the water out of your basement. A clothes dryer in the basement can also contribute moisture to the air, so make sure your dryer is vented properly.

Dehumidifiers and fans can help stop moisture, as can sealing the floor and walls with a low-VOC sealant. But these are only helpful if you've already found and addressed the cause of the moisture.

If your basement tends to be damp, avoid storing the following items. The moist environment can lead to mold and transform perfectly good pieces into more trash for the landfill. Carpet, upholstered furniture, books, papers, photographs, clothes, draperies, linens and other fabrics, wood, iron, or steel equipment, cans that can rust, and cardboard boxes.

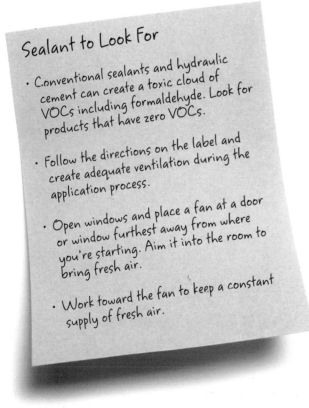

Sealant to Look For

- Conventional sealants and hydraulic cement can create a toxic cloud of VOCs including formaldehyde. Look for products that have zero VOCs.

- Follow the directions on the label and create adequate ventilation during the application process.

- Open windows and place a fan at a door or window furthest away from where you're starting. Aim it into the room to bring fresh air.

- Work toward the fan to keep a constant supply of fresh air.

Dehumidifier

- A dehumidifier can provide a short-term fix for a minor moisture problem, but not a long-term solution.

- Save energy and prolong the dehumidifier's life by not setting the humidistat higher than necessary.

- Clean the water container and replace the filter as needed.

- Once you've turned the unit off, wait at least 10 minutes before turning it back on. This will let the pressure equalize and keep the unit running longer.

CLEAN GARAGE

Neglected garages may be far from green

While there's no need to slip into the HazMat suit or dig out the gas mask, cleaning the garage does take some special precautions. Once you've cleared out the clutter and either disposed of or properly stored chemicals, the remaining concern for the environment is what's on the floor. Hosing down the floor can seem like a very logical and expedient way to clean, but it means that oil-tainted water flows down your driveway and into the storm drain or road, only to be washed into the surrounding environment the next time it rains. Just one drop of oil has the power to pollute 1,000 gallons of water. So think twice before you hose off that oil slick under the old Subaru.

Step 1: Cleaning Stains

- Cover the entire stain with a layer of kitty litter or sawdust about ½-inch deep.

- Lay down strips of paper or cardboard that are wide enough for your feet.

- Step onto the paper and do the twist! Grind the litter or sawdust into the concrete.

- Repeat whenever you have a minute to do it again. Add more litter or sawdust as needed. It may take up to 2 weeks of twisting to absorb the stain.

Step 2: Sweeping the Floor

- Discard the absorbent material and paper or cardboard as hazardous waste.

- Use a push broom to sweep the garage.

- Because the garage floor can be a collector of toxic debris from cars and household chemicals, don't just sweep the dirt out onto the driveway where rain can carry it into storm drains.

- Instead, sweep debris into piles and use a wet/dry vacuum to suck up the piles and dispose of it properly.

If your car is leaking oil or other chemical fluids, be proactive by strategically placing trays of kitty litter or sawdust to catch and absorb the leaks. When it's time to wash the floor, you'll be able to dispose of the oily litter safely, without risking the water supply. If you've caught it all and the garage floor is oil-free, then cleaning it is easy. You can wet the surface with the hose, apply a mixture of mild castile soap and water, and use a janitor's broom to scrub and guide the water toward the driveway.

For oil slicks directly on the floor, your best bet is to contain and absorb them by pouring on a generous amount of kitty litter or sawdust. Place strips of newspaper over the piles and proceed to do the twist—yes, the twist—to grind the sawdust into the floor and increase the absorption. If you do manage to get all of the oil up, then washing the floor with water is a possibility. Otherwise, stick to sweeping.

Step 3: Washing the Floor

- Mix a few squirts of phosphate-free detergent and a gallon of water in a bucket.

- In small amounts, pour the mixture onto the area you are cleaning.

- Use a push broom to scrub the floor and repeat in the next area.

- Use the hose and the push broom to rinse the floor and push the water out of the garage. Leave the door open for it to dry.

Preventing Stains

- Before pulling your leaky car back into your clean garage, place an old baking pan with sand or saw dust under the car to catch the leak.

- Be sure the pan is the right size and in the right position to catch all of the leak.

- And get your car fixed!

KEEPING IT CLEAN

Organized gear stations make cleaning easy and fast

If you have recently cleaned up your basement or garage, congratulations! Not only have you increased the usefulness and improved the appearance of these areas, but you also just increased the value of your home. In fact, real estate experts recommend cleaning out the garage as one of the cheapest things you can do to give a tremendous boost to the home's curb appeal. If you're not interested in selling your home anytime soon, just take a few more steps to organize these spaces, and they'll remain free of clutter and easy to clean over the long haul.

Setting up well-organized stations for the different types of gear stored there will save you time spent on searching

Off-the-Floor Storage

- The best use of space in your garage or basement is to build shelves to expand vertical storage.

- Install the bottom shelf about a foot above the floor to keep your stored items dry and make the whole room easier to clean.

- Designate sections of the walls for different types of items, and structure your shelving accordingly.

- Combine shelves with hooks and bungee cords to accommodate the different items you want to store.

Sporting Gear

- Store sporting goods where they won't get damaged by falling over or getting scratched from car doors.

- Surfboards, snowboards, wakeboards, and skis could get damaged or warped from the shelving itself; consider wrapping hard edges in old towels.

- Hang your most expensive gear where it is least likely to be damaged.

- Use milk crates, clean plant pots, or other recycled bins and containers to hold smaller objects like balls, gloves, surf wax, and bike tire tubes.

for the correct tool or soccer ball, as well as give you ample space for household projects like repotting plants or performing repairs. In essence, your garage and basement can actually be spaces you use instead of just parking and storing stuff in them. When all you have to do is back the car out and sweep and vacuum a few cobwebs, you'll be more inclined to tackle these projects more often.

Tools

- Organize tools so that you can easily see and grab whatever you need.

- Most pegboard is pressed wood and a source of formaldehyde and other VOCs.

- Look for companies who offer less-toxic choices (see the resources section).

- You can also use shelves, bins and hooks to achieve an organized tool area.

Crafts

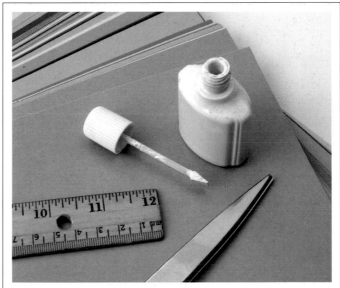

- Use a corner of your basement or other utility room to create a workspace for crafts, sewing, or other hobbies.

- Some glues, paints, dyes, and other craft supplies are toxic. Choose an area that can be ventilated easily.

- Keep all toxic supplies in a locked cabinet so children and pets can't get into them.

- Be sure to use the vertical wall storage space to give you more workspace.

EXTERIOR WASH

Get the dirt off without polluting the oceans

While washing your car every week will most likely help your car last longer, washing the car at home may not be your greenest option. All of that water running off the car as you wash contains oil, grease, mud, rubber, and gasoline, which will now enter the storm water system untreated, and eventually, the waterways and oceans.

On the other hand, professional car washes are required by law to drain the wastewater into sewer systems that will be treated, reducing the risk of contamination. Car washes can also save between 35 and 95 gallons of water per wash. These small details add up to huge benefits for the environment.

If you must wash at home, try a nontoxic soap such as the

Car Wash Suds to Avoid

Ingredients:

petroleum distillates

kerosene

silicone

mineral spirits

- All of these known carcinogens are found in car wash products.

- As you rinse your car, toxins including brake dust, exhaust fumes, and oils join the harsh detergents and carcinogens from the car wash solution.

- They get rinsed down your driveway and into the storm drains or the surrounding soil.

- Washing your car on the lawn acts like a filter, keeping the toxins out of the waterways, but they remain in your own yard.

Car Wash Suds Labels to Look for

- Petroleum-free

- Phosphate-free

- Kerosene-free

- Waterless

- Biodegradable

recipe you'll find here. Also, resist the urge to run the hose the entire time you're washing. Instead, use a hose attachment that enables you to turn the water on and off without having to run back to the faucet each time.

Eco-Friendly Car Wash

- Any car wash is greener than washing at home because wastewater goes into the sewer where it will be treated.

- Look for car washes that take extra steps to conserve water, such as separating the oil and water and reusing the water.

- A few car washes also use green building practices and alternative energy sources, like solar power.

- Above all, look for a car wash that uses nontoxic cleaners. If they don't tell you what they use, ask.

If You Must Wash at Home

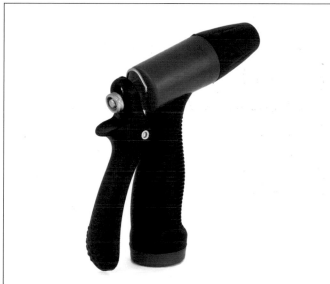

- Park the car in the shade or wash in the morning. You'll use less water because the sun won't bake on the soap. Use a hose attachment with a shut-off valve to wet the car.

- Suds up with a large sponge, and use a separate bucket to rinse the sponge so you minimize detergent use from changing dirty buckets.

- Rinse the car thoroughly but without going overboard and wasting water. If your car is fairly clean to begin with, try a waterless product (see resources).

211

CHROME

Keep your chrome looking showroom-new with a few items from your kitchen

If you're lucky enough to have a car that hasn't traded in all its classic shiny chrome parts for plastic, then you'll need something to bring out the shine. If you neglect them, oil or grease can bake into their surface, making cleaning them difficult. A better option is to clean chrome regularly so it maintains its shine. Before cleaning, look closely at the metal to be sure it's actually chrome. Some carmakers use polished aluminum, which resembles chrome but does not clean up the same way. If the surface has tarnish or pits in it, it's most likely aluminum.

Specialized chrome cleaners can contain ethylene glycol, a neurotoxin that can also damage the reproductive system, kidney, and liver. Of more immediate concern, it can irritate

Chrome Polish Ingredients to Avoid

Ingredients:
ethylene glycol
ammonia
1,1,1-trichloroethane
TEA
Fragrance

- Ethylene glycol is toxic to the nervous and reproductive systems, as well as a respiratory irritant that can cause kidney, blood, and liver damage.

- Ammonia is a respiratory irritant and 1,1,1-trichloroethane is a neurotoxin.

- TEA can combine with preservatives to form nitrosamines, which are carcinogenic.

- "Fragrance" represents a whole host of chemicals, including phthalates, a suspected endocrine disrupter.

Polish Technique

- For best results, use a soft flannel cloth to avoid scratching the chrome.

- Dip the cloth in apple cider vinegar.

- Move in the direction of the metal grain. Do not move in circles or you could scratch it.

- Use a second clean, dry, flannel cloth and buff the chrome to a shine.

your throat and lungs. These cleaners can also contain other irritants and neurotoxins along with carcinogens and synthetic fragrances. What's more, they're not even necessary when you have vinegar or lemons on hand. These nontoxic techniques will help minimize the impact of washing your car yourself by reducing the amount of toxic products you need to have on hand for the task.

Alternative Technique

- Cut a lemon in half, and cup it in your hand.

- Wipe the chrome with the lemon in the direction of the metal grain.

- Buff with a clean, dry flannel cloth.

Old Corroded Chrome

- If your chrome looks impossibly corroded, try this shine-saving technique:

- Use fine steel wool as coarse steel wool can damage the chrome further.

- Rub the steel wool across the chrome in the direction of the grain, and flip the wool often.

- Use some elbow grease for this task, and work it until it shines.

CAR

WINDOWS
Step-by-step tips to nontoxic, crystal-clear windows

Although the spatters on your car windows can be as different as bugs and milkshakes or tree sap and road salt, effectively cleaning them is easy. Club soda makes a perfect cleaner because its bubbles help break up the stuck-on goo, but it doesn't leave a residue when you're done like other glass cleaners. Other cleaners can also streak, especially when they come into contact with special water-repellent coatings on your windshield. Frequent cleaning will keep this job manageable without too much elbow grease. It will also help you avoid the always-dirty squeegee and toxic blue solution at the gas station.

If you live in a colder climate and constantly battle foggy

Step 1: Start at the Top

• Lower each side window just enough so you can clean the very top of it.

• Spray club soda on scrunched-up newspaper or a T-shirt rag.

• Do not use paper towels for this job—they can leave fuzz and waste paper.

• Wipe in straight lines from side to side.

Step 2: Work Your Way to the Bottom

• Raise the window so you can clean the very bottom of the window.

• Spray more club soda onto the newspaper and continue wiping in straight lines down the window.

• Take one more pass with a dry side of the newspaper to get rid of any streaks.

• Be sure to clean the frame around the window, as well.

windows and ice buildup on the windshield, here's another easy green solution: Mix ½ cup of white vinegar with 1½ cups water in a spray bottle. Spray generously on the windshield. Allow it to air-dry. Do this twice a week, and you'll notice that both the fog and the ice become much less of a problem. While other deicing products can harm your car's paint job, this basic solution will not.

Step 3: Exterior Windshield

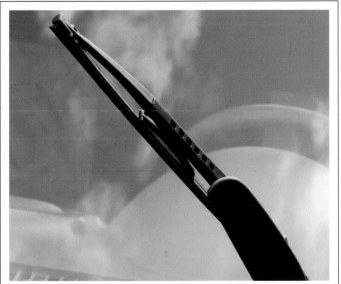

- Pull wiper blades off the window so they are sticking straight out.

- Start with the driver's side of the windshield. Spray club soda on your newspaper and wipe in long overlapping lines halfway across the windshield.

- Be sure to wipe below where you can see out of the windshield and around the wiper blades, which can catch a lot of dirt.

- Take another pass with dry newspaper to eliminate streaks and repeat on the other half.

Step 4: Interior Windshield

- Sitting at an angle on your knees in the front seat can help make cleaning the interior of the windshield a less awkward job.

- Spray the club soda on newspaper instead of the window and wipe in straight lines.

- Be careful around the rearview mirror. It is attached by glue and can be dislodged fairly easily.

- Split the window and do one side at a time. Take a final pass with dry newspaper to eliminate streaks.

CAR

SHINE AND PROTECT
Revive and preserve your car's finish with nontoxic polish

Regular cleaning and occasional polishing can protect your car so it looks newer longer. Unfortunately, many polishes contain chemicals that are irritants and can damage your central nervous system, cause dizziness, headaches, and nausea. But road debris, weather, and pollution do take their toll and protecting your car is still important. A growing awareness about toxins in the car industry is leading to new prod-

ucts that are less toxic to our bodies and the environment.

In the past, car polish and wax were completely different products. Polish was used to remove impurities, remedy surface scratches, and make your paint look brighter, while waxing protected the paint from chips and scratches caused by normal everyday use. As car paint technology advances, polish is less important and its abrasiveness can now actually

Car Polish to Avoid

- Like other polishes, car polish contains petroleum-based chemicals, such as petroleum distillates, a known neurotoxin.

- It has the second most serious hazard warning, "Danger," which means it could cause permanent tissue damage to the skin, mouth, throat, and stomach.

- This product is also "combustible" or able to catch fire and burn easily.

- Because paint technology has progressed so far, polish is less and less necessary. Using no polish is a better option than using this type of toxic product.

What to Look For

Ingredients:
water
coconut oil
beeswax
carnauba wax
banana essence oils
no petroleum distillates
no kerosene

- If you have a lot of plastic on your car, be sure to read the label. Some polishes are not appropriate for cars with plastic.

- To save water and reduce toxins, look for no-rinse cleaner-polish combo products (see resources). You save packaging, water, toxic

runoff, and time.

- These products are most effective for routine cleaning. If the car has not been washed in months, take it to the car wash and then wash every other week with the rinseless cleaner.

harm a car's clear-coated finish. The result is that polish and waxes have been combined into a single product designed for the new paint. The combination helps to reduce the number of products you need to buy and the plastic packaging they require. Yet the problem chemicals remain.

For the ambitious, try this homemade car polish and wax. It's a little more involved than other recipes you've found here, but works very well. Otherwise, look for nontoxic, biodegradable products.

Beads mean the car is well-protected.

Water Test

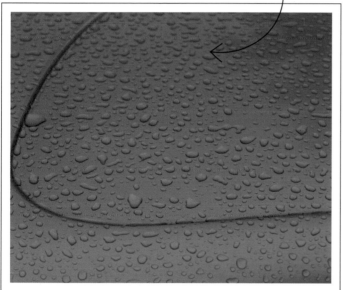

- If you see the water bead up on the surface, your paint is protected and you don't need to wax it.

- No beads means it might be time to take it to the car wash to have it professionally waxed.

- The more you wash your car, the less need you'll have for protective waxing.

- It is possible to overwax. If you do it too often, you can dull the finish on your car.

Homemade Polish/Wax Technique

- Before you begin polishing, the car should be out of direct sunlight and freshly washed.

- Working one section at a time, apply a quarter-size circle of polish to a clean flannel or microfiber cloth.

- Rub the polish on to the car in a circular motion and let dry so it looks cloudy.

- Use a dry flannel or microfiber cloth to buff the polish to a shine. Repeat on the next section of the car.

CAR

INTERIOR
Reinvent the "new car smell" by minimizing toxins

People either love or hate that "new car smell," but what is it exactly? Unfortunately, it's a toxic mix of chemicals that are offgassing from different parts of the car's interior. Even more unfortunately, a big part of this smell comes from PVC. You might expect that smell if you bought a car with vinyl seats, but even cars with leather or fabric seats usually contain PVC on the backs of seats, armrests, steering wheel, and door trim. As we've seen, PVC contains phthalates (see page 36) and is strongly linked to cancer as well as problems with reproductive development and fertility. Given that the typical American spends 100 minutes or more a day in their car breathing this stuff, it is definitely cause for concern.

Gearshift

- Attach the crevice tool to your household or wet/dry vacuum.

- Vacuum either from the top of the stick shift down or, for automatic cars, the length of the gearbox.

- If you have a soft leather or vinyl base to the gear-shift, use your other hand to stretch it taut as you vacuum.

- Finish by wiping down the area with a cloth dampened with castile soap and water. Wipe dry.

Interior Dash

- Your best tool is a micro-fiber cloth or a just damp T-shirt rag to make sure you are not just scattering the dust.

- Use a clean paintbrush to dust the vent slats, seams, and any other hard-to-reach places.

- After dusting, use a damp, clean sponge to wipe down the dash.

- Use club soda sprayed on a clean rag to wash glass surfaces.

If you're in the market for a new car, skip vinyl seats and look for cars with the least PVC content you can find (see the resource section). If you already have vinyl, try this recipe to minimize the smell and leave your car windows open in the garage so offgassing can happen without you there to breathe it.

Washing the interior of your car should not add toxins to the mix. Use your vacuum attachments to minimize dirt and dust and nontoxic cleaners like this vinyl deodorizer (right) for deeper cleaning.

MAKE IT EASY

Vinyl deodorizer:
¼ cup baking soda
1 gallon warm water
Dissolve the washing soda in water, saturate sponge, and wash. Wipe baking with a damp cloth.

"Baking Out" Vinyl

- To get rid of the vinyl car smell, try this: Leave the car in the hot sun for at least 3 hours with the windows open 1–2 inches. The heat speeds up the chemical emissions in the car.

- Next, open the windows all the way and let the car air out thoroughly without you in it.

- Vacuum thoroughly.

- Finally, use the vinyl deodorizer (above) with a microfiber cloth, and finish by wiping with a clean damp cloth.

Leather Seats

- Vacuum the seats and wipe with a microfiber cloth to ensure you've gotten up all the dust and debris.

- Skip the toxic leather cleaners and stick to the basics. Use the leather furniture cleaner (see page 123) as you would on your sofa and buff to a shine.

- Or, lather a bar of moisturizing soap on a clean wet cloth.

- Apply to the leather. Do not rinse. Buff with a clean cloth.

CAR

219

UPHOLSTERY AND CARPET
Vacuuming can reduce the need for cleaning products

Most car carpeting, as well as the glues and sealants used to install and protect it, is petroleum-based and contains offgassing VOCs that pollute interior air. Carpet and upholstery also trap dust and make an inviting home for dust mites. Avoid making matters worse by using more toxins to clean them.

Regular vacuuming with a quality filter can help reduce the toxins lingering in your car's dust. Vacuuming also helps reduce the need for cleaning products because dirt doesn't have time to get ground into the fibers. But for most people, ice cream cone drips and coffee spills are inevitable. Have a stain cleaning kit handy (see sidebar right) so you can treat the spill quickly when you'll have a better chance of removing it.

Maintenance: Clean Floor

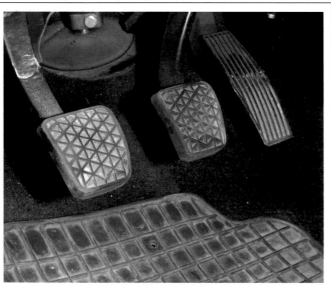

- Remove the floor mats from the car and shake them out.

- For rubber mats, hose them down and scrub with a brush and warm soapy water. Castile or dish soap works fine for this.

- For carpet mats, vacuum thoroughly. Sprinkle with baking soda and leave them out as you wash the rest of the car. Vacuum again before replacing them in the car.

- Using a flat tool and crevice tool, vacuum the entire floor of the car.

Maintenance: Clean Seats

Don't forget in here

- Vacuum your car frequently to keep the dirt from getting ground in or staining.

- Use the upholstery tool for flat surfaces. Pull the wand from top to bottom in long slow, overlapping strokes.

- Use the crevice tool for uneven surfaces and to get into tight spaces, including the space between the headrest and the seat back.

- Also use the crevice tool to get the areas on the floor alongside the seats where crumbs and other debris can fall.

When it is time to more deeply clean your upholstery, look for products that are fragrance-free to minimize your exposure to phthalates and other toxins. For an easy non-toxic deodorizer, sprinkle baking soda on your car's carpet and upholstery and leave overnight. Then use your vacuum's upholstery attachment, which includes a brush to vacuum up the baking soda. A vapor cleaner, or steam cleaner with a nontoxic solution, are great options for deepcleaning your car's carpet and upholstery (see page 123).

MAKE IT EASY

Easy spot stain removal kit:
Keep a clean rag and a small bottle of club soda in your glove compartment so you can treat stains immediately. Scrape off any of the spilled substance that has not yet absorbed into the material. Pour a small amount of club soda onto the stain and blot. Repeat several times.

Food Stains

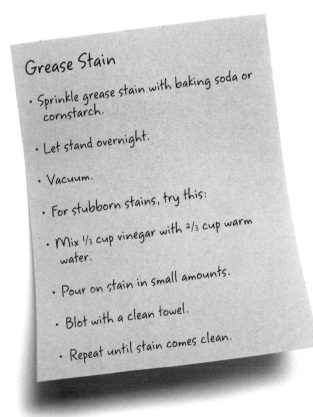

Grease Stain
- Sprinkle grease stain with baking soda or cornstarch.
- Let stand overnight.
- Vacuum.
- For stubborn stains, try this:
- Mix ⅓ cup vinegar with ⅔ cup warm water.
- Pour on stain in small amounts.
- Blot with a clean towel.
- Repeat until stain comes clean.

- Scrape off any unabsorbed spill with a knife. Pour club soda on the stain and blot with a clean towel. Repeat until the stain disappears.

- If it's still there, repeat process with white vinegar and water and another clean towel.

- For stubborn stains, mix ½ tsp dish soap in 1 cup water. Blot and repeat.

- As a last resort, repeat this mixture with hydrogen peroxide. Test first in a hidden area for discoloration.

CAR

OUTDOOR WOOD FURNITURE
Choose green and easy to clean

Wood furniture is the obvious choice for a natural and environmentally friendly backyard. It's a renewable resource and can be cared for with the ultimate in nontoxic cleaning products: mild soap and water. For some woods like teak, an occasional cleaning is all that is necessary, and the wood will age to a nice shade of silver. Some woods, like redwood and cedar, are naturally resistant to pests and rot, but look best with an occasional sealing. Still other woods, like pine, require yearly sealing to keep the moisture out and prevent rotting.

There are many different types of wood sealants and protective finishes available. Oil-based formulas are best for

Choosing

- Look for wood furniture that is FSC-certified to be confident you're buying a green product.

- Otherwise, look for non-exotic woods; skip the teak and go for western red cedar, which is naturally bacteria-, fungus-, and bug-resistant.

- Reclaimed or recycled wood furniture keeps wood out of landfills and the trees in the forest.

- Look for "secondary species" that are less popular and therefore less harvested woods like California oak, sweetgum, and madrone.

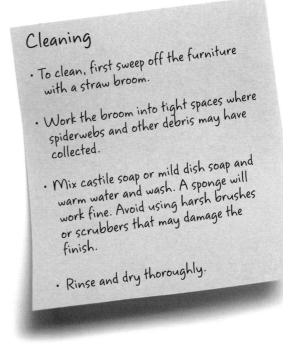

Cleaning

- To clean, first sweep off the furniture with a straw broom.

- Work the broom into tight spaces where spiderwebs and other debris may have collected.

- Mix castile soap or mild dish soap and warm water and wash. A sponge will work fine. Avoid using harsh brushes or scrubbers that may damage the finish.

- Rinse and dry thoroughly.

outdoor furniture, especially because the alternative, latex-based formulas typically contain ammonia and should not be exposed to direct sunlight. Many of the available products emit VOCs, which can combine with other substances in the air to produce hazardous gas like ground-level ozone, a big contributor to smog. These products also can contain 1,4-dioxane, a suspected carcinogen, and toxic solvents like xylene and toluene. Some also contain insecticides. Look for a Green Seal–certified product that has low VOCs and is plant-based.

Preserving

- To preserve your furniture, look for products that do not contain petroleum-based chemicals and are low-VOC.

- Some less-toxic products contain linseed oil, beeswax, or tung oil, but be sure these don't include toxic solvents and heavy metal dryers.

- Copper and zinc compounds are other less-toxic preservative ingredients.

- Follow the label for applica-tion, but most products suggest you clean furniture thoroughly and apply a thin coat of the oil. Wipe the furniture dry with a clean T-shirt rag.

Natural Aging

- If you already have teak furniture, you can oil it regularly and maintain its original coloring.

- But you can also let it age naturally and avoid using any product on it at all.

- When left alone with the weather, teak will age to a silver-gray color. Cracks can develop, but they will not weaken the structure of the wood.

- Cedar and redwood also do not need regular preserving.

OUTDOORS

OTHER OUTDOOR FURNITURE
Look for durable, recycled, or fast-growing materials

For covered decks or furniture that you're willing to pull in and store during the harsher weather months, fast-growing grasses like bamboo or vines like rattan transformed into wicker serve as alternative green options that deliver the natural look of wood. If you'd prefer furniture you can leave outside year-round without too much worry, recycled plastics and metal furniture are probably your best option.

Look closely at your wicker before cleaning. Much that is sold as outdoor furniture is actually not woven-vine wicker but woven plastic, like vinyl or resin. The most common wicker vine is rattan, but wicker is also made from cane, bamboo, and willow. Woven-vine wicker comes from renewable

Wood- or Vine-Based Wicker

- Wicker will last longer if not soaked either by rain or hose.

- To clean, use a brush vacuum attachment or a broom to remove dust deep inside the weave.

- Clean with a small amount of castile soap and water. Scrub with a brush to get into the fibers.

- Wipe with a clean damp cloth and leave in the sun to dry.

Resin- or Vinyl-Based Wicker

- If your furniture is very dusty or dirty, start with your vacuum or a broom to get dirt, dust, and spider-webs out from the fibers.

- Otherwise, use the water pressure from the hose to penetrate the fibers.

- Turn the hose off and scrub with castile soap and water.

- Rinse with another blast of the hose and leave out in the sun to dry.

resources so it qualifies as a green choice. However, it's not quite as durable as other options.

Both bamboo and natural wicker should be cleaned regularly because dust can build up in between the fibers and cause wear, and mold can develop in these spaces as well. Vacuuming with a brush attachment is your best option for routine cleaning. You can also wash the furniture with a damp sponge or rag and mild soap. Avoid soaking with a hose unless absolutely necessary.

Metal Furniture

- Aluminum, steel, and iron are your primary choices for metal outdoor furniture.

- Aluminum is durable and can handle being wet.

- Iron and steel are more inclined to rust, especially if you live near the ocean. Care should be taken to store furniture in dry places during rainy seasons. If rust begins to develop, sand area with 600-grit sand paper until you see the metal again.

- Wash with castile soap and water, but be sure to dry thoroughly.

Plastic

- Recycled plastic outdoor furniture is extremely durable and closes the recycling loop for recycled milk jugs and other HDPE plastic.

- To clean, hose down and then scrub with castile soap and water and a brush.

- Rinse with the hose and leave to dry in the sun.

- Plastic furniture can stay out in harsh weather, but if you know you won't use it for an entire season, it's best to store it out of the elements.

OUTDOORS

GRILLS AND FIRE PITS

Whether you use gas or charcoal, regular cleaning reduces pollution and increases efficiency

Another seemingly eternal debate amongst the environmentally conscious is whether to go with gas or charcoal for grilling. Although the debate is far from over, it's clear that neither option is perfect. Charcoal releases greenhouse gases, produces ground-level ozone, and contributes to deforestation. Typical charcoal grill accessories like lighter fluid and self-lighting briquettes can give off petrochemical VOCs as well. On the other hand, gas grilling, which includes either propane or natural gas options, requires a nonrenewable resource. Gas contributes pollution on its own, but far less than charcoal.

If you prefer charcoal, look for briquettes that don't have

Proactive Step

- To reduce the need to clean the grill often, take this simple step each time before you use it.

- Fill a pump spray with a high-heat oil, such as safflower or grapeseed oil.

- Before you turn the grill on to cook, spray the cooking grates with oil so food will not stick to it.

- Or brush the oil on, but be careful not to pour the oil into the grill itself.

Easy Clean

- Once you finish cooking your meal, turn off the gas or extinguish the flame and shut the top of the grill to keep it hot while you serve the food.

- After your meal, come back to the grill and use the grill brush. You could also use aluminum foil for this —a great way to recycle used aluminum foil.

- Brush or scrub the heated grates to rid them of any grilled-on food.

- Tap the brush a few extra times to ensure that it's clean when you finish.

chemical additives, and use a chimney starter instead of lighter fluid to get it going. It's also important to keep the grill as clean as possible to prevent extra smoke, which means extra pollution. For both gas and charcoal, regular cleaning and maintenance of your grill will keep it functioning efficiently and safely.

Deeper Clean

- Remove grates and soak in warm soapy water.

- Remove coal grate for charcoal and everything but the burner for gas grills. Brush out the inside of the grill.

- Dip a stiff wire brush in soapy water and gently scrub the inside of the grill, removing any debris. For gas grills, brush the briquettes and metal flame shield in warm soapy water.

- Scrub and rinse cooking grates, reassemble, and leave the top open to dry.

Fire Pits

- Clean fire pits regularly to reduce the particulate matter they release as pollution into the air. Cleaning also helps keep them safe.

- Remove any leftover wood and add the ash to your ornamental garden soil.

- Spray the pit with water and scrub gently with a soft brush and warm soapy water.

- Rinse the pit and leave it in the sun to dry.

OUTDOORS

DECK CARE
Practice eco-friendly seasonal cleaning and take protective steps

A deck can offer the promise of carefree, peaceful days spent reading or barbecuing with family and friends. Yet, some decks require a few extra steps before they can be entirely worry-free. Until recently, many decks were constructed out of arsenic-laden pressure-treated wood—chromated copper arsenate (CCA)—and many of us still have those decks.

The problem is that they leach arsenic and other toxins into the earth, groundwater, and your body. If you do have CCA wood, it's important to seal it regularly with a low- or no-VOC sealant to reduce the leaching.

If you decide to replace your deck, look for reclaimed wood. It's easy to clean, but does require additional care, such as fin-

Winter Proactive Step

- Winter neglect can make a lot more spring work for you.

- Weight from snow and debris can harm your deck, as can months of exposure to moisture. To prevent damage, shovel your deck after each snowstorm.

- Dig the shovel into the snow in shallow layers rather than digging all the way to the bottom.

- As you get closer to the wood, shovel more gently so you don't nick and cut into the deck with the shovel.

Summer Scrub

- Sweep your deck and railings weekly to get rid of any debris that may trap moisture and cause mold.

- Use a knife or screwdriver to remove any debris caught between boards.

- Wet the deck with a hose. Power washers are effective but can strip and damage the wood.

- Scrub with castile or dish soap and water using a push broom or deck brush. Be sure to follow the direction of the grain. Do this early in the morning so it can dry in the sun.

ish and sealants. Composite plastic lumber is another green option. It's made with recycled wood and plastic and doesn't require extra maintenance. It also resists moisture, has a long life, and is fully recyclable.

For regular wood decks, it's important to remove any accumulated debris to prevent mold and rot. Cleaning your deck is a great opportunity to inspect for loose boards or soft or rotting wood and replace any that you find. Pay attention to any signs of infestation. Termites and carpenter bees can ruin your wood deck. For regular cleaning use mild castile soap and water, scrub with a janitor's broom, and rinse off with the hose.

Deck Sealer to Look For

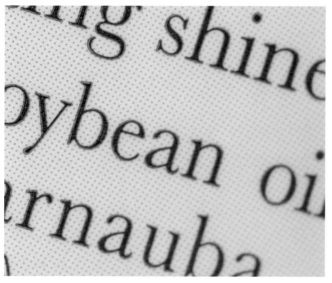

- You know it's time to seal your deck when water no longer beads up on the surface.

- It's important to choose a safe sealant.

- Deck sealers contain pesticides and petroleum-derived ingredients to pen-etrate and weatherproof the wood.

- Less-toxic products rely on plant-derived oils, safer solvents like isoaliphate, and contain no preservatives. (see the resources section for ideas)

Sealing the Deck

- Check the weather forecast to ensure it won't rain for at least two days.

- Follow the label instructions. Most products suggest you strip the old sealant off the deck by sanding it. Wash the sanded deck, and give it time to dry completely.

- Use a paint roller with a long handle to apply an even coat to your deck.

- Remember to start furthest away from your exit and work your way off the deck.

YARD WORK

Smart planning makes green yard care a breeze

Typical yard chores can take a toll on the environment. According to the EPA, gas-powered mowers, trimmers, and other landscaping tools are responsible for 5 percent of our urban air pollution. Homeowners tend to use pesticides more frequently and strongly than farmers, resulting in disrupted ecosystems and contaminated land and water. And having a perfectly manicured lawn and velvety grass requires tons of water and additional fertilizers and pesticides to stay healthy.

"Beneficial landscaping" is key to changing this situation. It means choosing plants and grasses that are native to your region and, therefore, typically need less supplemental watering. Native plants are also more resistant to pests on their own, without the need for pesticides. Keeping your lawn area to a

Grass Alternatives

- Look for drought-tolerant grass varieties that are native to your area. They'll require less water and less pest control.

- Skip or reduce the size of the lawn and plant a vegetable garden to help feed your household.

- Plant native, drought-tolerant bushes, grasses, and trees instead of a lawn. Plant them strategically to help heat and cool your home by providing shade where you need it.

- Use rain barrels to catch water and use it to irrigate your yard.

Eco Grass Cutter

- Push mowers with spinning blades are perfect for small lawns and require only you for power.

- Mower blades need sharpening periodically. Check your area for sharpening services before buying this type of grass cutter.

- Electric mowers pollute less than gas. Although they are more expensive than gas up front, they require less than half the cost to operate over 10 years.

- Skip the bag feature, and leave grass cuttings as mulch for your lawn to help it hold in moisture and need less water.

minimum makes it possible to switch from an energy-intensive gas mower to a person-powered push mower. Letting the grass grow longer between mowings also helps because deeper root systems mean less watering and healthier grass.

While fertilizing is important, look for nonsynthetic and non-fossil-fuel-based options that won't add nitrates and phosphates to our waterways. Contamination can kill fish and birds that inhabit those areas. Using your own compost is the best and most effective fertilizer you can use, and it doesn't cost you more than the bin and the compost starter.

Fertilizers to Avoid

- Studies show that fertilizers contain many of the most toxic heavy metals, along with dioxins.

- Synthetic fertilizers dump all of the nutrients at once and in large doses.

- Fertilizer chemicals contribute heavily to algae blooms in our waterways that kill fish and vegetation because the algae reduces the oxygen in the water.

- Avoid fertilizers that also contain pesticides. Applying toxic pesticides every time you fertilize is not good for your health or the environment.

Organic Fertilizer

- Overfertilized lawns are not healthy lawns.

- Instead of synthetic fertilizers, let the grass grow to at least 3 inches so it absorbs more sun and will develop a deeper root system. Deeper roots mean less watering over time.

- If you're composting, you have all you need for a healthy lawn.

- Leave the grass clippings on the lawn as mulch and try seeding the lawn with dutch clover, which naturally fixes nitrogen in the soil.

OUTDOORS

PEST MANAGEMENT
Choose ladybugs over carcinogens for effective pest control

With an integrated pest management approach (IPM), garden pest control does not have to be toxic. Instead of neurotoxins and carcinogens, your pest management arsenal can consist of nontoxic products like liquid soap, cooking oil, horticultural-grade (as opposed to pool-grade) diatomaceous earth (DE), neem oil, and ladybugs.

To prevent infestation, beneficial landscaping can be key. Any new plants you add to your yard should be native to your area and, therefore, naturally resistant to pests. Providing appropriate care without overwatering or overfertilizing also helps because the plants are healthier and better equipped to resist pests.

Aphids

- Aphid infestation is not pretty, but the damage is largely superficial. From an Integrated Pest Management (IPM) approach, toxic intervention is not worth the risk.

- Check plants before you buy them to make sure you're not bringing home aphids.

- Reduce the use of fertilizer because new growth attracts aphids. Sustained, slow growth is healthier and makes plants less vulnerable to this pest.

- Introduce ladybugs, lacewings, or syrphid flies, who like to feed on aphids.

Mites

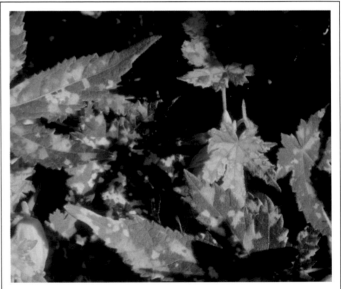

- Plants that are hot and dry are particularly vulnerable to spider mites.

- To test for mites, look for yellow or white specks on leaves. Or hold a piece of paper under a plant's leaves. Shake the plant. If tiny bugs appear on the paper, you have mites.

- Remove infested leaves immediately.

- Wipe both sides of each remaining leaf with a damp cloth once a week to eliminate the dust and webbing the mites use to protect their eggs.

Strategic planting is another IPM approach if you do find pests accumulating on specific plants. For example, plant nasturtiums, which black aphids love, right next to a plant you want to be aphid-free. When the nasturtiums fill up with aphids you can pull them out and take the aphids with you. Introducing beneficial bugs that eat destructive pests are also an easy and effective solution. For example, ladybugs love to dine on aphids, chinch bugs, alfalfa weevils, whiteflies, and mites among others. Green lacewings prefer aphids, mealy bugs, spider mites, and whiteflies. Do some research before introducing your beneficial bug of choice to make sure your garden and climate is well-suited for their needs.

Snails and Slugs

- These pests can cause major damage to your garden by eating leaves and sometimes the entire plant.

- Pick off snails and slugs whenever you see them.

- Look for them in the dark spaces of your garden -- the undersides of leaves as well as walls shielded by plants, inside or underneath containers, your compost heap, etc.

- Some research has shown caffeine to be toxic to slugs. Use your coffee grounds as a mulch and see if the slugs retreat.

Deer

Deer Resistant Plants	
Boxwood	
Coneflower/Echinacea	
Holly	
Iris	Spruce
Marigold	Strawflower
Nasturtium	Yucca
Snapdragon	Zinnia

- There are a million techniques for trying to defend your garden from munching deer, including fencing, scents, dogs, and rotten eggs.

- Even when they do work, it's usually a temporary fix. Then the deer are back munching your tomatoes.

- The best defense is to choose plants that the deer don't like.

- You may still have the pleasure of seeing them pass by, without the frustration of knowing what they just did to your garden.

OUTDOORS

RESOURCES / ADDITIONAL READING

Green Resources

Annie Berthold Bond's Healthy and Green Living: www.care2.com/greenliving

Bond, Annie B. *Home Enlightenment: Practical, Earth-Friendly Advice for Creating a Nurturing, Healthy, and Toxin-Free Home and Lifestyle.* Emmaus, PA: Rodale Books, 2005

Body and Soul magazine: www.marthastewart.com/body-and-soul

E Magazine www.emagazine.com

Healthy Child, Healthy World: www.checnet.org

Lime: www.Lime.com

Mother Jones magazine: motherjones.com

National Geographic *Green Guide:* www.thegreenguide.com

Natural Home magazine: www.naturalhomemagazine.com

Plenty magazine: www.plentymag.com

Rocky Mountain Institute: www.rmi.org

Rogers, Elizabeth and Thomas M. Kostigen. *The Green Book: The Everyday Guide to Saving the Planet One Simple Step at a Time.* NY: Three Rivers Press, 2007

General Information

The Fly Lady: www.flylady.net

Stewart, Martha. *Homekeeping Handbook: The Essential Guide to Caring for Everything in Your Home.* NY: Clarkson Potter Publishers, 2006

Household Products

Blanc, Paul D. *How Everyday Products Make People Sick: Toxins at Home and in the Workplace.* Berkeley and LA: University of California Press, 2007

Campaign for Safe and Affordable Drinking Water: www.safe-drinking-water.org

Department of Health and Human Services Agency for Toxic Substances and Disease Registry: www.atsdr.cdc.gov

Dickey, Philip. *Buy Smart, But Safe: A Consumer's Guide to Less-Toxic Products.* Washington Toxics Coalition, 1994

Environmental Working Group: www.ewg.org

Greenfeet: www.greenfeet.com

Green Nest: www.greennest.com

Gaiam: www.gaiam.com

Healthgoods: www.healthgoods.com

Imus, Deidre. *Green This!* NY: Simon & Schuster, 2007

Is It In Us? - Study of toxins in our bodies: isitinus.org/home.php

National Geographic Green Guide's: www.thegreenguide.com

National Institutes of Health and National Library of Medicine's Household Products Database: householdproducts.nlm.nih.gov

Real Green Goods: www.realgreengoods.com

Shapiro, Mark. *Exposed: The Toxic Chemistry of Everyday Products and What's at Stake for American Power.* White River Junction, VT: Chelsea Green Publishing, 2007

U.S. Environmental Protection Agency: www.epa.gov

Washington Toxics Coalition: www.watoxics.org

Personal Care Product

American Dental Association: www.ada.c

Campaign for Safe Cosmetics: www.safecosmetics.org

Cancer Prevention Coalition: www.preventcancer.com

Environmental Working Group's Skin Dee Project: www.cosmeticsdatabase.com

Fluoride Action Network: www.fluoridealert.org/

Food and Drug Administration: www.fda.g

Malkan, Stacy. *Not Just a Pretty Face: The U Side of the Beauty Industry.* Gabriola Island British Columbia: New Society Publishers 2007

Silent Spring Institute: www.silentspring.

Indoor Air Quality

Allergy Consumer Review: www.allergyconsumerreview.com

American Lung Association: www.lungusa.org

Asthma and Allergy Foundation of Amer www.aafa.org

Bond, Annie B. *Home Enlightenment: Practical, Earth-Friendly Advice for Creating Nurturing, Healthy, and Toxin-Free Home a Lifestyle.* Emmaus, PA: Rodale Books, 2005

Environmental Protection Agency Indoor Air Quality pages: www.epa.gov/iaq

National Radon Safety Board: www.nrsb.org

Wolverton, B.C. *How to Grow Fresh Air: 50 Houseplants that Purify Your Home or Office.* NY: Penguin Books, 1997

Pesticides, and Integrated Pest Management (IPM)

Beyond Pesticides: www.beyondpesticides.org

Green Methods IPM resource: greenmethods.com

Northwest Coalition for Alternatives to Pesticides: www.pesticide.org

PesticideWise www.pw.ucr.edu

Seabright Labs Smart Mouse Trap: seabrightlabs.com

U.S. Center for Disease Control: www.cdc.gov/drugresistance

U.S. Environmental Protection Agency – Indoor Air Quality: Pesticides: www.epa.gov/iaq/pesticid.html

University of California IPM Online: www.ipm.ucdavis.edu

Energy Efficiency and Global Warming

Atmosfair – offset air travel: www.atmosfair.com

California Urban Water Conservation Council's H2Ouse Water Saver Home: www.h2ouse.org

Carbon Counter – offset carbon emissions: www.carboncounter.org

Consumer Energy Education Group: manageenergycosts.com

Native Energy - offset carbon emissions: www.nativeenergy.com

Natural Resources Defense Council: www.nrdc.org

Sustainable Travel International – My Climate project to offset travel emissions: www.my-climate.com

Terrapass – offset carbon emissions: www.terrapass.com

US Department of Energy - Energy Efficiency and Renewable Energy: www.eere.energy.gov

DIY Green Cleaning

Bond, Annie Berthold. *Better Basics for the Home: Simple Solutions for Less Toxic Living.* NY: Three Rivers Press, 1999

Bond, Annie Berthold Healthy and Green Living Web site: www.care2.com/greenliving

Green Labels

Carpet and Rug Institute Green Label: www.carpet-rug.org

Consumer Reports Eco-labels resource center: www.greenerchoices.org/eco-labels/eco-home.cfm

Energy Star: energystar.gov

Forest Stewardship Council: www.fsc.org/en

Green Seal: www.greenseal.org

Leaping Bunny: www.leapingbunny.org

USDA Organic: www.usda.gov

Find Green Products

Consumer Reports Greener Choices www.greenerchoices.org

Cradle to Cradle: www.mcdonough.com/cradle_to_cradle.htm

National Geographic Green Guide's Smart Shopper Cards: www.thegreenguide.com

Cleaning Supplies

Baking and Washing Soda

Arm and Hammer: www.armandhammer.com

Borax

www.20muleteamlaundry.com

Herbs and Essential oils

Lavender Fields Farm: www.lavenderfieldsfarm.com

Olympic Lavender Farm: www.olympiclavender.com/farm.cfm

Monterey Bay Spice Company: www.herbco.com

Vegetable-based Soap

Dr. Bronners castile soap: www.drbronner.com

Vinegar

Heinz: www.heinzvinegar.com

Spectrum Organic Vinegar: www.spectrumorganics.com

The Vinegar Institute: www.versatilevinegar.org

Non-petroleum Candles

Bear Creek Candle Company: www.bearcreekcandlecompany.com

Cleaning Tools

Sponges and Scrubbers

Our Green House: www.ourgreenhouse.com

Eco Choices – Eco Kitchen: www.ecokitchen.com

Twist Sponges: www.twistclean.com

Mabu cloths: www.mabu.com

Green Cleaners

Earth Friendly Products www.ecos.com

Ecover Cleaning products: www.ecover.com

Hope's Homecare metal polishes: www.hopecompany.com

Howard Naturals cleaning products: www.howardsnaturals.com

Method Cleaning products: www.methodhome.com

Seventh Generation: www.seventhgeneration.com

Kitchen

Crate & Barrel: www.crateandbarrel.com

Preserve recycled plastic kitchen products: www.recycline.com

Totally Bamboo: www.totallybamboo.com

Vivaterra: www.vivaterra.com

Clean Food

Environmental Working Group's "Shopper's Guide to Pesticides in Produce": www.foodnews.org

US Department of Agriculture (USDA) Organic: www.usda.gov

Humane Farm Animal Care: www.certifiedhumane.org

Food Alliance certification program: www.foodalliance.org

Pollan, Michael. *The Omnivore's Dilemma: A Natural History of Four Meals.* NY: Penguin Books, 2006

Environmental Working Group's Safe Fish List: www.ewg.org/safefishlist

Institute for Agriculture and Trade Policy – Smart Guides: www.iatp.org/foodandhealth/

Monterey Bay Aquarium Seafood Watch: www.mbayaq.org/cr/seafoodwatch.asp

National Geographic Green Guide Product: www.thegreenguide.com

Bed and Bath

Anna Sova: annasova.com/

Coyuchi: www.coyuchi.com

Earthsake: www.earthsake.com/puregrow.html

Eco Choices - Eco Bathroom: www.ecobathroom.com

Eco Choices - Eco Bedroom: www.ecobedroom.com

Gaiam: www.gaiam.com

Greenfeet: www.greenfeet.com

Heart of Vermont: www.heartofvermont.com/

Kushtush Organics: www.kushtush.com/

Lifekind: www.lifekind.com

Apparel

American Apparel: www.americanapparel.net

Patagonia: www.patagonia.com

Rawganique hemp products: www.rawganique.com

Gaiam: www.gaiam.com

Personal Care

Aubrey Organics: www.aubrey-organics.com

Dr. Hauschka Skin Care: www.drhauschka.com

Ecco Bella: www.eccobella.com

Natracare: www.natracare.com

Preserve recycled products: www.recycline.com

Seventh Generation: www.seventhgeneration.com

Babies

Born Free glass baby bottles: www.newbornfree.com

Bum Genius cloth diaper system: www.bumgenius.com

Burt's Bees - baby care: www.burtsbees.com

California Baby - baby care: www.californiababy.com

Diaper Jungle: www.diaperjungle.com

Eco Choices – Eco Baby: www.ecobaby.com

G Diapers flushables: www.gdiapers.com

Green Nest: www.greennest.com

Healthy Toys: www.healthytoys.org

Klean Kanteen steel water bottles and sippy cups: www.kleankanteen.com

Kushtush Organics: www.kushtush.com

Mothering magazine: www.mothering.com

National Association of Diaper Services www.diapernet.org

National Resource Defense Council's "Healthy Milk, Healthy Baby: Chemical Contamination and Mother's Milk": www.nrdc.org/breastmilk

Naturepedic clean mattresses and bedding: www.naturepedic.com

Organic Gift Shop: www.organicgiftshop.com

Poppywood Recycled Wood Toys: www.poppywood.com

Quiet Hours Toys: www.quiethourstoys.com

Seventh Generation disposable diapers and wipes: www.seventhgeneration.com

Tushies Disposable Diapers: www.tushies.com

Under the Nile organic cotton diapers, clothes, and toys: www.underthenile.com

U.S. Consumer Products Safety Commission: www.recalls.gov/ or www.cpsc.gov

U.S. Public Interest Research Group "Tips for Toy Safety Report": www.uspirg.org/html/TipsforToySafety2006.pdf

Laundry

Project Laundry List: www.laundrylist.org

Seventh Generation: www.seventhgeneration.com

Ecover: www.ecover.com

BioKleen: www.bi-o-kleen.com

www.findco2.com

www.revolutioncleaners.com/

Furniture/Decor

Furniture

Eco Choices – Eco Sofa: www.ecosofa.com

Flor carpet tiles: www.flor.com

Gaiam: www.gaiam.com

Green Culture furniture: www.eco-furniture.com

Reforest Teak: www.reforestteak.com

Summit Views – greener firelogs: www.summitviews.com

Vivaterra: www.vivaterra.com

Vivavi: vivavi.com

Office Products

Better World Books: www.betterworld.com

Dolphin Blue Environmentally Responsible Office Supplies: www.dolphinblue.com

Green Earth Office Supply: www.greenearthofficesupply.com

Greenline Paper Company: www.greenlinepaper.com

Re-Product: www.reproduct.net

Twisted Limb: www.twistedlimbpaper.com

Pets

BioBag: www.biobagusa.com

Doggyarchy dog beds: www.doggyarchy.com

Earth Bath: www.earthbath.com

Eco Choices – Eco Animal: www.ecoanimal.com

Environmental Working Group's "Pets for the Environment" site: www.petsfortheenvironment.org

Environmental Working Group's "Polluted Pets" Report: www.ewg.org/reports/pets

Feline Pine: www.felinepine.com

Humane Society of America: www.hsus.org

Only Natural Pets: www.onlynaturalpet.com

Purina's Yesterday's News recycled newspaper kitty and small animal litters: www.yesterdaysnews.com

Swheat Scoop Natural Wheat Litter: www.swheatscoop.com

World's Best Cat Litter: www.worldsbestcatlitter.com

Worldwise Pet Products: worldwise.stores.yahoo.net

Recycling Resources

Act (Alternative Community Training) Recycling: www.actrecycling.org

Brides Against Cancer: www.bridesagainstbreastcancer.org

Carpet America Recovery Effort: www.carpetrecovery.org

Collective Good Mobile Phone Recycling: www.collectivegood.com

Computers for Schools: www.pcsforschools.org

Craigslist: www.Craigslist.org

Earth 911: www.earth911.com

EBay: www.ebay.com

Electronics Take-back Coalition: www.computertakeback.com

Freecycle: www.freecycle.org

Goodwill: www.goodwill.org

Habitat for Humanity: www.habitat.org

International Book Project – donate books: www.intlbookproject.org

Lamp Recycle: www.lamprecycle.org

National Cristina Foundation – donate used technology: www.cristina.org

Nike's athletic shoe recycling program: www.letmeplay.com/reuseashoe

Patagonia's Common Threads program: www.patagonia.com

Rechargeable Battery Recycling Corporation: www.rbrc.org

Salvation Army: www.salvationarmyusa.org

Share the Technology – computer recycling: www.sharetechnology.org

Composting

Gaiam: www.gaiam.com

Nature Mill composters: www.naturemill.com

Planet Natural: www.planetnatural.com

Soil Soup : www.soilsoup.com

Worm's Way: www.wormsway.com

Basement/Garage

DPI – Source for greener pegboard: www.decpanels.com

EarthSource Forest Products: www.earthsourcewood.com

Paints, Etc.

AFM Safecoat: www.afmsafecoat.com

Bioshield Healthy Living Paints: www.bioshieldpaint.com

Eco-House: www.eco-house.com

Sherwin Williams Green Sure Initiatives and Harmony Line: www.sherwin-williams.com

Soy Guard wood protection: www.biopreserve.com

Car Products

Easy Wash: www.easywash.com

Eco Touch: www.ecotouch.net

Ecology Center Clean Car Campaign: www.ecocenter.org

Healthy Car – Consumer Guide to Toxic Chemicals in Cars: www.healthycar.org

Sierra Antifreeze/Coolant: www.sierraantifreeze.com

Outdoor Products

Arbico Organics – garden products: www.arbico-organics.com

Bradfield Organics fertilizer: www.bradfieldorganics.com

CITES – Convention on International Trade in Endangered Species of Wild Fauna and Flora: www.cites.org

Cowboy Charcoal – greener charcoal for the grill: www.cowboycharcoal.com

Dagoba Organic Chocolate – great for s'mores: www.dagobachocolate.com

EarthSource Forest Products – FSC certified decking materials: www.earthsourcewood.com

Eco Choices - Eco Patio: www.ecopatio.com

Extremely Green garden products: www.extremelygreen.com

Forest Stewardship Council – certifies wood from well-managed forests: www.fsc.org/en/

Neptune's Harvest fertilizer: www.neptunesharvest.com

Northwest Builders Network: www.nwbuildnet.com/stores/gm/

Organic Gardening magazine: www.organicgardening.com

Planet Natural lawn and garden supplies: www.planetnatural.com

Rawganique - hemp hammocks and other hemp products www.rawganique.com

Reforest Teak – Responsibly grown and harvested teak with profits benefiting reforestation projects in Central America: www.reforestteak.com

Safe Lawns: www.safelawns.org

Soy Guard wood protection: www.biopreserve.com

Summit Views – greener firelogs and charcoal: www.summitviews.com

Sunlawn human powered mowers: www.sunlawn.com

Terracycle worm casting fertilizer: www.terracycle.net and www.gardeners.com

Theodore Payne Foundation Wildflowers and Native Plants: www.theodorepayne.org

Wild Ones – Information promoting use of native plants and landscapes www.for-wild.org

PHOTO CREDITS

p. xii (left) Stasys Eidiejus/shutterstock; p. xii (right) Carsten Reisinger/shutterstock; p. 1 (left) Bomshtein/shutterstock; p. 1 (right) oblong1/shutterstock; p. 2 (left) © Scott Van Blarcom | Dreamstime.com; p. 2 (right) © Krzysztof Wiktor | Dreamstime.com; p. 3 (left) © Feng Yu | Dreamstime.com; p. 3 (right) Johanna Goodycar/shutterstock; p. 4 (left) Graca Victoria/Shutterstock; p. 4 (right) stocksnapp/shutterstock; p. 5 (left) © Karin Lau | Dreamstime.com; p. 5 (right) © Randy Mckown | Dreamstime.com; p. 6 (left) Courtesy United States Department of Agriculture; p. 6 (right) Courtesy Green Seal; p. 7 (left) Courtesy Leaping Bunny; p. 7 (right) Courtesy Forest Stewardship Council; p. 8 (left) photos.com; p. 8 (right) © Kirill Roslyakov | Dreamstime.com; p. 9 (left) Courtesy of The American Soybean Association; p. 9 (right) Yusaku Takeda/shutterstock; p. 10 Liz Van Steenburgh/shuttterstock; p. 11 Elena Elisseeva/shutterstock; p. 12 (left) Carole Drong; p. 12 (right) Jonathan Vasata/shutterstock; p. 13 (left) Domenico Gelermo/shutterstock; p. 13 (right) Carole Drong; p. 14 (left) Courtesy of Gaiam; p. 14 (right) © Shaday365 | Dreamstime.com; p. 15 (left) Wikipedia; p. 15 (right) matka_Wariatka/shutterstock; p. 16 (left) Liette Parent/shutterstock; p. 16 (right) HomeStudio/shutterstock; p. 17 (left) K Chelette/shutterstock; p. 17 (right) Courtesy of Gaiam; p. 18 (left) serthom/shutterstock; p. 18 (right) rj lerich/shutterstock; p. 19 (left) R McKown/shutterstock; p. 19 (right) © beth ponticello | Dreamstime.com; p. 20 (left) © Flashon Studio | Dreamstime.com; p. 20 (right) Bashkirova Marina /shutterstock; p. 21 (left) Ruben Enger/shutterstock; p. 22 (left) photos.com; p. 22 (right) Deborah Reny/shutterstock; p. 23 (left) rebvt/shutterstock; p. 23 (right) Liv friis-larsen/ shutterstock; p. 24 (left) photos.com; p. 24 (right) IoanaDrutu/shutterstock; p. 25 (left) K Chelette/shutterstock; p. 25 (right) photos.com; p. 26 (left) oblong1/shutterstock; p. 26 (right) Carole Drong; p. 27 (left) Aleksei Potov/shutterstock; p. 27 (right) Hugo de Wolf/Shutterstock; p. 28 (left) Courtesy of Kohler Co; p. 28 (right) Courtesy of Kohler Co; p. 29 Courtesy of Kohler Co; p. 30 (left) UrosK/shutterstock; p. 30 (right) ©Varyaphoto1000 | Dreamstime.com; p. 31 (left) Courtesy of Kohler Co; p. 31 (right) Courtesy of Marble.com; p. 32 (left) Courtesy of Maytag; p. 32 (right) Sandra Rugina/Shutterstock; p. 33 (left) © Pat Choinski | Dreamstime.com; p. 33 (right) © Thesupe87 | Dreamstime.com; p. 34 (left) Stephen Coburn/shutterstock; p. 35 (left) TheSupe87/shutterstock; p. 35 (right) Carole Drong; p. 36 (right) photos.com; p. 36 (right) © Design56 | Dreamstime.com; p. 37 (left) © Rafa Irusta | Dreamstime.com; p. 37 (right) R. Gino Santa Maria/shutterstock; p. 38 (left) Mark Stout Photography; p. 38 (right) © Igor Terekhov | Dreamstime.com; p. 39 (left) Courtesy of Ikea; p. 39 (right) photos.com; p. 40 (left) FSC Trademark ® FSC Forest Stewardship Council; p. 40 (right) Stasys Eidiejus/Shutterstock; p. 41 photos.com; p. 42 Patricia Hofmeester/shutterstock; p. 43 © Kotiki | Dreamstime.com; p. 44 (left) Courtesy of Ik ea; p. 44 (right) Courtesy of Build Direct; p. 45 Courtesy of Ikea; p. 46 felix casio/shutterstock; p. 47 (left) Carole Drong; p. 47 (right) Graca Victoria/shutterstock; p. 48 Kiselev Andrey Valerevich/shutterstock; p. 49 (left) Courtesy Certified Humane; p. 49 (right) ahkim/shutterstock; p. 50 (left) Courtesy of Kohler Co.; p. 50 (right) Courtesy of Kohler Co; p. 51 Courtesy of Kohler Co; p. 52 © Milanlj | Dreamstime.com; p. 53 © Edward Sporbert | Dreamstime.com; p. 54 (left) photos.com; p. 54 (right) Marie C. Fields/shutterstock; p. 55 Anthony Berenyi/shutterstock; p. 56 (left) Courtesy of American Standard; p. 56 (right) © Marc Pinter | Dreamstime.com; p. 57 (left) photos.com; p. 57 (right) Carole Drong; p. 58 (left) photos.com; p. 58 (right) Konstantin Sutyagin/shutterstock; p. 59 (left) Courtesy of Gaiam; p. 59 (right) photos.com; p. 60 (left) Carsten Reisinger/shutterstock; p. 60 (right) photos.com; p. 61 photos.com; p. 62 (left) Courtesy of White Lotus Home; p. 62 (right) Factoria singular fotografia/shutterstock; p. 63 (left) Courtesy of Coyuchi; p. 63 (right) Courtesy of VivaTerra; p. 64 (left) shutterstock; p. 64 (right) Piotr Skubisz/shutterstock; p. 65 (left) shutterstock; p. 65 (right) Courtesy of Gaiam; p. 66 Courtesy of Gaiam; p. 67 (left) Courtesy of VivaTerra; p. 67 (right) Courtesy of Gaiam; p. 68 Svetlana Larina/shutterstock; p. 69 Courtesy of VivaTerra.; p. 70 (right) Deborah Reny/shutterstock; p. 71 (left) Andrew Kroehn/shutterstock; p. 71 (right) Pattie Steib/shutterstock; p. 72 (left) © Heide Hibbard Reed | Dreamstime.com; p. 72 (right) Gravicapa/shutterstock; p. 73 shutterstock; p. 74 Ali Ender Birer/shutterstock; p. 75 (left) Steve Cukrov/Shutterstock; p. 75 (right) Milan Vasicek/Shutterstock; p. 76 (left) Brett Mulcahy/shutterstock; p. 76 (right) Lev Olkha/Shutterstock; p. 78 Carole Drong; p. 79 (left) matka_Wariatka/shutterstock; p. 79 (right) Carole Drong; p. 80 (left) Carole Drong; p. 80 (right) Carole Drong; p. 81 (left) Carole Drong; p. 81 (right) Elke Dennis/shutterstock; p. 82 (left) Michal Kram/shutterstock; p. 82 (right) Carole Drong; p. 83 (left) Serghei Starus/shutterstock; p. 83 (right) wheatley/shutterstock; p. 84 holligan78/shutterstock; p. 86 (left) Elena Schweitzer/shutterstock; p. 86 (right) Marcel Mooij/shutterstock; p. 87 elaine hudson/shutterstock; p. 88 (left) Kim Ruoff/shutterstock; p. 88 (right) Annmarie Young/shutterstock; p. 89 (left) Courtesy of G Diapers; p. 89 (right) Anita Patterson Peppers/shutterstock; p. 90 Ramona Heim/shutterstock; p. 91 Losevsky Pavel/shutterstock; p. 92 (left) Oleg V. Ivanov/shutterstock; p. 92 (right) Galushko Sergey/shutterstock; p. 93 Artem Efimov/shutterstockp. 94 (left) Alexan66/shutterstock; p. 94 (right) The Mary Cordaro Collection™; p. 95 (left) Courtesy of Coyuchi; p. 95 (right) MalibuBooks/shutterstock; p. 96 (left) ostromec/shutterstock; p. 96 (right) evan66/shutterstock; p. 97 (left) shutterstock; p. 97 (right) Barbara Delgado/shutterstock; p. 98 Courtesy of Maytag; p. 100 (left) Glenda M. Powers/shutterstock; p. 100 (right)Péter Gudella/shutterstock; p. 101 (right) Stephen VanHorn/shutterstock; p. 102 (left) Carole Drong; p. 102 (right) Johanna Goodyear/shutterstock; p. 103 (left) Sarah Bossert/shutterstock; p. 103 (right) STILLFX/shutterstock; p. 104 Courtesy of Maytag; p. 105 (left) shutterstock; p. 105 (right) Abel Leão/istockphoto; p. 106 Chris Howey/shutterstock; p. 107 (left) Dan Bellyk/istockphoto; p. 107 (right) Bocos Bene-

239

INDEX

243

INDEX